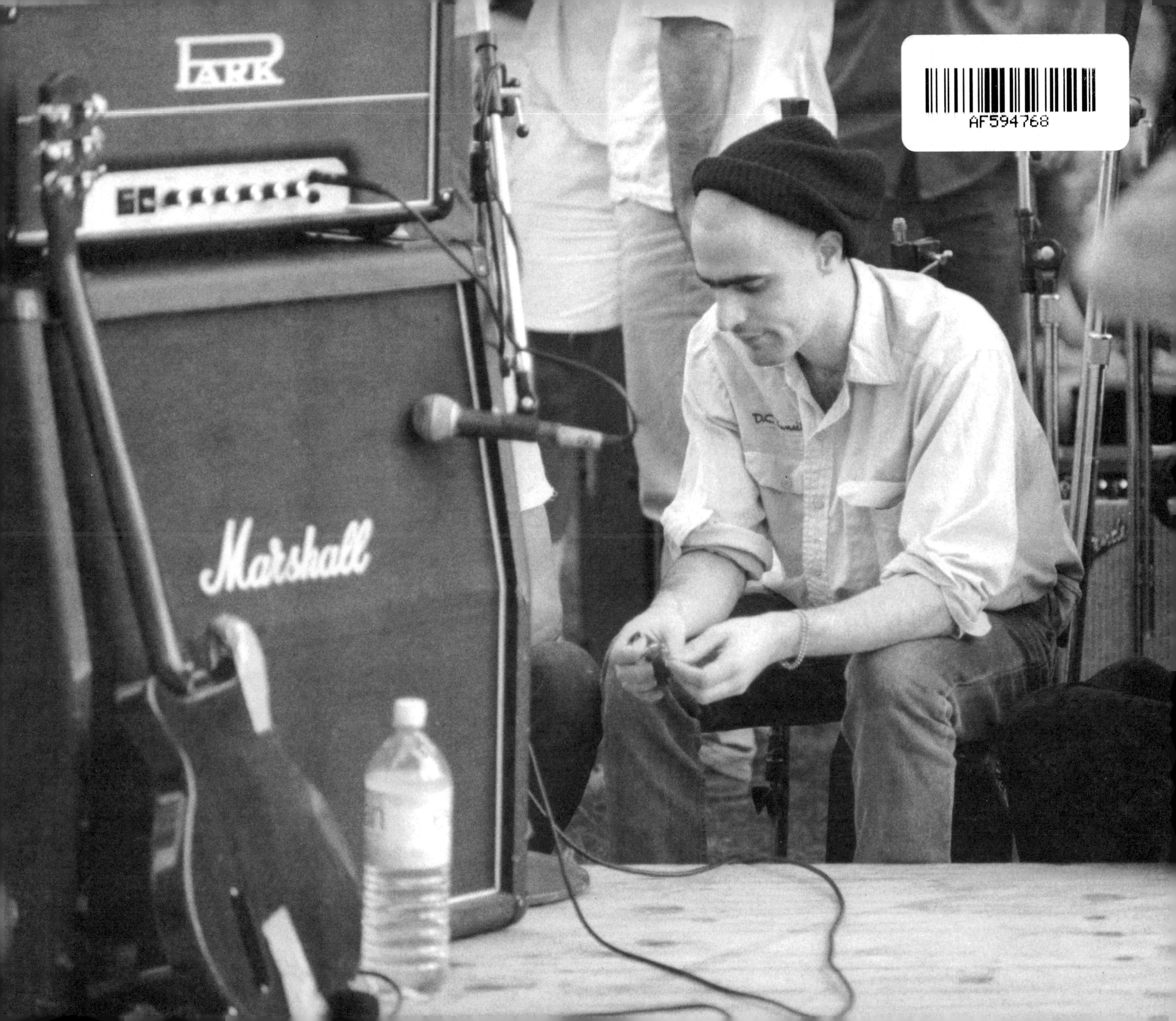
PARK
Marshall

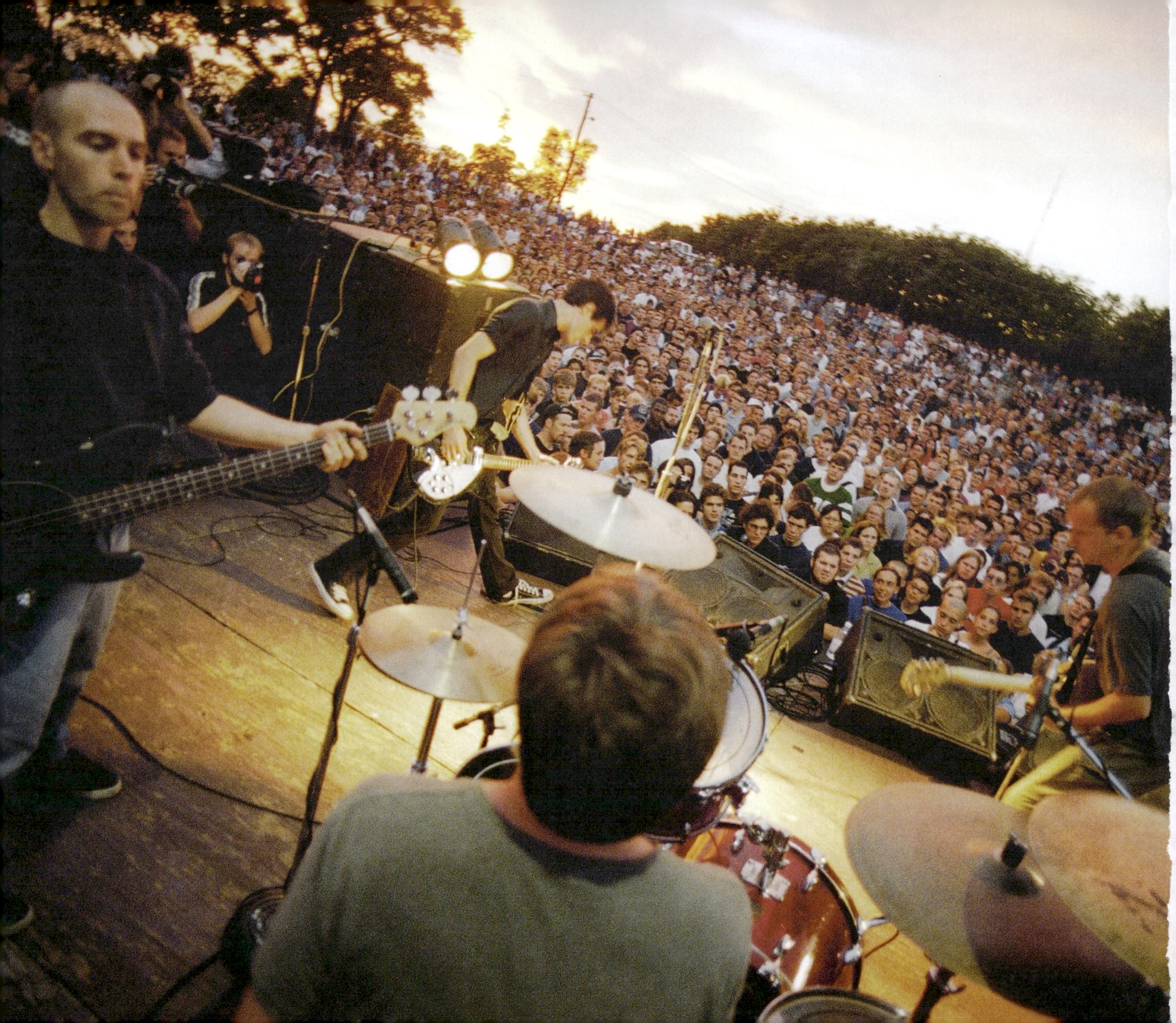

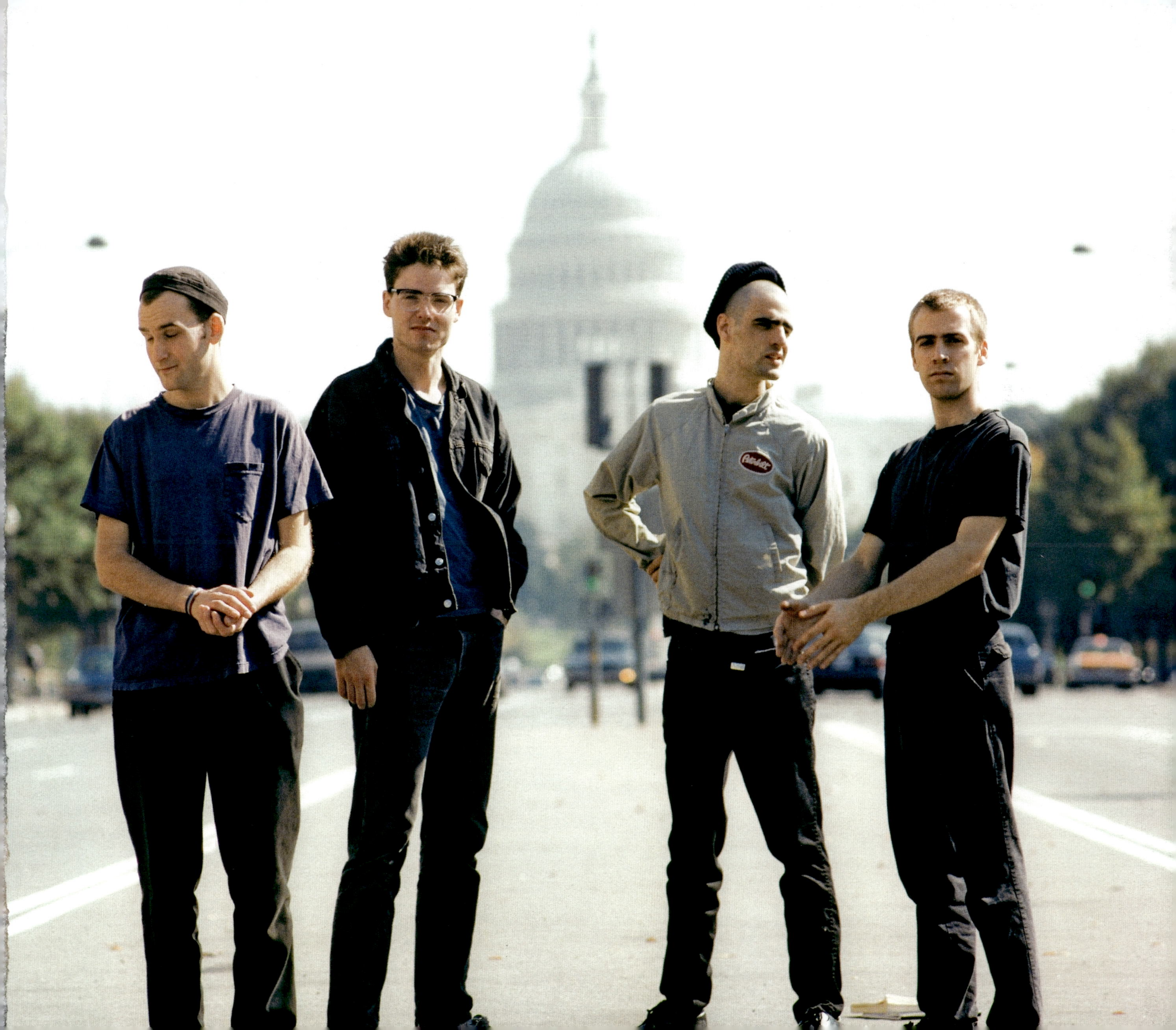

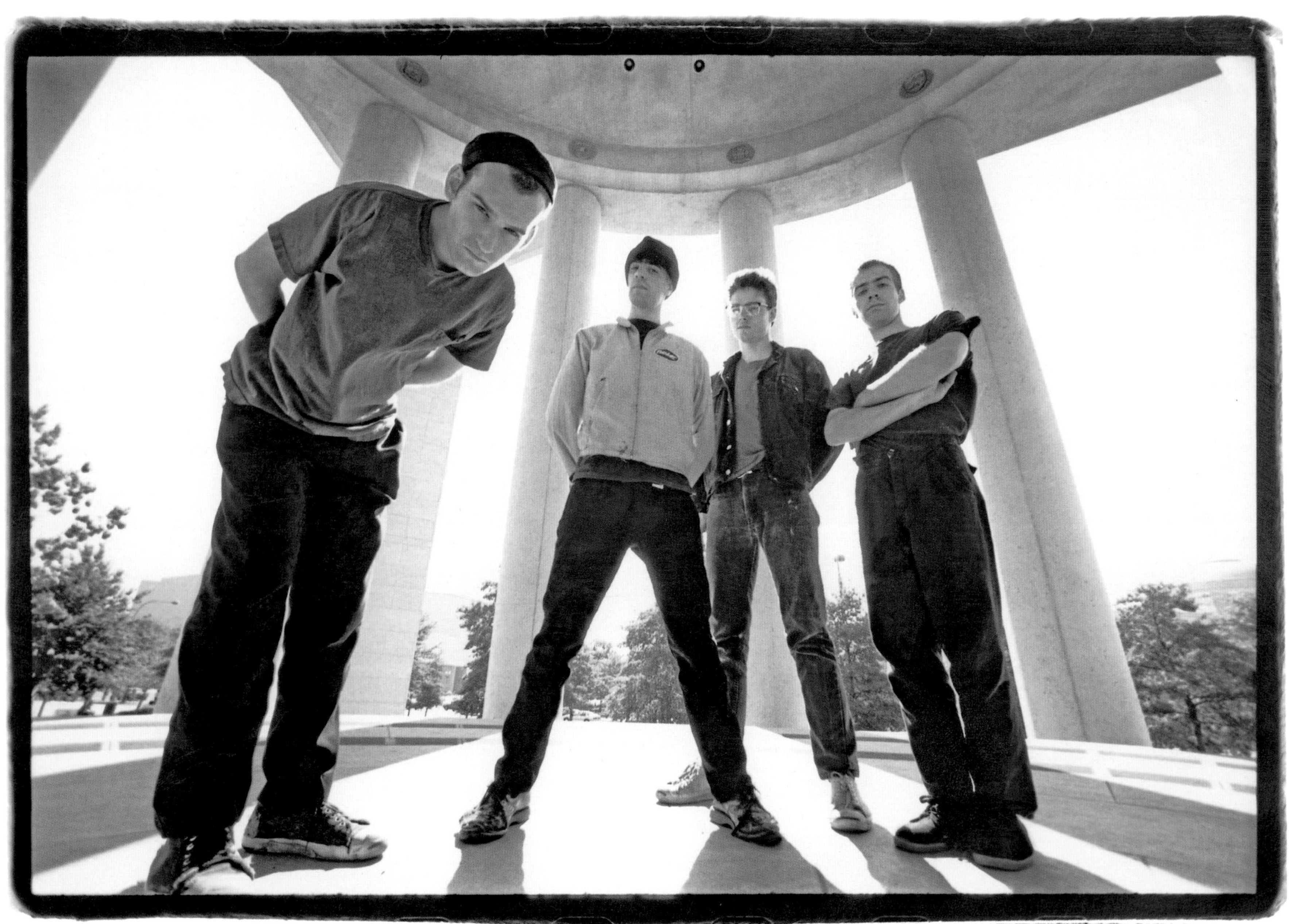

keep your eyes open

FUGAZI

glen E. friedman

KEEP YOUR EYES OPEN

THE FUGAZI PHOTOGRAPHS OF GLEN E. FRIEDMAN

SECOND EDITION

PUBLISHED BY AKASHIC BOOKS

ISBN: 978-1-61775-700-6
LIBRARY OF CONGRESS CONTROL NUMBER: 2018960898

SECOND PRINTING OF THE AKASHIC BOOKS EDITION

PRINTED IN CHINA

ESSAY ON FUGAZI BY
IAN F. SVENONIUS

Fugazi song and album titles used as page markers courtesy of Dischord Records.
This book was edited and designed by Glen E. Friedman, with Sohrab Habibion (second edition).

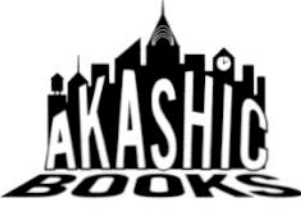

Akashic Books, Brooklyn, New York, USA
Instagram, Twitter, Facebook: AkashicBooks
info@akashicbooks.com, www.akashicbooks.com

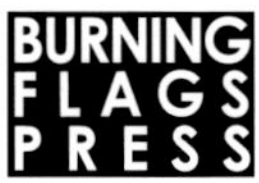

Burning Flags Press
PO Box 69, New York, NY 10003
www.BurningFlags.com

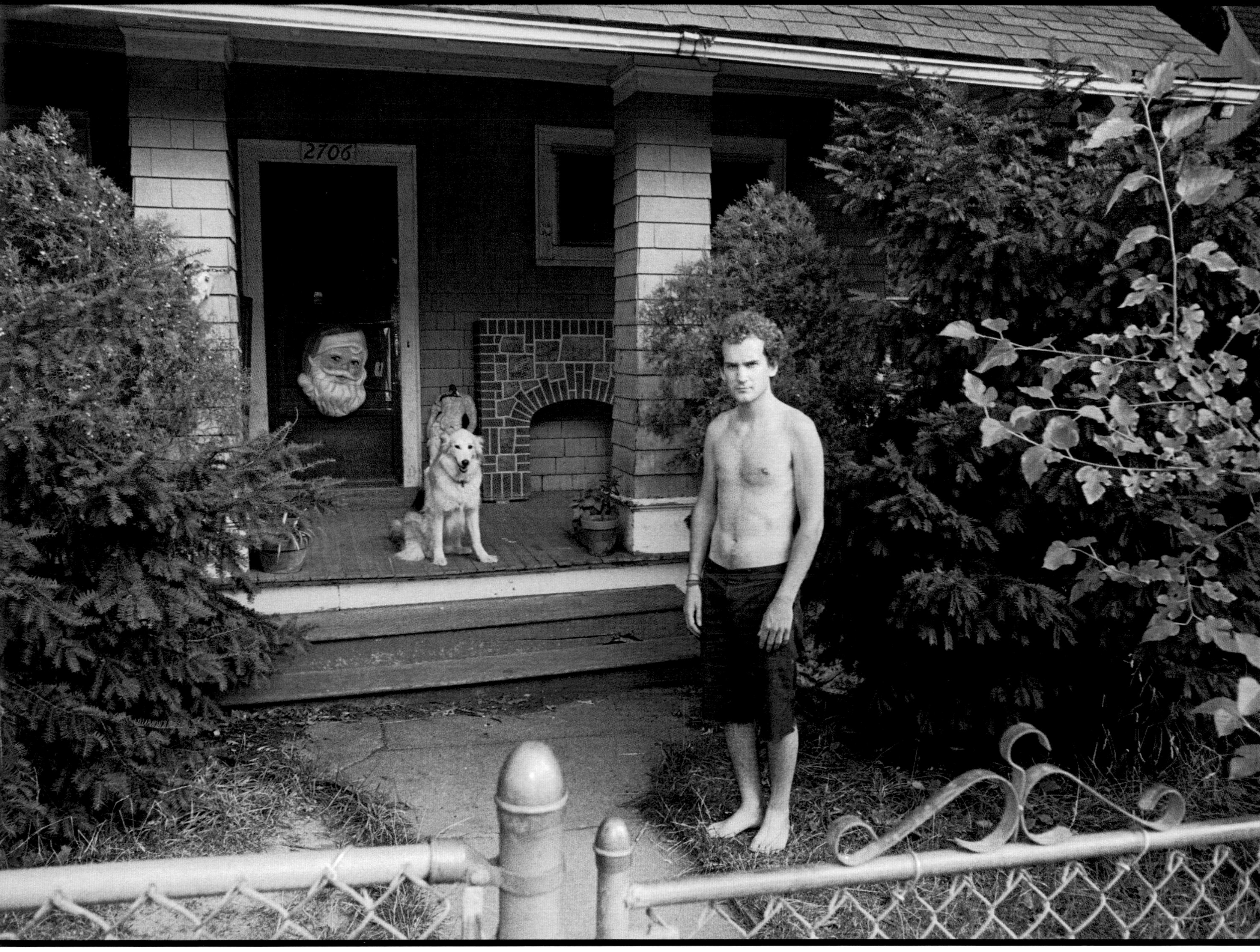

Ian in front of Dischord House, midsummer 1986.
Less than two weeks later he sat down with Joe and they had their first talks about starting a new band that would become Fugazi.

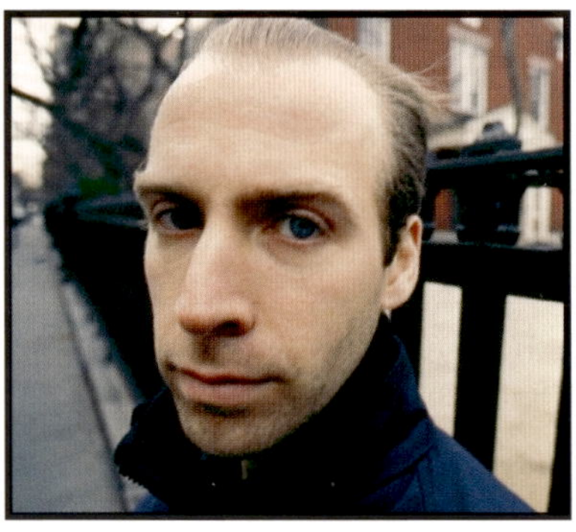
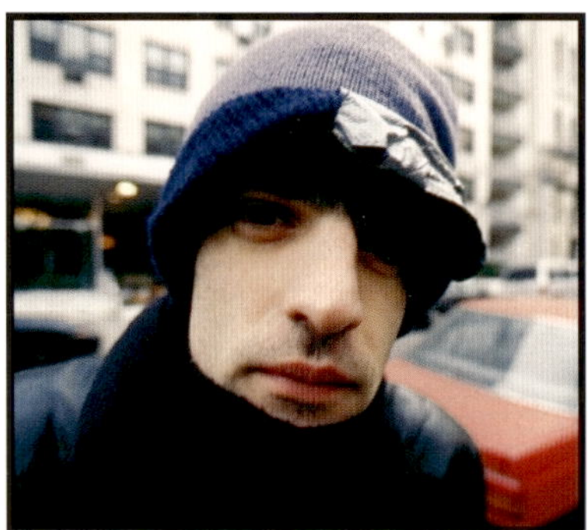
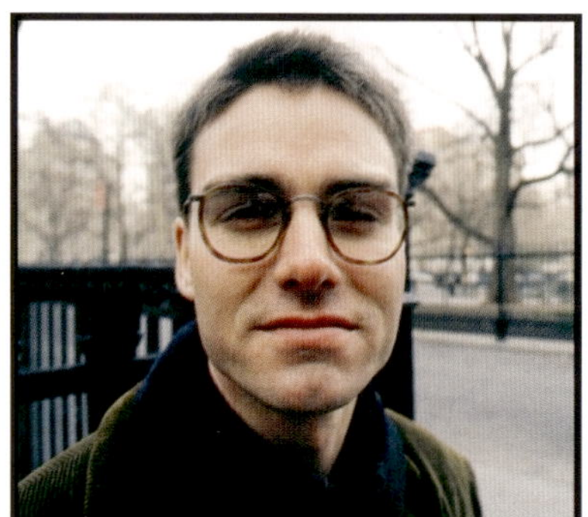
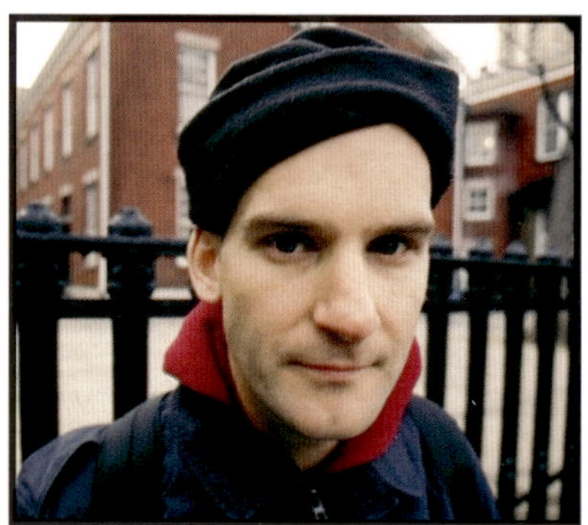

Fugazi and Rock 'n' Roll

Rock 'n' roll is riddled with contradictions. No one has resolved them, though many have tried. In fact, the history of rock 'n' roll has been, for the most part, a struggle to define its as-yet-unclear meaning. As battles are fought over this issue, different ideological fronts are constituted and abandoned. Every participant, whether they know it or not, is involved. Perhaps no one has been as influential or as perverse in their attempts at resolution of this riddle as the group Fugazi.

As we have said, "rock" is, in essence, a contradiction. The name itself, on examination, presents difficulties: "to rock" means "to sway to and fro," while "to roll" is defined as "to move along a surface by revolving or turning over and over, as a ball or a wheel." Since these actions can't happen simultaneously, we see that "rock 'n' roll" is beset by internal contradictory impulses at its very core. This is borne out by an observation of the medium itself. Rock 'n' roll is marked by a thematic celebration of nihilistic excess on the one hand (typically a celebration of sexual/sensual gratification), and by a powerful inclination toward social responsibility on the other.

Indeed, for every Bill Haley–style maniac, exhorting his acolytes to rend and rip society without conscience, there is a group like Rudimentary Peni, printing antivivisection screeds in their sleeve notes. And it's not just the explicitly expressed ideologies that are beset by paradox, but the art itself. Rock defies easy stylistic classification because as soon as one progenitor of the form expresses a single urge in a song or a record, another equally sincere devotee smashes that paradigm in rude defiance.

This perversity is expressed in music styles, aesthetics, and presentation, et al. If a curious alien were to ask, "What is rock 'n' roll, what does it say, and what is its use?" we would be hard-pressed to reply. Though we each have an emotional response to this question, as science, the answer is increasingly remote. The tangle of negation gets more snarled each day, whenever Lee Atwater plays rock guitar at the Republican National Convention or Bob Dylan performs especially for the pope. In fact, negation and contradiction is, at this point, the defining quality of rock, not the exception. Consider the dualism of the medium: the production values of the modern rock record or performance contrasted with the supposed primitivism of the form, rock's glam plasticity offset by its pretension of authentic experience, the democracy of "pop" vs. the elitism of "art," the proletarian origins of a form used as a signifier of individualism by the most privileged classes in history, and the utilization via export of this music by capitalism's rulers to exhort the world toward their sordid directives.

These crossed signals don't discourage rock 'n' roll's base from embracing it though. The incoherence of rock seems to make it more bewitching, more impervious to obsolescence. Its workforce, laboring to create something beautiful out of a template so lousy with essential problems, dodders over an eternal oxymoron; like architects constructing a grand monument on a syphilitic, rotted infrastructure.

The early "punks" tried to resolve rock's incoherence by propagating a "do it yourself" ideology and by enforcing a primitive aesthetic that could be mass-produced at a local level by amateurs, but were quickly hobbled by an entrenched record industry's draconian control over distribution and promotional channels. The first wave of punk groups were almost immediately compromised by Faustian bargains they entered into with the very same dark forces they had initially rebelled against.

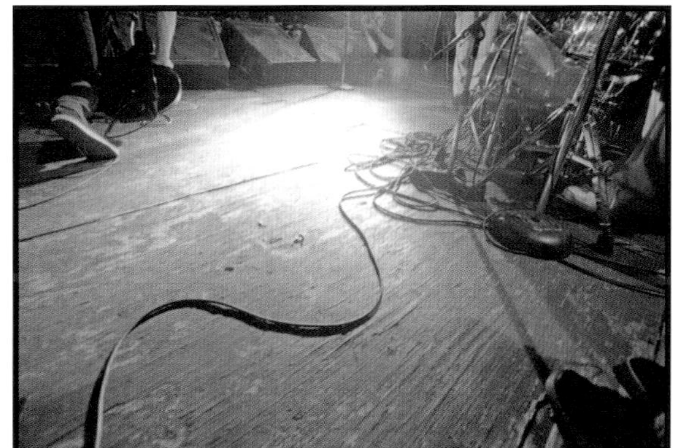

Photo used on *End Hits* lyric sheet

This apparent sellout—and relative commercial failure—by the punk bands precipitated "hardcore," an extremist sect. This was a people's insurrection against punk's apostates, whose initial revolt against rock's establishment had ended with them subsumed and indistinguishable from their supposed foes. Hardcore, like punk, retained the formal qualities of rock 'n' roll presentation: aggressiveness, humor, simple "pop" composition—but contorted it through speed, incompetence, artlessness, and tribal inscrutability. Beats per minute were often sped up substantially. Fashion was stripped down to essential signifiers. Typical hardcore regalia was a cropped hairdo, a hand-decorated tee emblazoned with a cryptic symbol (e.g., the Black Flag bars), and jeans or work pants; an American refutation of early punk's Anglo-dandy trappings. Like punk, HC was apocalyptic; though the lyrics were often political, hope was mostly absent.

Hardcore was an uncompromising cult form; groups made records directed to the movement's acolytes without pandering to squares or music business envoys. This was partially based on disgust with contemporary rock and pop (i.e., groups like Foreigner, Journey, and Lionel Richie), but also by resigned acceptance of an impenetrable status quo. At the time (1980–1983), there was no longer any hope of "making it" in music, except through the most corrupt prefab machinations of the major label "industry," those specters of degeneracy who had corrupted the original punks. Like its punk antecedent, hardcore celebrated self-reliance in business and production. This was actually necessary since, at the time, there was no patronage or interest in the corporate world for underground or "difficult" music. Fanzines and record labels were formed, many of which had their own aesthetic and/or ethos of behavior based on a vague ideology of fairness or antiexploitation.

When punk and hardcore squared off, it was one of those Talmudic discussions that seems inscrutable to the outsider, and yet it was concerned with the very fate of not only music, but also the world itself. This was its conceit at least, and, since belief for humans is tantamount to reality, the industry was brought into this discussion and responded as it always does, with milque-toast variants designed to make themselves seem less irrelevant to the conversation; in this case "political" songs like "99 Luftballons," "Undercover of the Night," and particularly "We Are the World," a disgusting declaration of ruling-class supremacy disguised as a paternalistic, Kipling-esque "save the savages" statement.

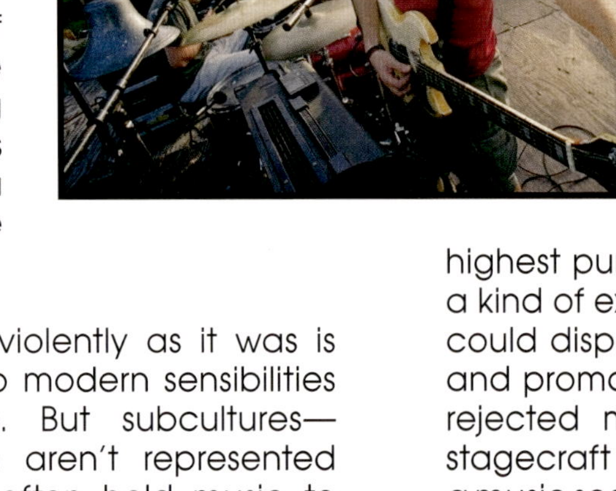

That music was debated as violently as it was is something that is so foreign to modern sensibilities as to be incomprehensible. But subcultures—meaning communities which aren't represented through mainstream media—often held music to be the primary totem of their tribe, and considered it sacrosanct. Every subcultural tribe or sect had an inferred (rarely explicitly declared) ideology and aesthetic, and the music groups and star personalities who were part of these milieus—whether they were called metal, punk, psychobilly, hip-hop, ska, or goth—were beset by enormous expectations from their partisans. The "star" characters weren't cult leaders, but more like priests, dispensing interpretations of an overarching dogma. Behavior was closely monitored, and a step out of line wasn't just the band shaming themselves, but the band dishonoring its attendant scene. Failure to uphold standards was harshly denounced. The groups instinctively understood the bond of trust and expectation as well.

Soon the limitations of hardcore and its own contradictions forced the form to mostly disintegrate, and it was eventually shunned, even by its progenitors, as being uninteresting, simplistic, or dumb. The groups that it spawned, however, carried on the intensity of the movement and many of its conceits as well. One of these conceits was that playing live was the highest purpose of a band and must be treated as a kind of exorcism or rite. Another was that concerts could dispense with the promotional cabal of yore and promote a new, more egalitarian ethos, which rejected many of the "spectacular" aspects of stagecraft (i.e., "showbiz"). Hardcore dissipated, but a music scene followed it featuring many of the same personnel. These new groups retained the aggression, the perverse humor, and the obliqueness of HC, but embraced music instead of trying to destroy its tenets in a savage death rite. Bands like the Jesus Lizard, the Minutemen, the Laughing Hyenas, Big Black, and hundreds of other groups grew from hardcore's roots, transcending that scene's orthodoxy but carrying on its spirit of brashness, innovation, self-sufficiency, and contempt for the music industry and star system.

The most notable of these groups was Fugazi, who in particular carried a radical hardcore ethos into the next era while also forwarding the music. When Fugazi appeared, it was after a thousand permutations of rock, punk, and their various offspring. Since underground music has always consisted of a community of self-styled nonconformists, it features a highly critical and discerning audience. Typical was the reaction of longtime Fugazi associate Mac Lozenge, who spoke with me at a café in Washington, DC.

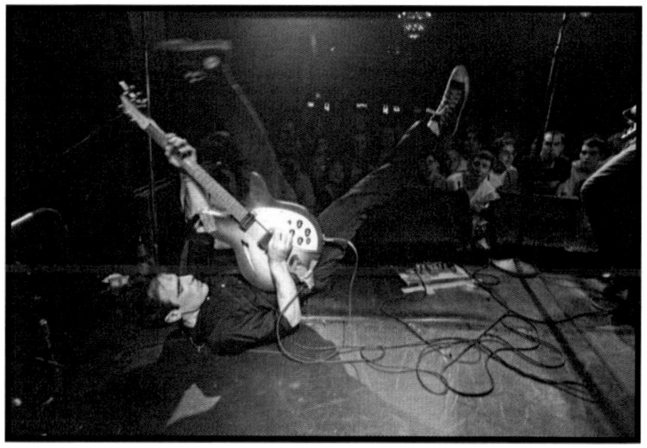

"I'd been hanging around clubs for a while when Fugazi burst on the scene," Lozenge recalled. "They immediately drew notice for their compelling performance style. At first I ignored them, but with all the rumbling, this became difficult. People were citing them in conversation, recounting their vivid shows, humming their tunes. It became annoying. Reluctantly, I attended one of their concerts.

"'Fugazi,' I remember saying on my way to the show, 'surely just another crew of puffed-up pretenders; another . . . *rock band.*'"

Lozenge deliberately emphasized these last two words and summoned his most satirical tone of voice, in case anyone in the café overheard him. I asked him why.

"Perhaps it will spur them to think about why I—who resemble a rock fan—would be so outspoken in criticizing the vast majority of rock groups. Maybe then they will go about educating themselves on the sad state of the medium and do something about it. But probably not; their passivity is maddening." With this, he turned and fixed a withering stare at the patrons nearby. "If they did, however, they would be rewarded with the revelation that rock 'n' roll has become just another weapon of the ruling class; a covert device for mind control and misinformation."

Turning back to me, Lozenge summarized: "Spectacular diversions such as rock, collectively called 'entertainment,' are the elite's principal mechanism for hypnotizing their hapless, drooling pawns."

This sense that rock 'n' roll has gone off track from pure intentions is typical with underground rock 'n' roll aficionados. Lozenge continued with his story.

"The first Fugazi show I saw was held in some church crypt or mausoleum." I prodded him to describe the place; I had compiled a thorough list of Fugazi shows through the years, based on FBI surveillance records. "I forget the precise spot, but I do remember it was five dollars to get in. It seemed like a lot; at the time, I was barely surviving on warmed-up pretzels left over from a sporting event and rescued from a landfill."

I offered him a half of my sandwich, which he put in his bag.

"When the group got onstage, I was toying with just hanging out in the bathroom as a protest of their popularity. Such nonconformity was not only my trademark, but also a fiercely guarded birthright. Only laziness, another inalienable right, precluded me from doing so.

"After a quick tune-up and the announcement, 'Hello, we're Fugazi from Washington, DC,' the group started playing, and . . . I was blown away!" Lozenge hunched over conspiratorially. "You see, I had endured years of disappointment and betrayal by groups I'd put my faith in. It had left me twisted . . . with bitterness. Cranky. Hard to please. But that night, I was finally seeing a group that I knew wasn't bullshit."

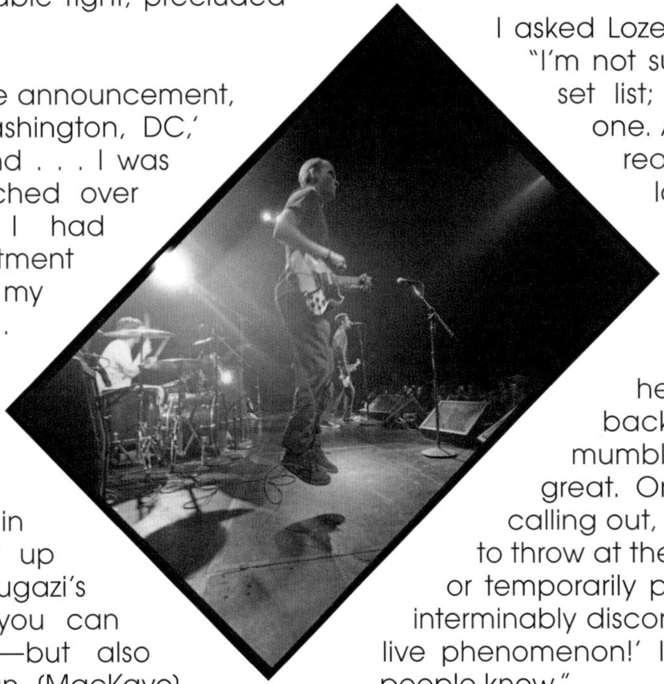

I asked him what it was in particular. Lozenge's eyes lit up as he described the event: "Fugazi's show was really dynamic—you can hear that from the music—but also outrageous; even strange. Ian (MacKaye) and Guy (Picciotto) moved around the stage with real intensity . . . like hungry animals. Joe Lally and Brendan Canty are this crazy rhythm section; they stand right next to each other while all this mayhem is happening around them." As Lozenge spoke he seemed to go into a trance. "Even though there were four of them, the group seemed to form a composite whole; a larger organism. The two guitars were this creature's arms, while the drums were the legs and the bass was the pelvic thrust. While Fugazi was playing, this golem ran around the room and consumed everyone. But instead of screaming out in terror, the audience was complicit in their being eaten, like a plant that is willingly chewed by a rabbit."

I asked Lozenge what songs they played. "I'm not sure. I remember there was no set list; apparently they never used one. And after a few years that was really something, as they had a lot of songs! The performance seemed spontaneous, wild, led by instinct rather than intellect. Songs merged into one another seamlessly. And they sang—you could hear words and even sing along, back when almost everyone was mumbling incomprehensibly. It was great. On the bus home, I remember calling out, 'Finally, not just another morsel to throw at the baying dogs of consumerism, or temporarily placate the easily dazzled but interminably discontent insatiables . . . but a real, live phenomenon!' I wanted to reach out, to let people know."

Lozenge's experience was typical. The group immediately had a cachet, simultaneously popular with nonconformist politicos like Lozenge, and also more trend-conscious creatures such as his alter ego Per Hamsson. Like most people, Mac Lozenge suffers from multiple personality disorder. I got the chance to interview some of his other identities about seeing

Fugazi as well, and while Lozenge was content with his experience, his opportunistic dual personality wanted more.

"Well, since Fugazi were clearly something special, I immediately looked for some way to profit from an association with them," Hamsson told me. "I offered to produce them, to introduce them to record company representatives, to get them drugs, legal advice, jewelry, guns, you know—all the perks traditionally awarded the culture's heroes. Though the band was quite polite about it, they didn't seem interested. In fact, they seemed almost obsessively concerned with making music and playing shows. Kind of a turnoff. That didn't faze me, though; I was a fairly savvy operator at the time. I told them I could get them (an amount I'm not at liberty to discuss) in exchange for (an undisclosed number) of nights at the (so-and-so), and that I would take (such-and-such) as a cut; the details escape me, but it was a sweet deal, one I would have betrayed my children and their children's children for. All to no effect—Fugazi's members politely declined."

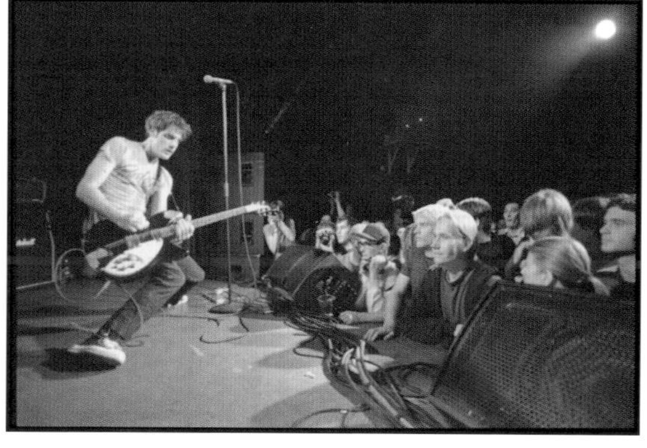

Hamsson admitted that, at first, this made him resentful. "I scratched my head and pouted for a while, plotting my spectacular revenge, until I was told that it was nothing personal."

As he was to learn, Fugazi are remarkable not only for their music and performance, but also for the attention they put into controlling their live context. In fact, of any band ever, none has tried to activate the fantastic myth of rock's rhetoric quite like them. There have been half-hearted attempts (e.g., the Beatles' Apple Corps, the Clash's *Sandinista!* (3 LPs for the price of one), the Stones' concert at Altamont), but for the most part, the medium's populist prattling and high-minded pronouncements have been accepted as theatrical hyperbole and empty rhetoric by almost everyone—especially after the corporate subjugation of punk in the late seventies.

As opposed to the aforementioned bands' faux-populist stunts, Fugazi uses the ideas of "punk rock" as a working model. This manifests itself in part as concern for the mundane details of show business: the "brass tacks" which are typically the domain of managers, production companies, and stagehands. Fugazi's much-cited cheap ticket price—almost always five dollars—is just one example.

Instead of playing in clubs, the band routinely rented halls for their live events. At first these were community centers or the ritual lodges of Masonic orders. Later, when the group was "bigger," they hired the sorts of beautiful historic theaters that developers love to transform into parking lots or expensive college dorms. This gave the concerts a sense of occasion.

Since so much of a modern group's success seems to hinge on marketing, I called an expert in marketing and sales to discuss the group's unique sense of presentation. Nanker Phelge of Horizon Marketing, who has approached the group about assisting them with their promotional problems—and who is coincidentally another one of Lozenge's multiple personalities—had this to say: "Fugazi always brought their own sound system with them on tour, and they traveled with an experienced team of sound engineers. So the low door price was infuriating to me, as I justly felt that the group was denying the audience the right to pay boutique prices for what was, in fact, a luxury product. Without these price differentials in the culture, there is no way to tell what is what, who is who, and why someone is who they are in relation to someone else."

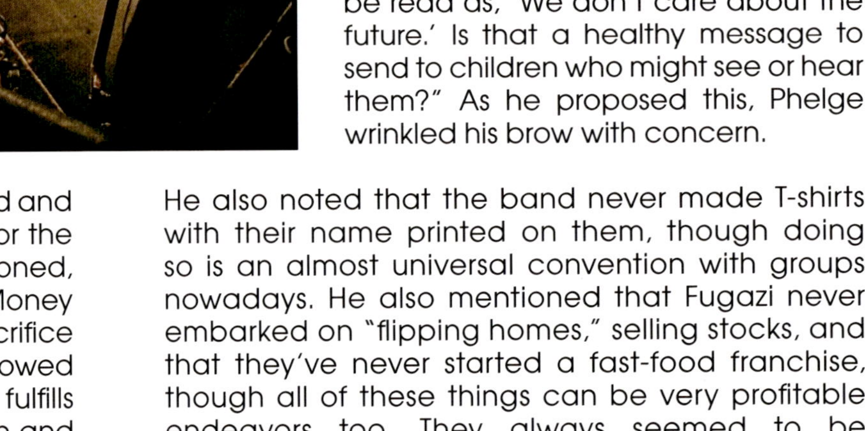

Phelge felt strongly that the group was indeed threatening the whole system of exchange, all due to their intransigence in maintaining an "irrational" reductionist economic model. "I tried to make them understand that, under capitalism, people actually LIKE to be exploited. In fact, the amount that people pay for a show is directly proportionate to the amount that they enjoy the show. Ask any impresario: raising entry fees is a time-tested and easy way of making a show more enjoyable for the audience. If Fugazi set their door at $100, I reasoned, people would dig it twenty times as much. Money spent on a concert ticket, in fact, is a ritual sacrifice that fans make willingly to their idols, a hallowed ceremony enacted since pagan times, that fulfills humanity's basic urge toward self-degradation and servility. In antiquity, people made these sorts of sacrifices for a pantheon of spirits or gods; now the deities are rock groups."

Nevertheless, Fugazi concerts have maintained an extraordinarily equitable price arrangement. And it does seem generally appreciated. By refusing to exploit the audience members' need to see the group by charging a high ticket price, Fugazi are saying, "We aren't interested in cheating you," and, "We are challenging the traditional consumer-producer relationship."

"But," countered Phelge, "charging just enough to pay for the complicated machinery of putting a show on, and then expending enormous amounts of energy in performance, Fugazi gigs are, for all intents and purposes, free of charge. By playing for what is essentially nothing, are Fugazi also sending a message of apocalypticism? 'We don't care about money' could easily be read as, 'We don't care about the future.' Is that a healthy message to send to children who might see or hear them?" As he proposed this, Phelge wrinkled his brow with concern.

He also noted that the band never made T-shirts with their name printed on them, though doing so is an almost universal convention with groups nowadays. He also mentioned that Fugazi never embarked on "flipping homes," selling stocks, and that they've never started a fast-food franchise, though all of these things can be very profitable endeavors too. They always seemed to be preoccupied by things besides making T-shirts.

Because of this, I can't say what their impetus was in ignoring the lucrative textile trade. "They're like conquistadors who, having been driven mad by the ocean crossing, have lost their taste for gold," remarked Phelge.

Fugazi's attitude about merchandise was just one aspect of their disregard for the kind of commodification of everything that William Burroughs once remarked "degrades both the seller and the buyer." It marked a refusal to be part of the sort of product fetishism that encourages wearing a particular T-shirt (for example) as a signifier, a talisman, or an announcement of who one is. Fugazi wasn't content to be another Nike logo or some similar touch-stone of modernity's ubiquitous "branding." On hearing this possible explanation, Phelge sighed. "One throws one's hands in the air at such bewildering logic."

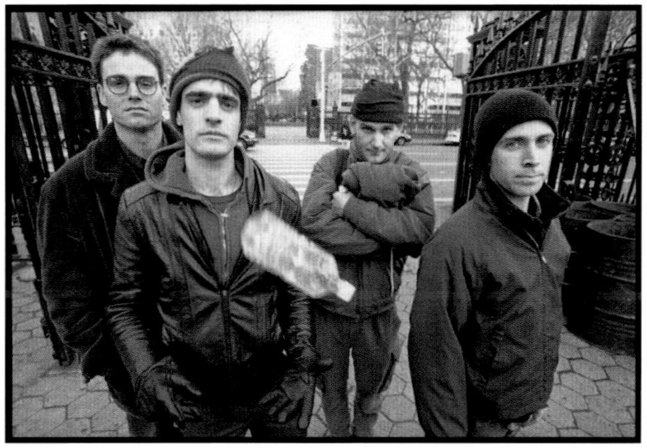

When I mentioned the music, it touched a nerve. "Their records," Phelge explained angrily, "are another misfire on their part. Twelve-inch remix 'maxi singles,' limited-edition ten-inch runs, picture vinyl, and interview discs are intelligent ways of maximizing output and keeping a group 'out there' on the charts and in the radar screens of consumers. Studies have shown that the same record buyer can sometimes be induced to purchase the same song up to fourteen times if repackaging is done in a cunning way. Hapless cows!"

Phelge is right. From the beginning Fugazi have shown no interest in these time-tested schemes, and so their records vary significantly one to another, charting a progression from their origins as a stripped-down, bass-driven group, to noisy forays, dub excursions, and brittle, soaring melodies. Said Phelge: "This laziness on their part in not diversifying their product line is certainly regrettable."

Fugazi tried to build up the underground network of which they were a primary part, and so they favored interviews with amateur "fanzines" to being featured in big rock rags. This led to a certain antagonism toward them for a time by the most influential (i.e., widely distributed, glossy, and publicly traded) magazines. Throughout Fugazi's existence, these establishment organs have given only the most cursory coverage to the group, preferring instead to hype bands who don't challenge the synergy and cross-promotional strategies of the Time Warner–Elektra-Atlantic arrangement. Phelge explained this oversight: "Though this seems like poor form on the part of certain editors, it is simply the product of hurt feelings. Executives at irrelevant magazines are very insecure about their roles as promulgators of filth and nonsense and understandably punish those who refuse to genuflect at their arbitrary power."

In fact, Fugazi's inexorable ascendancy and popularity, occurring in spite of an industry-wide moratorium on their music by major print and radio, underlined the sad irrelevance of official or corporate rock media. The group's success has been deeply humiliating for these wretched institutions.

Fugazi emerged as the most articulate and charismatic scion of what was called "punk." According to some, like Phelge, "The reckless abandon of their performance, combined with their apparent disregard for money, is a fresh take on punk's first love: nihilism." To others, like Lozenge, "Fugazi behave like social workers, raising tens of thousands of dollars at benefit concerts for a variety of worthy causes, like homeless shelters, free clinics, and the like. They've also performed at protests in the shadow of the White House, playing songs that grapple directly with social and political concerns." Is this kind of contradiction intrinsic in rock 'n' roll's design? Lozenge, Hamsson, and Phelge shrugged their shoulders.

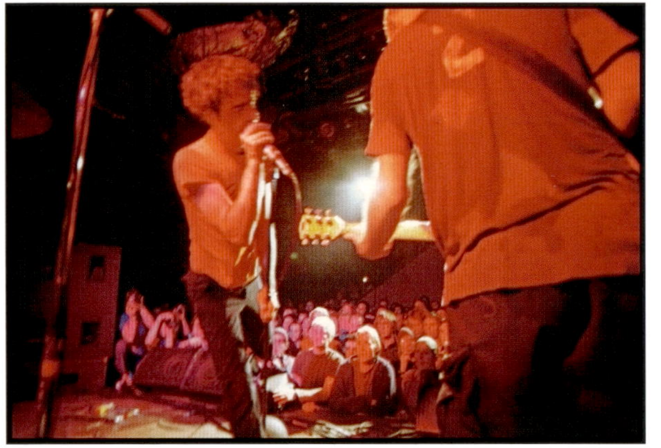

At the café, I tried to discuss with Lozenge "what makes them good." Knowing that I'm a fan, he refused. "That is laboring the point. Nice work maybe for a boor or a nitwit—neither of which I am." He seemed scared that articulating something which is almost magical will rob it of its power. And I understand. But here's something I've learned from trying to investigate the daily life of the Egyptians by studying smudged hieroglyphs on ancient papyrus scrolls: when one is writing about something—even if it seems perfectly obvious at the time—one must consider the plight of those people reading it thousands of years in the future; people who live perhaps on a space station or in a nuclear bunker or in a nest in a hole in the ground. Are they to be denied an explanation? Are they expected to subsist on a wink and a nod by those "in the know"? For these poor creatures of tomorrow, stuck in an atomic winter or being sucked up at any moment by a black hole, one must attempt to explain what makes Fugazi such a special group.

When it was put to Lozenge in this way, he relented. After thinking awhile he spoke: "First, I suppose it's the music. Many exciting live groups have been underestimated as 'songwriters,' since the spectacle of their show becomes the mainstay of the conversation about them. This is the case with Fugazi, perhaps, whose songs have that vital component, missing from so many otherwise competent groups' compositions, called 'personality.'"

I agree with Lozenge on this point. This sense of the group as narrator of a story (and the story might have no words) is what music people respond to in a band, beyond whatever styles or fads may come and go. Great groups don't just have an identity or aesthetic, but a sense of a narrative that goes through their work, a mythic trajectory which marks a search for meaning, not just by the group, but also for the listener. The "fans" utilize the group as a guide for their own aesthetic and moral journey.

The records, examined one against another, give a sense of evolution, and therefore echo the listener's own journey.

"A group with this quality is immediately recognizable when you hear them, regardless of who is actually singing," Lozenge said. It's true. When you hear a Fugazi song, it's recognizable as being them—even the instrumentals. However, while there is this unity in Fugazi's work, it's not because the group is the exponent of one particular vision. All four members are engaged in composing the music. Fugazi's egalitarian show ideal is indeed a direct extension of their creative working relationship. From sources close to the group and electronic bugging devices, this writer has learned that band practice is a loose exchange of ideas, with equal parts jamming and preconceived compositions. Though Canty is ostensibly the drummer, he might write a guitar line. Bassist Lally might suggest a drum fill or guitar arrangement, and so on. These are not precious "specialists" but creative workers engaged in making things, with only a tenuous relationship to aesthetic orthodoxy. Because of an openness to external influences, Fugazi have sometimes enlisted other players (e.g., guitarist Eddie Janney) and incorporated a part-time fifth member, Jerry Busher, on drum kit, percussion, and trumpet, to enhance their dynamism and range.

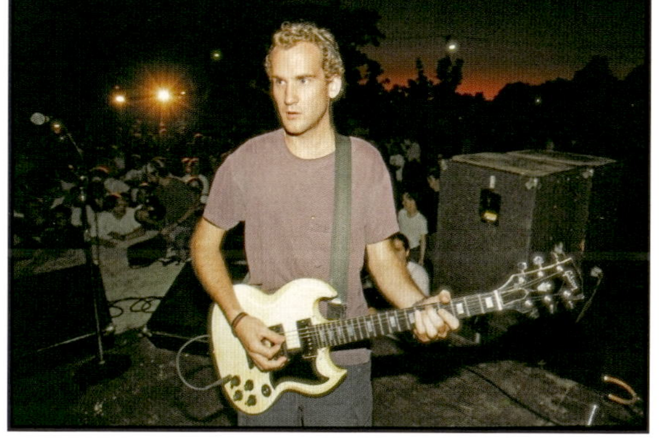

Lozenge continued, "Then there's their performances . . . I mean, from the very beginning!" He stared, nonplussed. And he's right. Fugazi stands with few rivals in terms of pure energy. "And it's important that you mention that Fugazi use their microphones not only for 'vocals,' but as a public address system for actual communication!" He pounded his fist on the table. "This is an important distinction to make, since most rock 'n' roll bands pantomime their way through performances which are exactly the same whether they're playing before five thousand Romans or thirteen Vermonters." I nodded my head as I jotted down his remarks. "Fugazi are doing sort of a Living Theatre thing, like Jim Morrison, but combining it with a kind of round-table discussion. And . . . they reinvent their songs every night. Every composition is continually beaten, stretched, and reconfigured . . . Fugazi shows are expected to be cathartic both for the group and for their audience. And it's really rare to have any expectation at all these days," he sighed.

Lozenge then took a sip of water and looked into the palm of his hand. He glanced wearily in disgust at the other patrons. "And be sure to mention their role as catalyst and inspiration for a new era of independent underground music." I assured him that this is central to my thesis, which I started to read aloud and which explains the group's context. When Fugazi started in the late 1980s, the underground scene in the USA was straddling the melee of hardcore on the one hand and the death-trip art rock coming from New York and the Midwest on the other. Both of these movements were marked by nihilism—a Germanic sense of death destiny and depressed fatalism—both in sound production and in lyrics. Though the bands from these scenes were committed to an "independent" ethos, this came as much from an FTW (fuck the world) paradigm as any idealism. Fugazi's actionism rejected the defeatist narrative, which in some ways defined the underground. They replaced a tragic parochialism with the insistence that bands could maintain control (i.e., independence) but also transcend the limitations of the microcosmic basement-show circuit.

Fugazi thus has toured all over the world, through Asia, Europe, South America, the North Pole, and all fifty states. They've also sold millions of records through singer MacKaye's independent (i.e., not a corporate subsidiary) label, which sells music at significantly cheaper prices than major-label competitors. Remember that the price-gouging exploitation of the "CD revolution" is what led directly to the disastrous, anemic state of the record business in the twenty-first century. (Note to those reading this in the future: CD stands for "compact disc," an ugly, intrinsically flawed device designed for transporting recorded sound. CDs were introduced by the music industry in the mid-1980s, but were then abandoned for aesthetic and pragmatic reasons in the twenty-first century. Despite their egregiousness, CDs briefly replaced records as the primary mode for listening to music.)

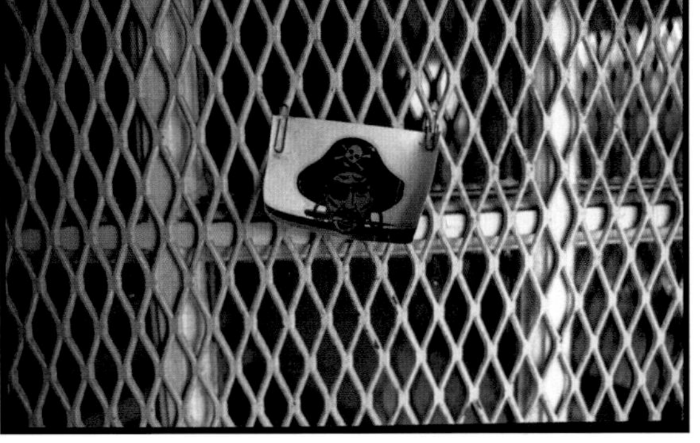
Front door at the Pirate House, circa 1994

Talking about music is always perilous territory and unsatisfying for the reader, but an attempt must be made for future generations who've lost their hearing from the atomic explosions they will endure nearly every day. In Fugazi the influences of dance music (funk, hip-hop, disco), reggae (dub), and proletarian glam (anthemic sing-along music such as British prole-punk) are often cited. Though all of that is probable, Fugazi's most apparent antecedents are English postpunk art bands like Wire, This Heat, and the Fall, with their oblique lyrics, textural Eno-isms, and "fractured" R&B-rooted guitar, playing over deceptively simple compositions. Since Fugazi are North Americans, though, their expression is different, perhaps more visceral. Contemporaries like the Ex, Public Enemy, Autoclave, and all sorts of other aggregates also influenced them; rumor has it the group members were employees at record stores at some point, though this has never been confirmed. There is, however, fairly indisputable proof that they had played in other musical groups.

Washington, DC, has been an axis of innovation since the punk era began, with bands like Bad Brains, Void, Half Japanese, Slickee Boys, S.O.A., Velvet Monkeys, Scream, Faith, Obsessed, Teen Idles, Unrest, G.I., No Trend, Pussy Galore, Black Market Baby, 9353, and the group Minor Threat, which featured Ian MacKaye and Jeff Nelson, founders of Dischord Records. Minor Threat were among the most influential hardcore bands ever, in part because MacKaye was a charismatic, articulate ideologue, who helped give form to the vague community called "hardcore." His pronouncements were the most marked departure from the nihilist "punk" tradition that had informed hardcore music, especially his signature philosophy, called "straight edge." After Minor Threat disbanded, MacKaye and Nelson collaborated on a record called Egg Hunt, which carried on their former groups' lean, melodic approach. MacKaye also sang for avant-punk group Embrace (with members of the Dischord group Faith), and Pailhead was the name of his brief collaboration with Chicago industrial-music impresario Al Jourgensen.

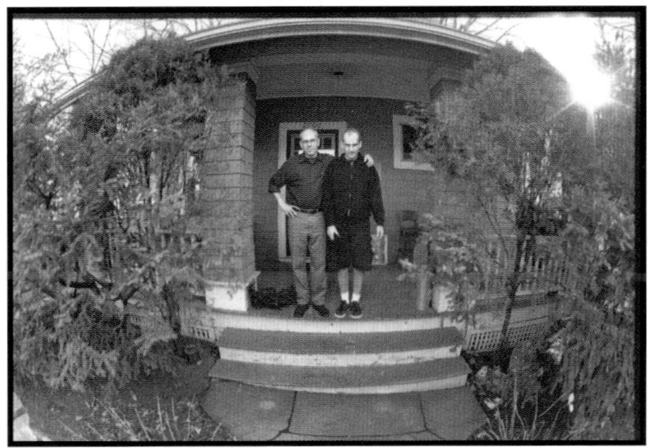
Dischord Records founders Jeff and Ian, twenty years on, outside Dischord House, 2001

Though Fugazi was his first touring band, bass player Joe Lally had roadied for Dischord band Beefeater. Beefeater, perhaps the most eclectic group to appear on the label, created an art-skronk indebted to Hendrix, noise, and "inspirational" or gospel music. Beefeater singer Tomas Squip lived at one point in the communal Dischord House, whose other residents included, at one time or another, Ian MacKaye, Jeff Nelson, Kingface singer Mark Sullivan, artist Cynthia Connolly, Rites of Spring guitarist Eddie Janney, Iron Cross' Sab Grey, and Joe Lally. Such group houses marked the DC music landscape through the eighties and nineties and were hotbeds of cross-pollination between bands and artists. Pirate House was another such institution, where Fugazi's Guy Picciotto and Brendan Canty lived. They also recorded bands in a studio set up in the living room and basement.

It should be noted that Picciotto and Canty collaborated extensively before Fugazi, beginning with the Venom-esque Insurrection. They also played together in the folk group Black Light Panthers, the Manc-funk One Last Wish, and the psych-fop Brief Weeds. Most significantly, they were one half of Rites of Spring, who wedded rock savagery with a transcendentalist/romantic–era aesthetic. Rites of Spring were shaggy-haired and Byronic, a reaction to the austere HC aesthetic of stylized violence and poverty. Their presentation was ecstatic and hallucinatory, with lots of smashed musical gear punctuating out-of-control performances.

Rites of Spring were, like Minor Threat, a phenomenon, a shift in aesthetic for the underground on a national level. Their widespread renown was signaled by their 1985 interview in *Flipside* magazine. This influential LA punk organ had gone to DC to dig a story up and had hit pay dirt, since the scene at the time was undergoing what Communists would call "autocriticism"—an auditing of belief systems and orthodoxies—which resulted in the "Revolution Summer" of bands (primarily ROS, MacKaye's Embrace, and the aforementioned Beefeater) creating art and initiating activism. The idea was to demolish the fetid body of punk while retaining its constructive aspects. ROS morphed into

One Last Wish and then into the Brit-art postpunk combo Happy Go Licky, whose shows were each absolutely different from the next. Though prolific, HGL were broken up after only a few seasons of gigs.

Soviet filmmaker Sergei Eisenstein once wrote, "Heraclitus observed that no man can bathe twice in the same river. Similarly, no aesthetic can flourish on one and the same set of principles at two different stages in its development." Necessarily, therefore, Fugazi was different from the members' previous groups. Always melodic, Fugazi combined a community (i.e., dance) aspect with Happy Go Licky's art-rock and the heaviness of Joe Lally and Ian MacKaye's favorite acid-rock bands. Since Fugazi put out their own records through the Dischord imprint, which had grown since Minor Threat to be an influential and well-distributed indie label, they were completely self-sufficient and never had to "demo" or sell themselves to any company.

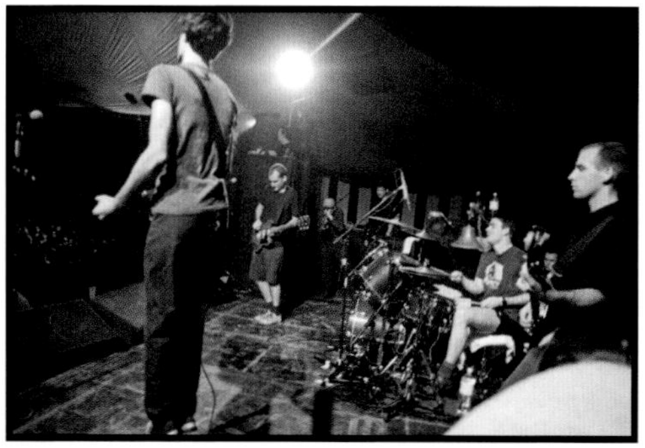

Considered either in terms of hardcore and underground music or with regard to mainstream or popular groups, Fugazi has been absolutely ambitious in terms of transformational intent—a counterpoint and response to many of rock 'n' roll's contradictions over the years.

At this point, Mac Lozenge stopped me. "Yes, but what about the touring? They brought their stringent ethos of nonexploitation EVERYWHERE THEY WENT! That is an achievement in itself. You must let the people know!" I assured him that I would, and asked him not to interrupt me again.

When the group began, they immediately instituted an aggressive touring schedule inspired by Black Flag and the SST label groups of the hardcore years. Black Flag had been the ones to really codify the network that had sprung up organically around the loosely defined punk labels, fanzines, and makeshift show venues inspired by punk and HC. Fugazi booked all their own shows (at that time not unusual) and insisted on an all-ages door, whereby people were admitted regardless of their ability to purchase alcohol. This was a standard in the DC of Mayor Marion Barry, with its lax cabaret laws and pro-youth legislation. Such regulatory principles, which the band brought with them everywhere, were an attempt to present the idea that the group was actually in control if they wanted to be, a "buck stops here" ideology that served to shine a light on the hands-in-the-air haplessness of bands who were oblivious to exploitation of themselves and their fans.

Indeed, Fugazi's performances, records, and music were often about who was in control. Hardcore and punk had been marked by a victim complex, the expression of a caste who felt perpetually underrepresented. The Fugazi ethos countered this with the idea that the group—and by extension the audience (since the punk announcement was that they were one and the same)—could be at the reins if they so desired.

Because the group had such a direct and personal connection to punk and hardcore, Fugazi has been, from the beginning, followed by a partisan base bewitched by the antiauthoritarian ethos of that scene. They were also admired by those attracted to the punk aesthetic due to that milieu's idolatry of street culture and stylized violence. Therefore, though the group had transcended punk's attendant internecine feuds, provincialism, and orthodoxy, their shows were marked sometimes by the same sorts of delinquent and unreconstructed behavior which had typified the latter half of the hardcore era. Since a major aspect of a Fugazi gig was about who was in control—of security, door price, environment, lights—the group personally dealt with antagonistic elements and melees, creating a theater of confrontation that entirely dissolved the "fourth wall."

This kind of attention paid to interlopers had the perhaps unintended effect of codifying violence at Fugazi concerts, which therefore maintained the energy of the bygone hardcore era, even as the epoch changed to a new nonconfrontational "indie" paradigm. "Indie rock" was most notable for an emphasis on unobtrusive groups and petit bourgeois small-business management. While Fugazi's music wasn't parochial or "punk," per se (though they would perhaps call it that), a tiny but noisy recalcitrant element meant Fugazi shows retained an atmosphere of anarchic, freewheeling energy, while their peers' gigs often became, despite their attempts otherwise, staid and conventional.

Although Fugazi was the punk favorite, for their perverse disavowal of rock 'n' roll's corporate malfeasance, they had turned punk on its head by also refuting the nihilistic death-trip aesthetic and empty posing that had often typified that scene.

At this point Mac Lozenge, in a bickering internal dialogue with one or more of his other personalities, begged me to finish up. "Hamsson needs to go to the bathroom, you understand."

A bit miffed, I skipped to my conclusion:

Thousands of workers over half a century have spent their entire lives trying to hammer this undefined monstrosity—rock 'n' roll—into a shape that embodies their ideological concerns, but no one has succeeded in finalizing its meaning or finishing its sentence. In fact, legend has it that when this is finally done, the world will break into a thousand pieces, the largest of which will form a meteorite that will smash heaven and destroy its idiotic, self-satisfied population once and for all. God will be toppled from His seat of despotism and the universe will rejoice.

Fugazi seems the best equipped to bring this conclusion forth, both through the precedents they have set and whatever they choose to do in the future. Glen E. Friedman's photographs, taken over many years of association with the group, present the energy, excitement, and emotion of Fugazi in an inspiring way. People looking at these from a future, whether it's squalid or Arcadian, will see something beyond the context of punk or rock 'n' roll, or even entertainment, and also be driven to bring their own righteous underdog narrative to life.

Ian F. Svenonius
Washington, DC
2007

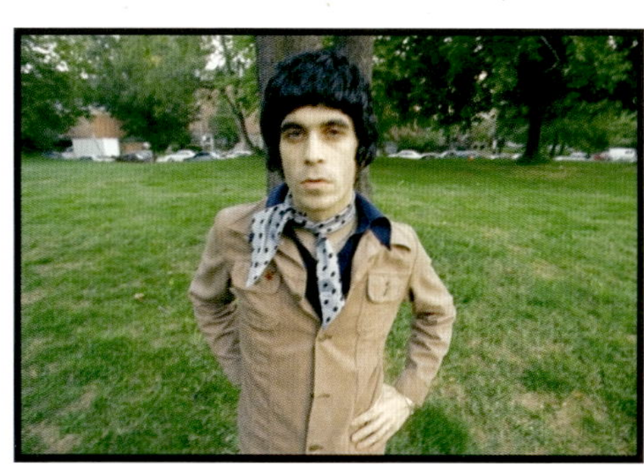

I.F.S. before a Fugazi show at Fort Reno

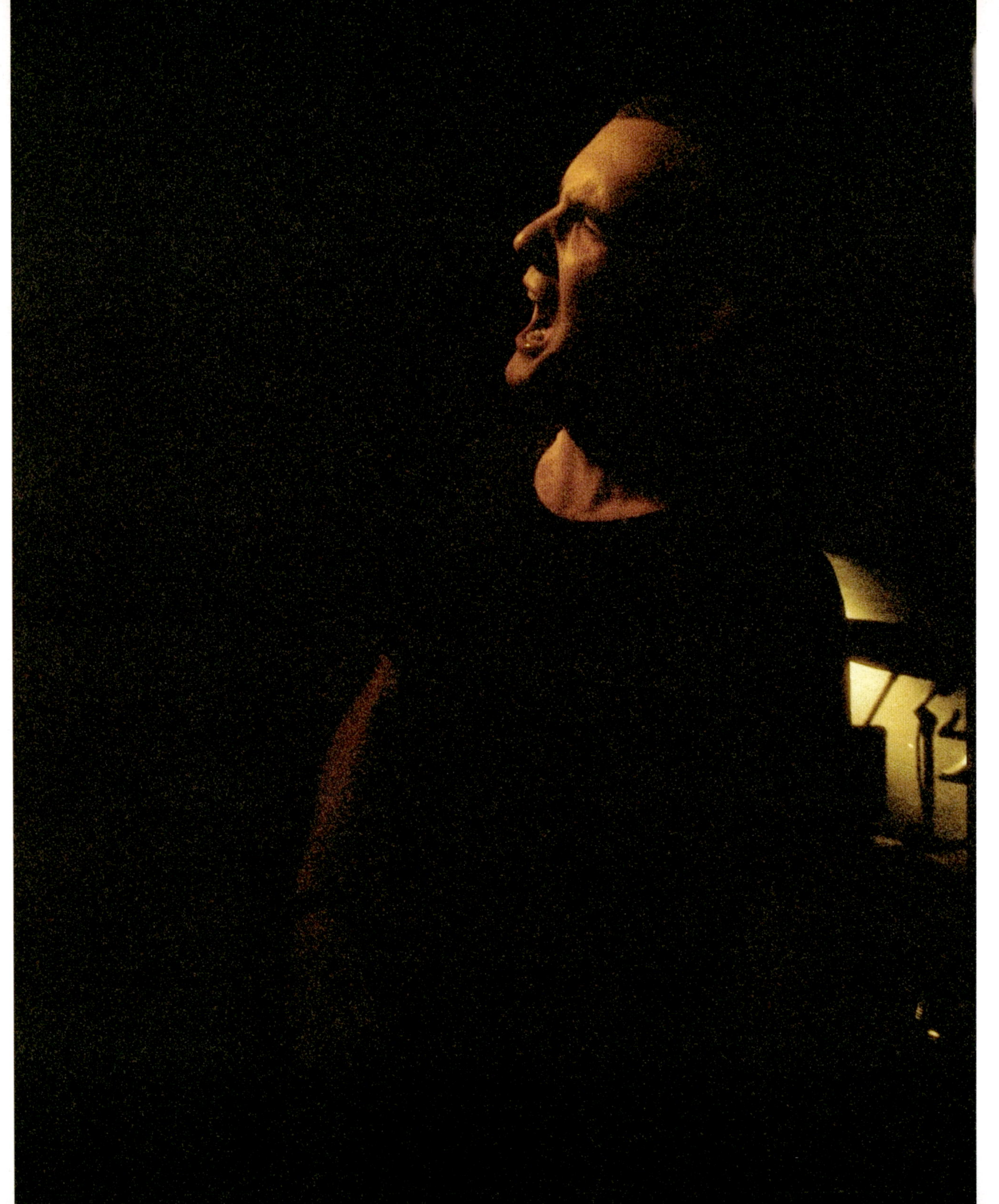

HOBOKEN, NEW JERSEY, 1988

joe #1

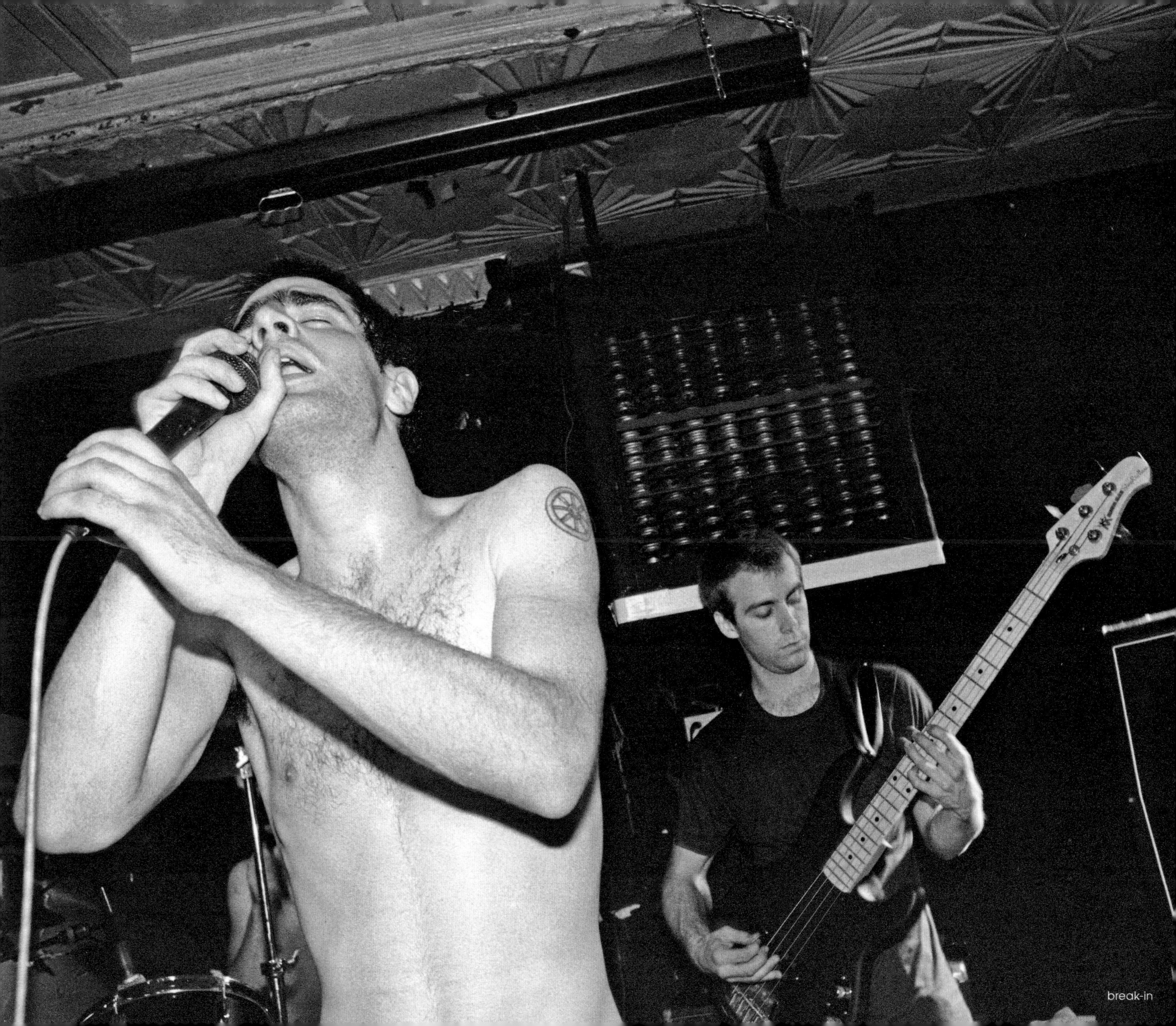

break-in

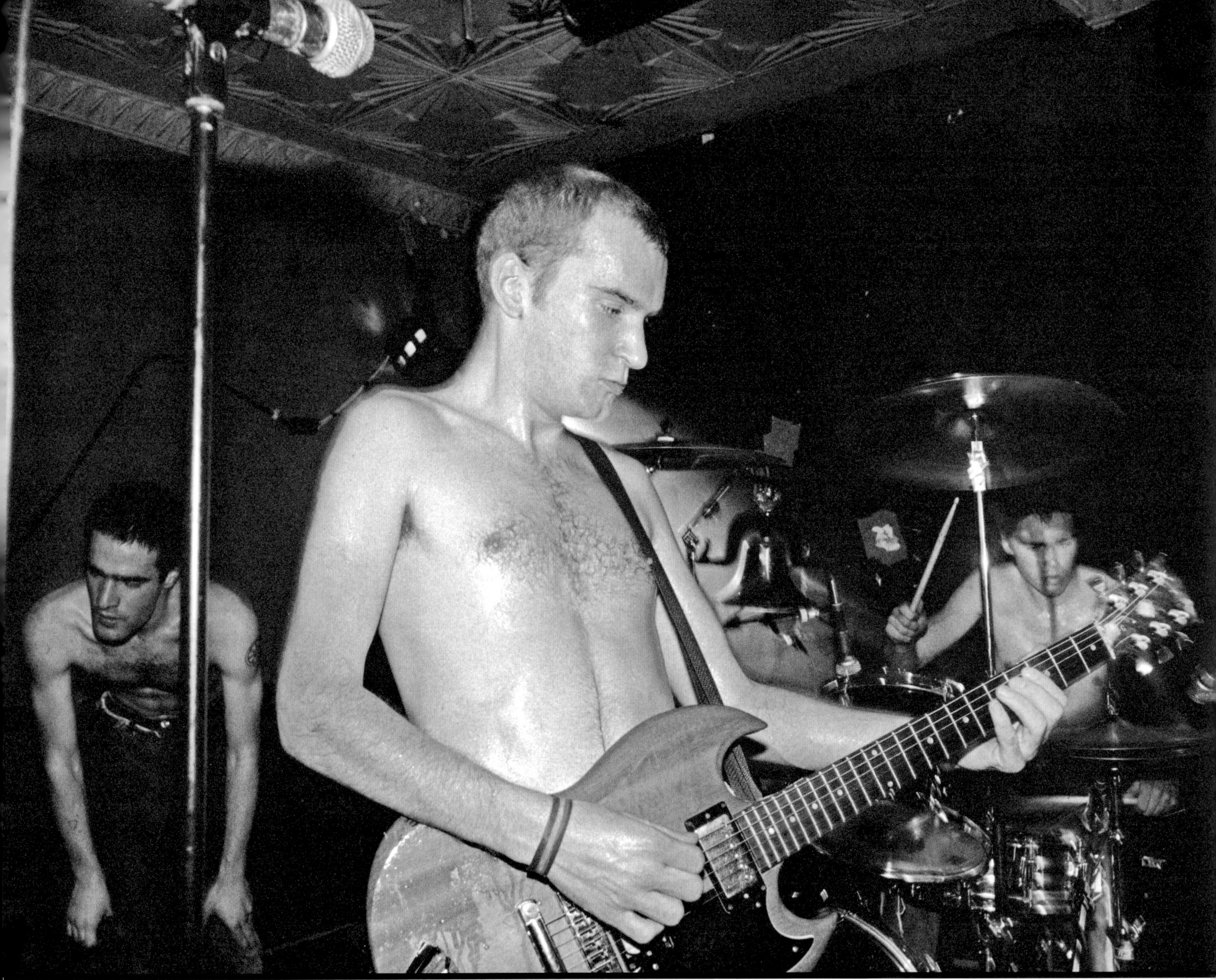

turnover

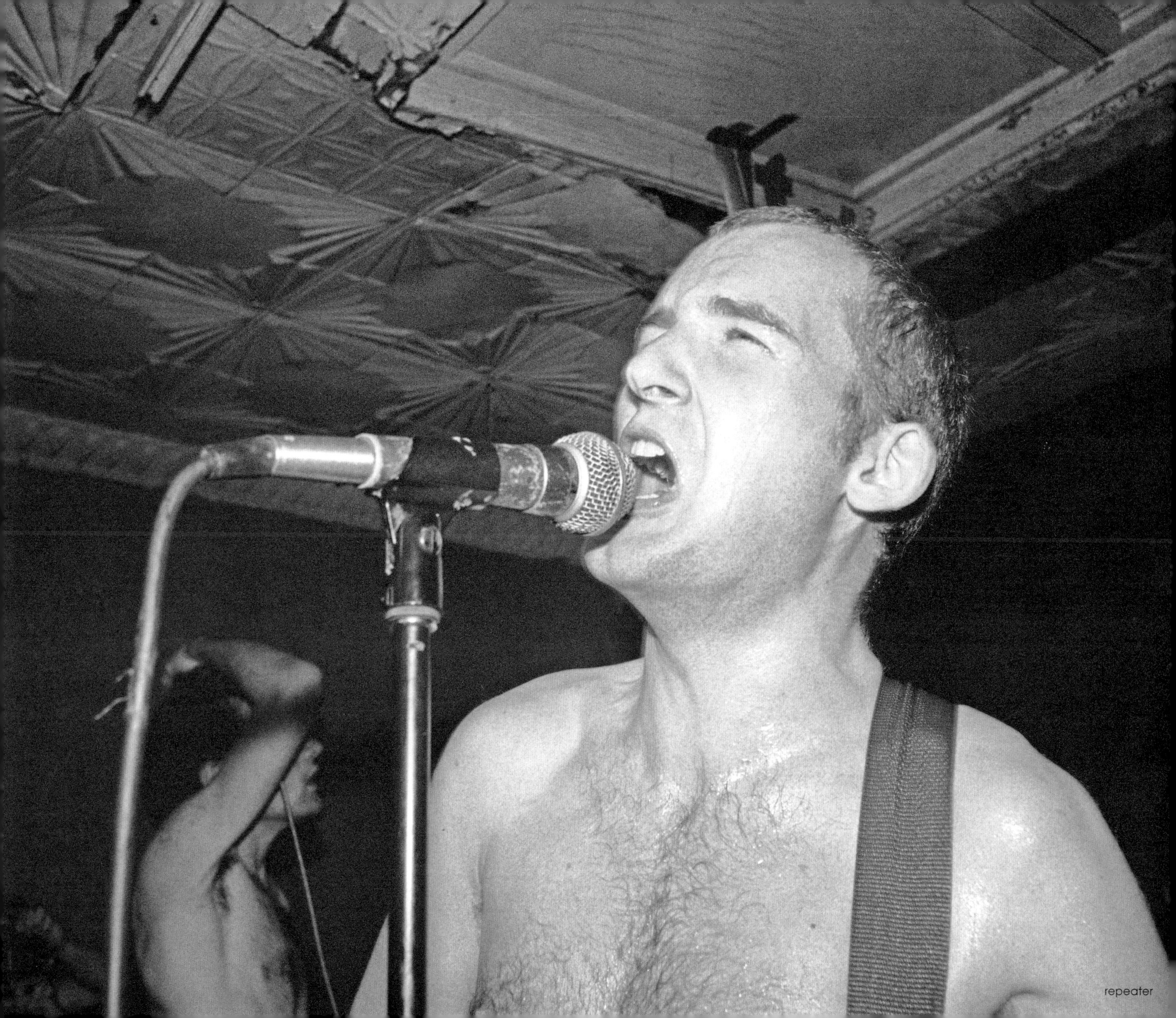

repeater

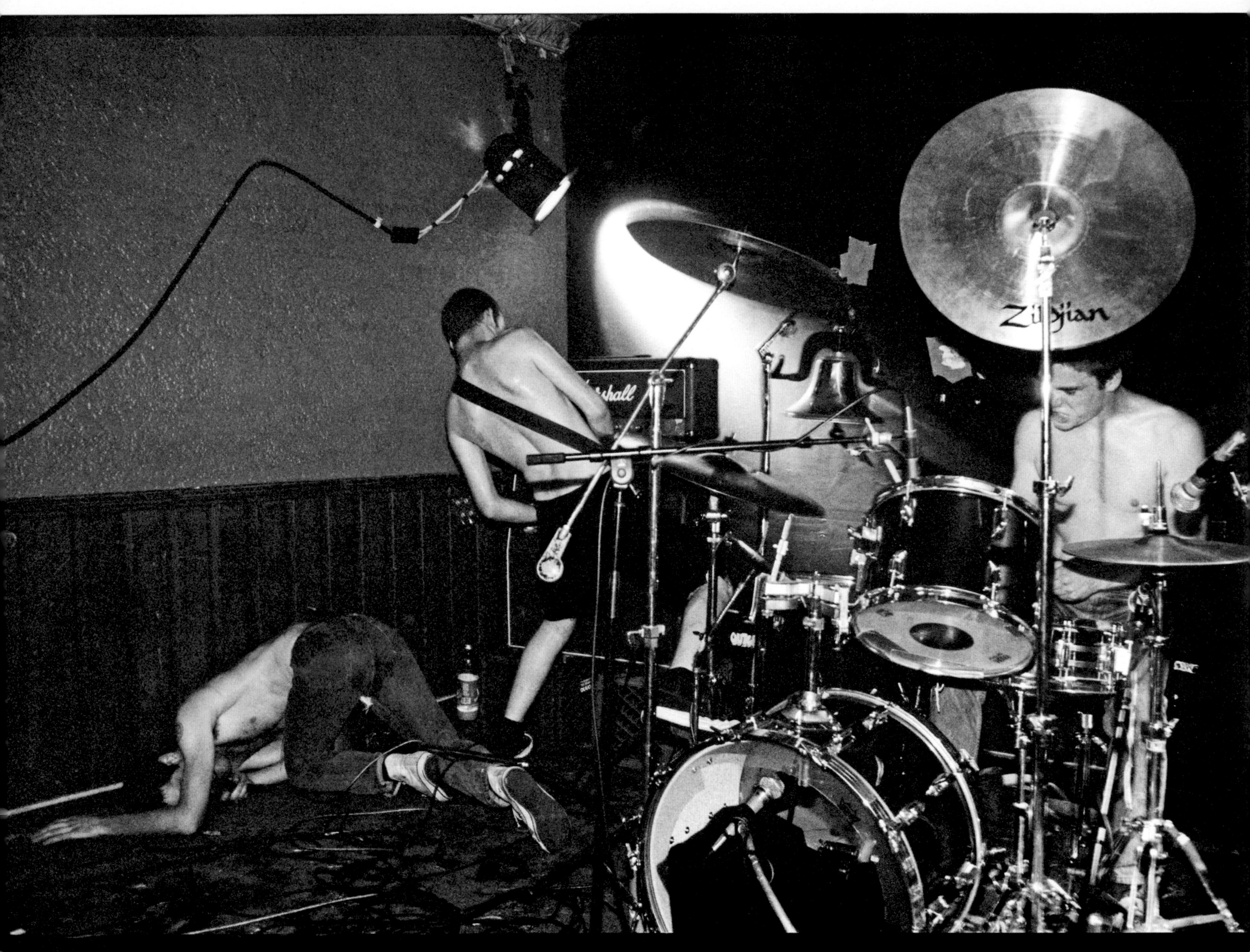

Of course I had seen Fugazi play before this evening, but this was the first time I shot them, on one of their first northern tours.
"Fresh" was a word being used in hip-hop a lot at this time, but the way it could be applied to this Fugazi show was an entirely different matter.

brendan #1

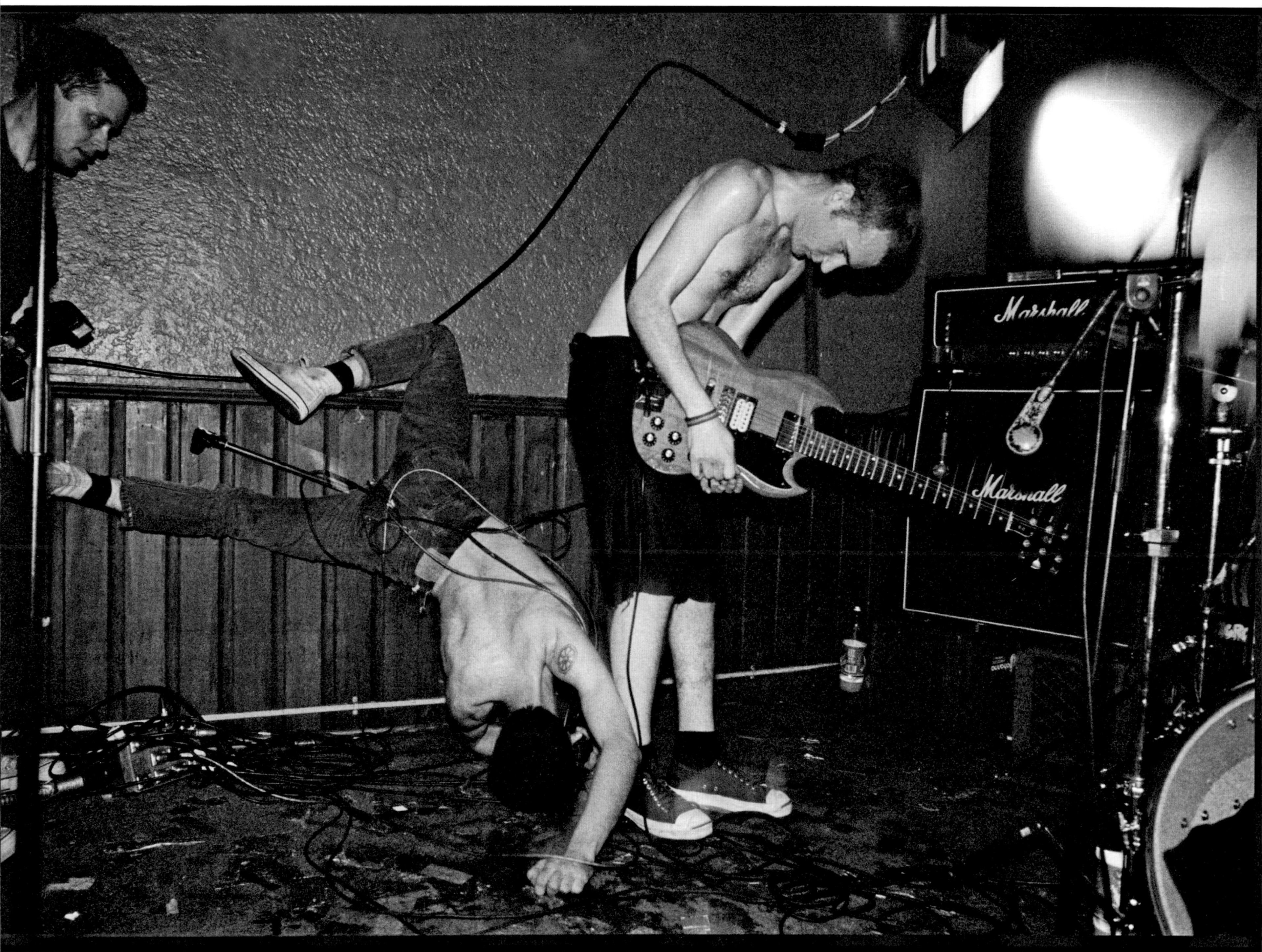

This photo was used on the inner sleeve of the first EP.

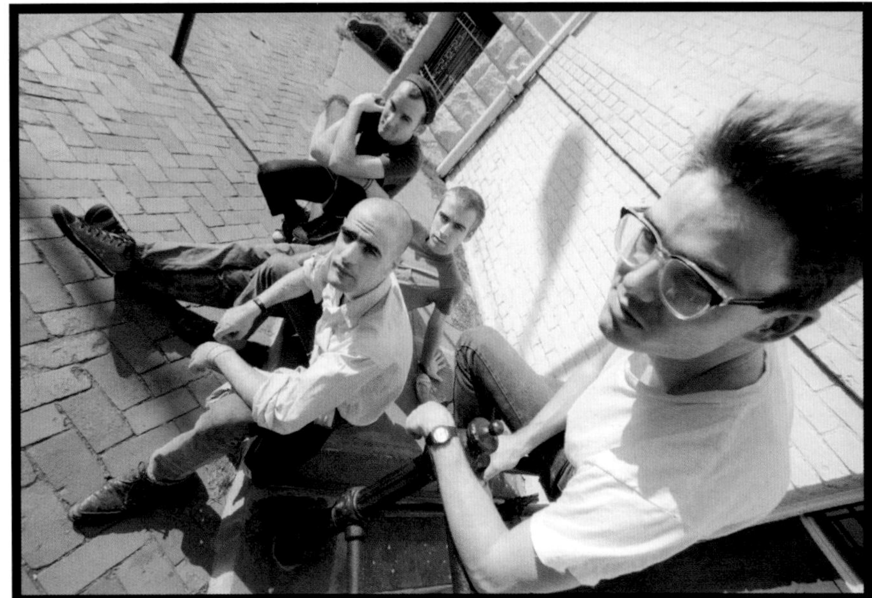

This photo was used on the back cover of the first LP.

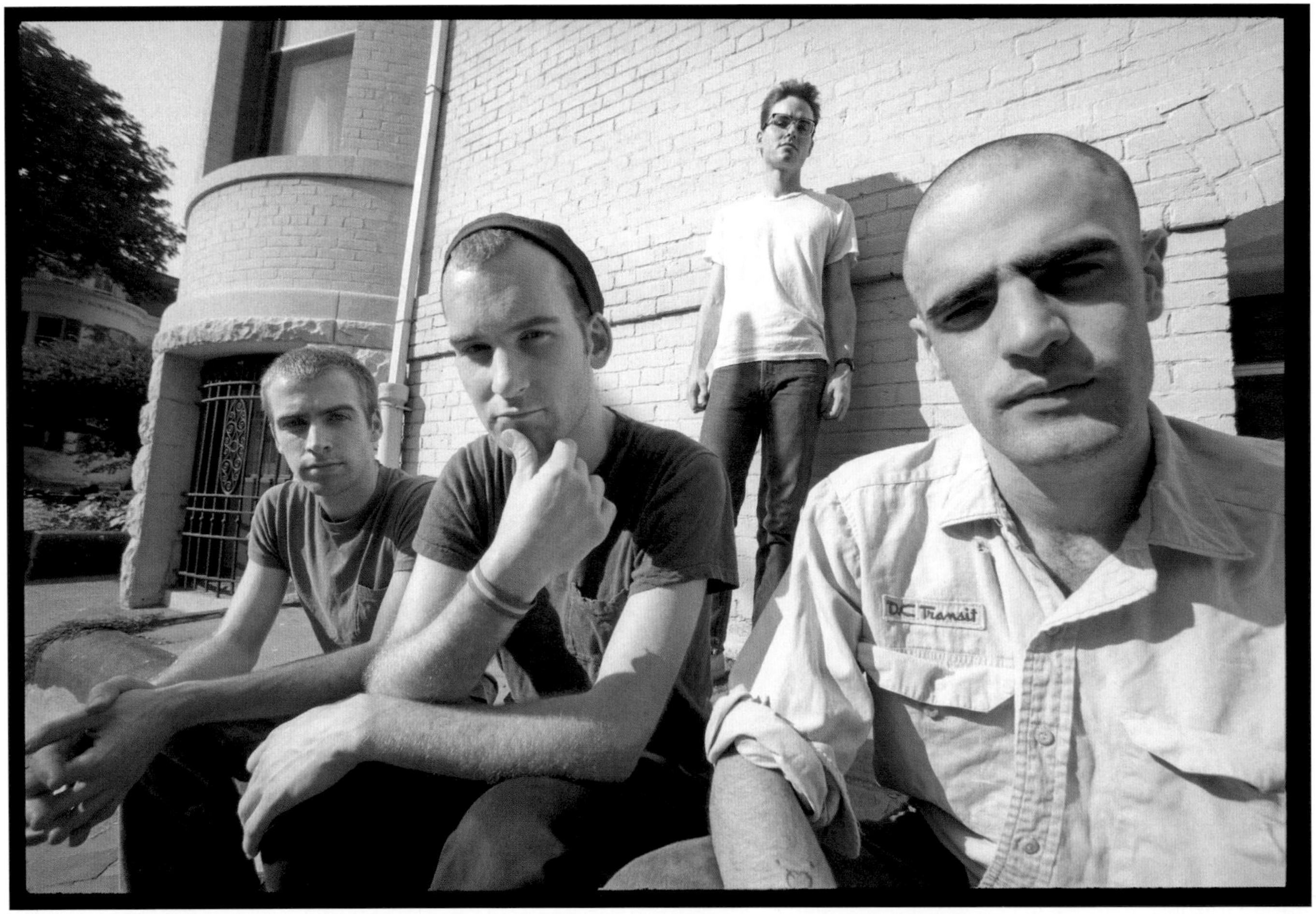

WASHINGTON, DC, 1989

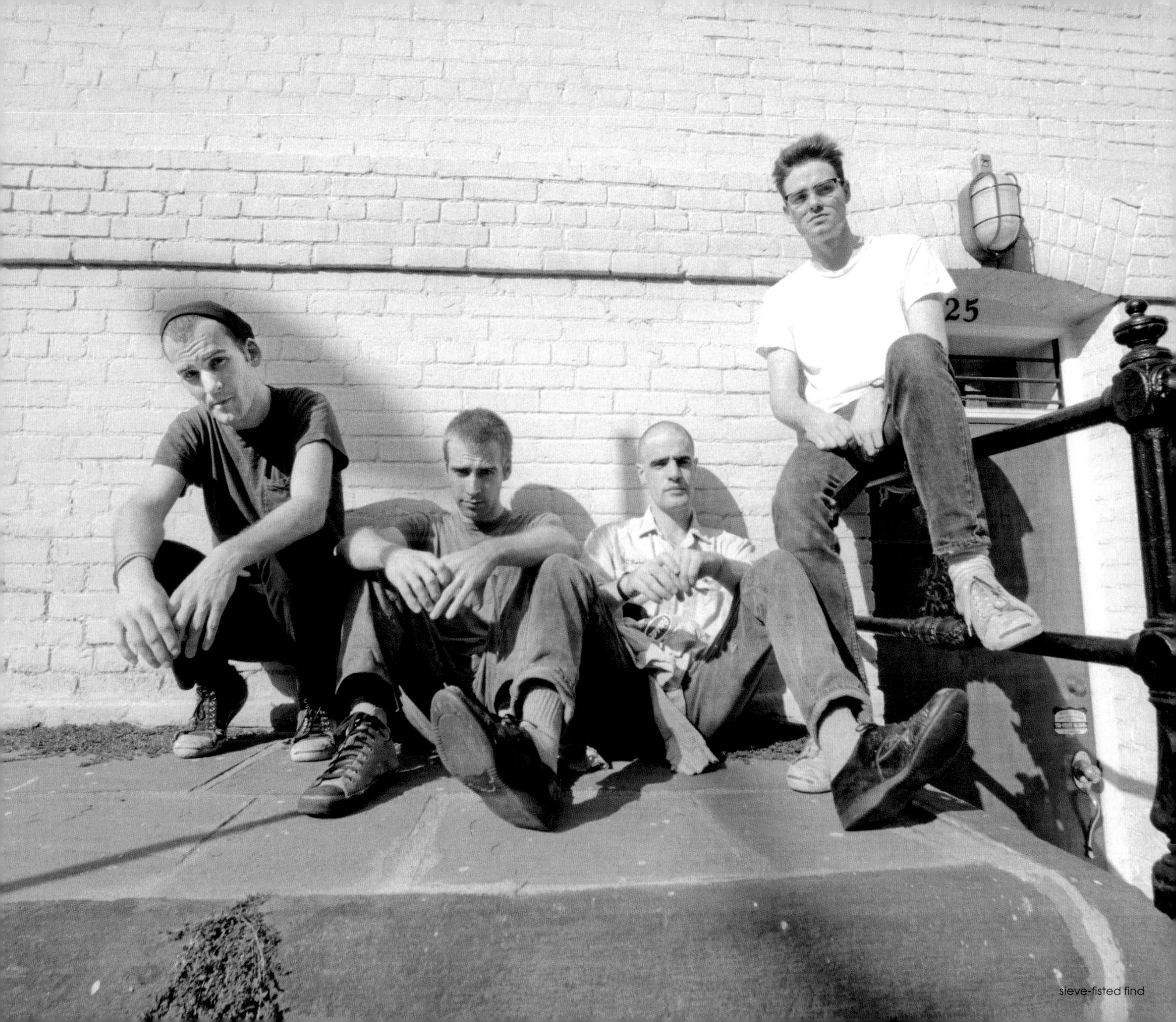

sieve-fisted find

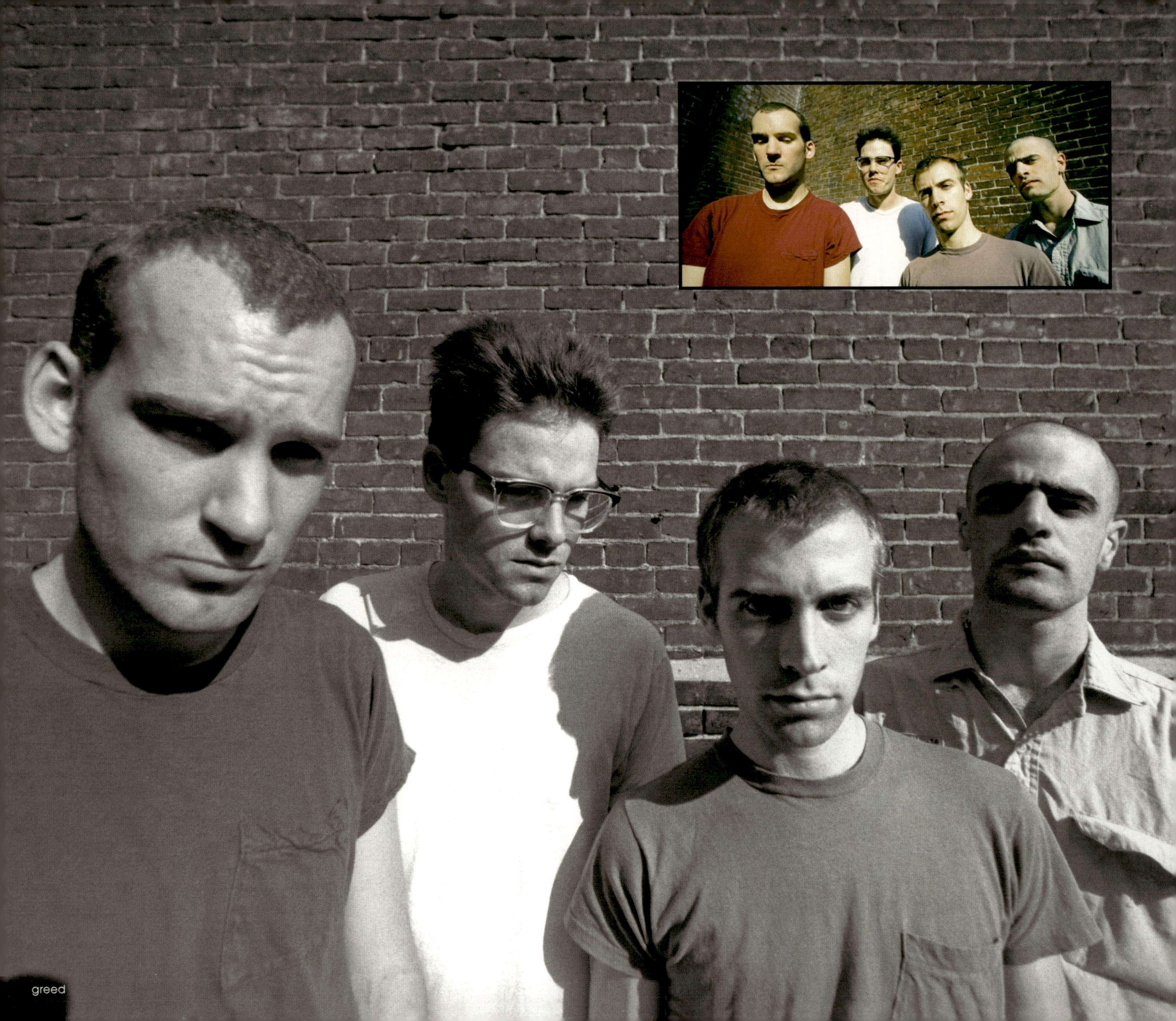

greed

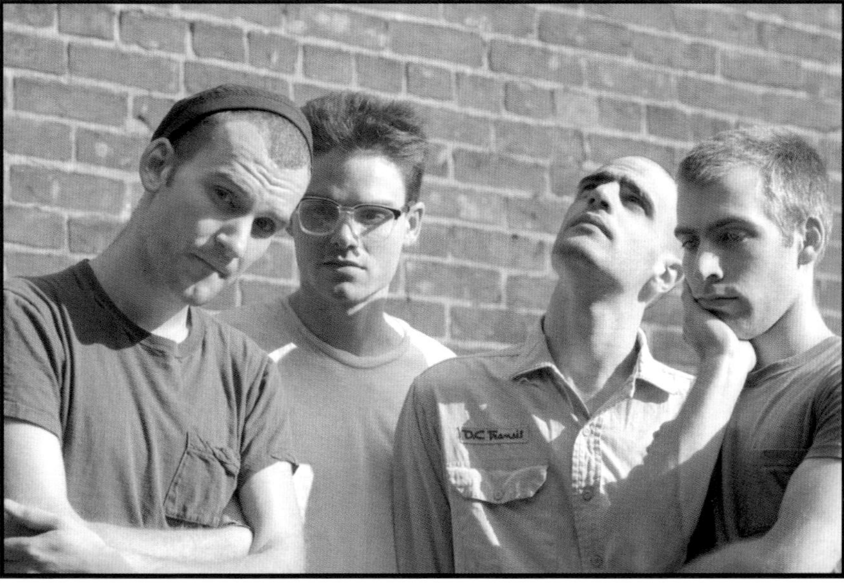

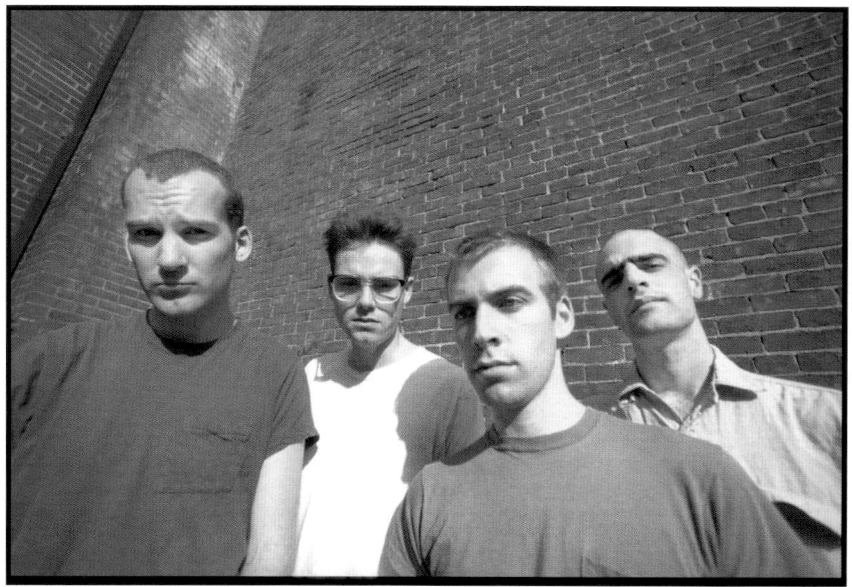

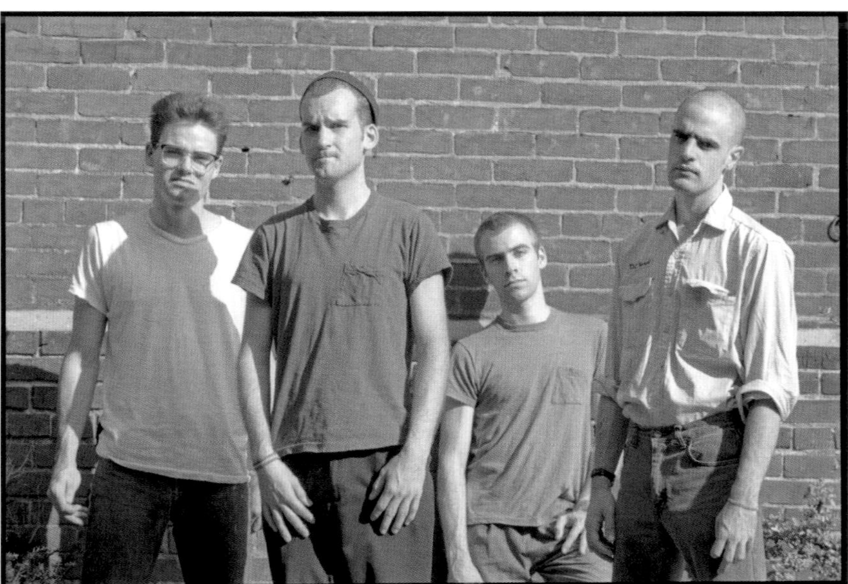

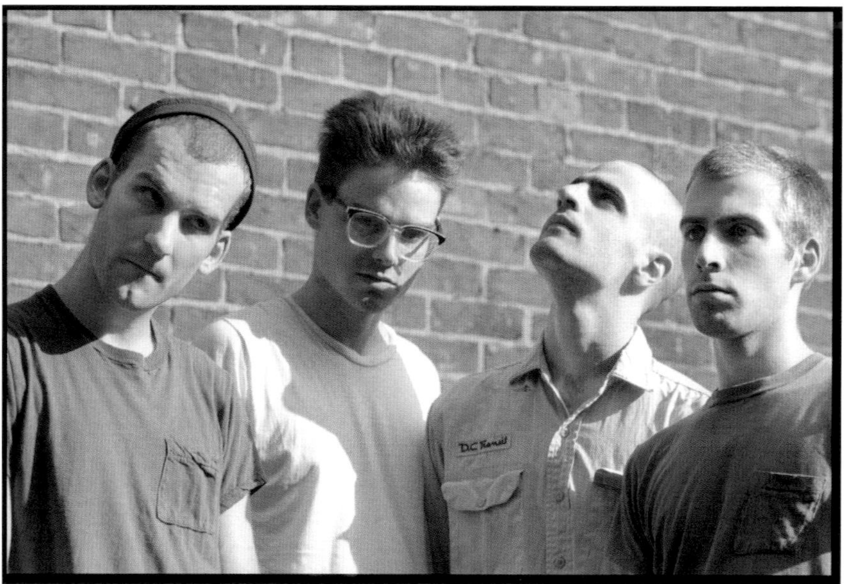

Almost every time we would shoot pictures of a live performance, if we had the opportunity we would take a couple of portraits before the show. This being the first time for three of the guys to be shuffling in front of my lens, it was not too easy or comfortable, but considering they had a gig in the park to play just an hour later, I think they did pretty well. After all, they were punks from the start, and attitude always works well on film.

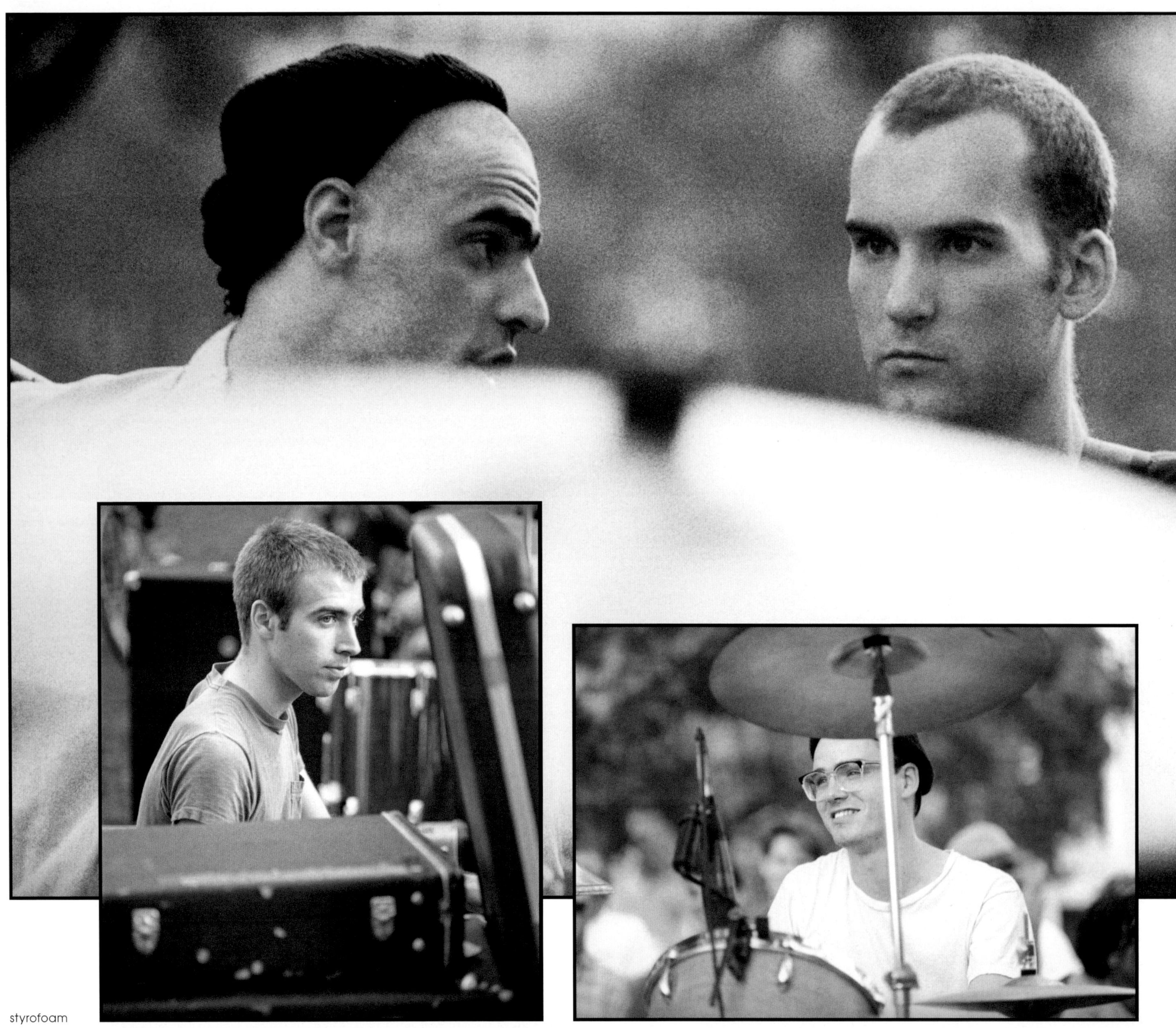

styrofoam

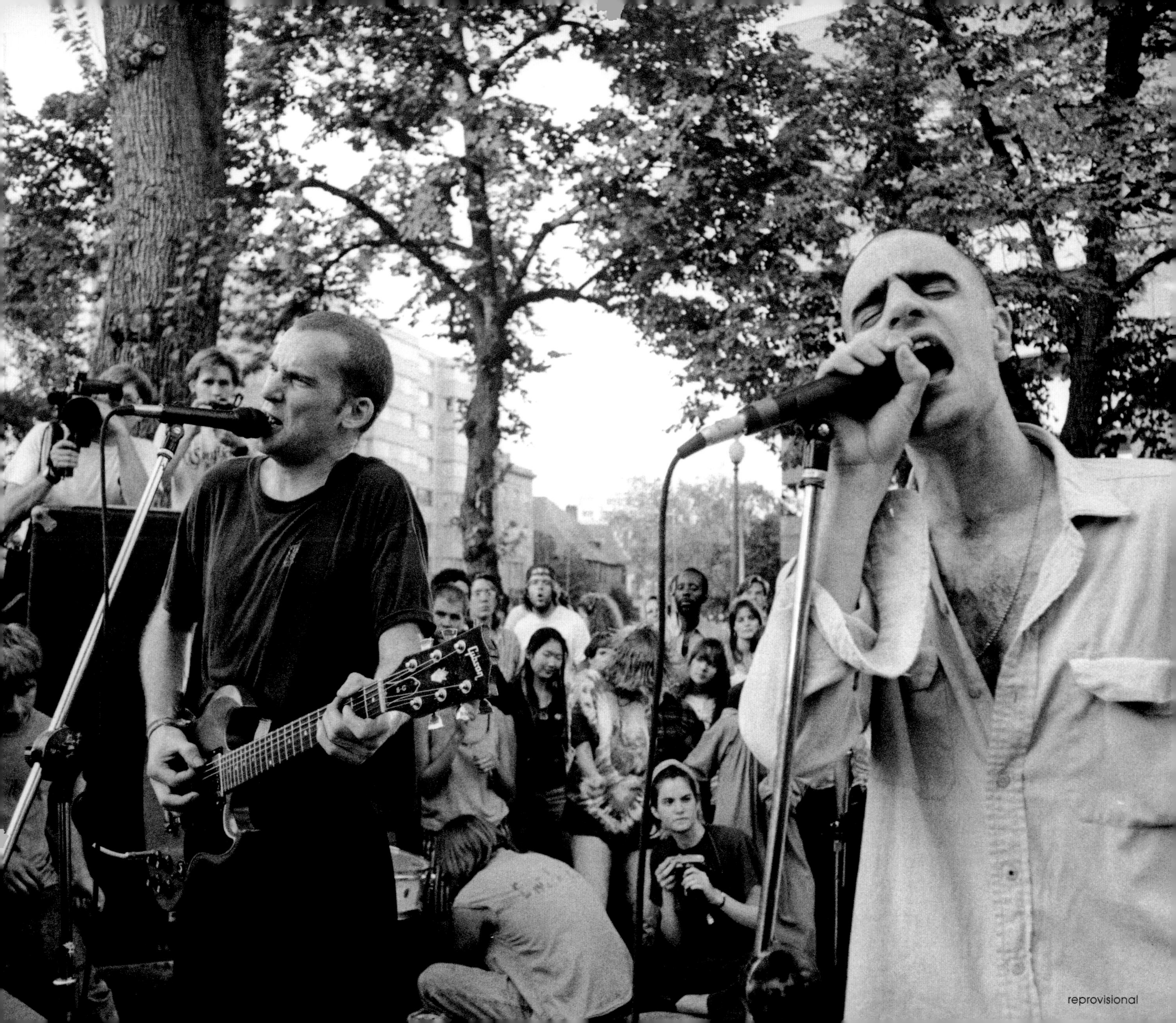

reprovisional

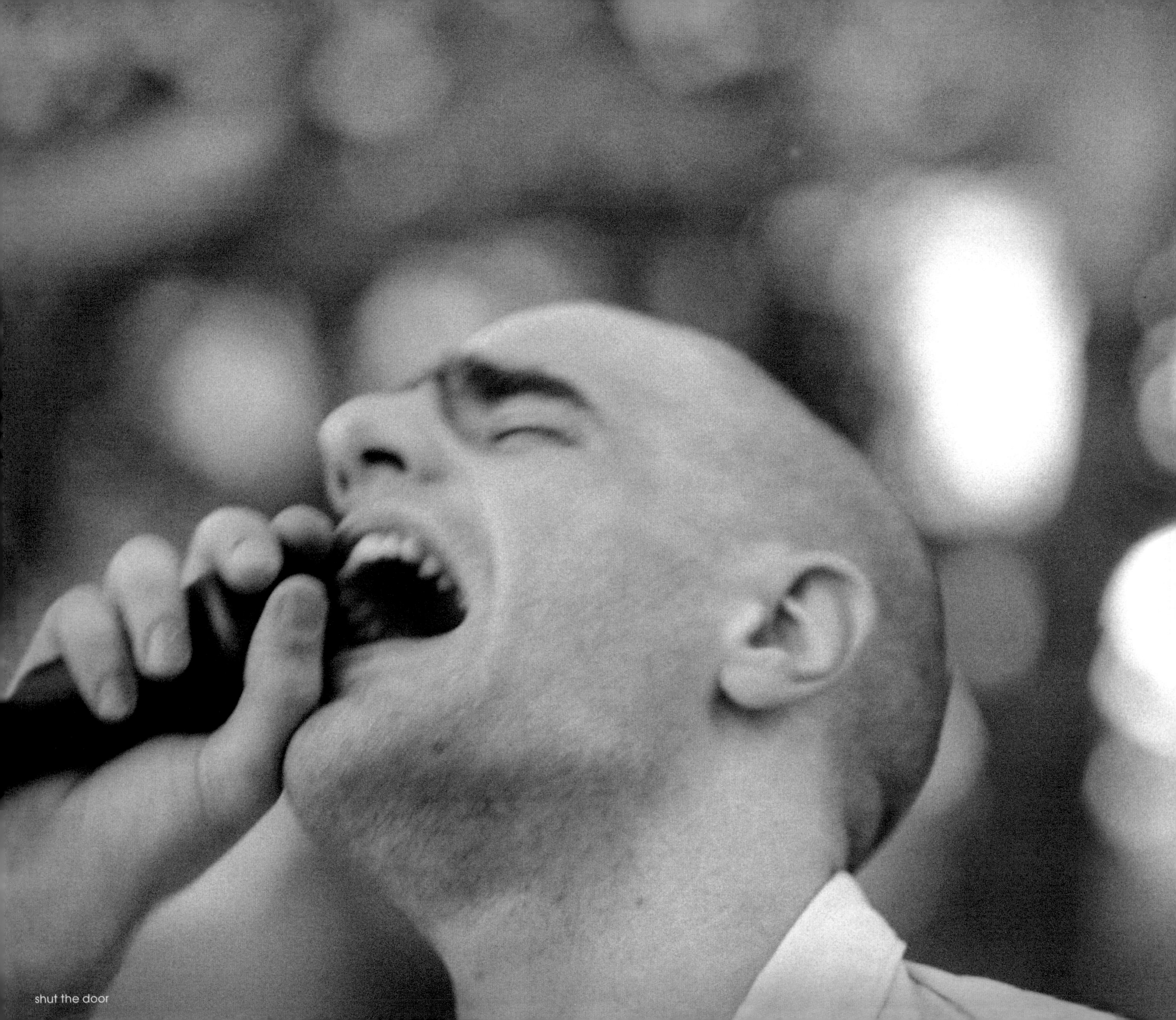

shut the door

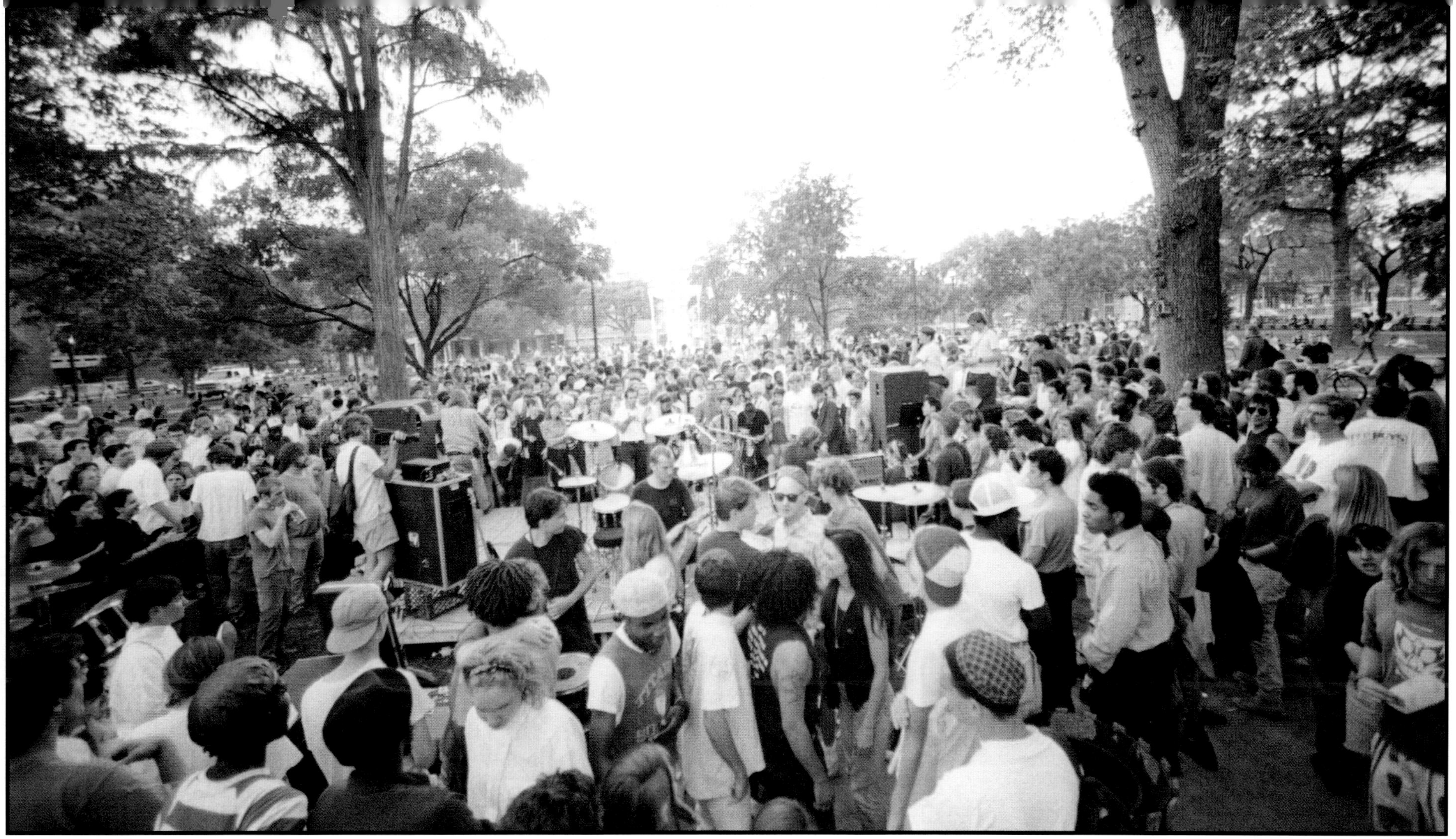

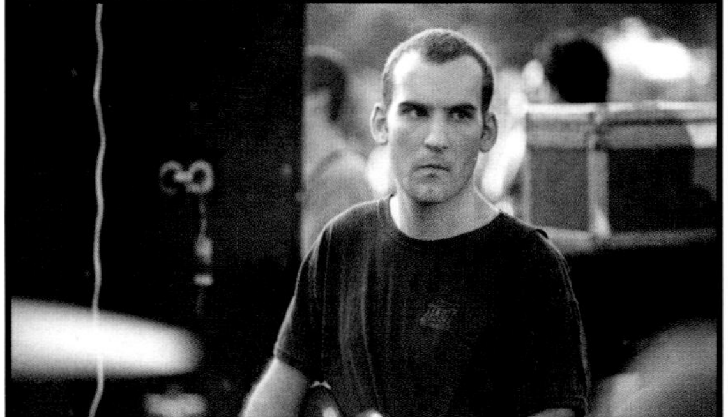

Shows are always serious, but in DC
a lot of friends and family are usually there.

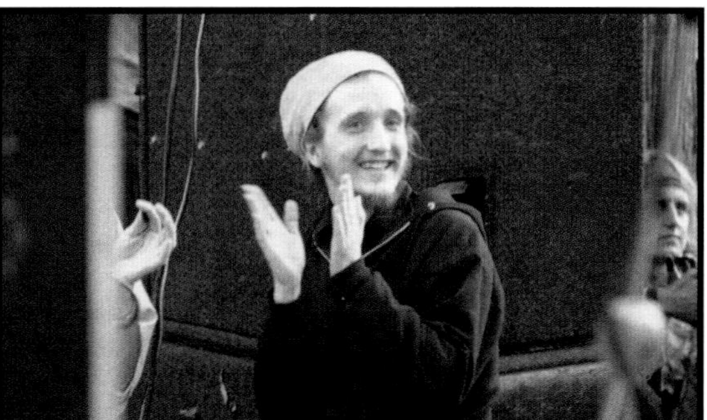

Tomas Squip

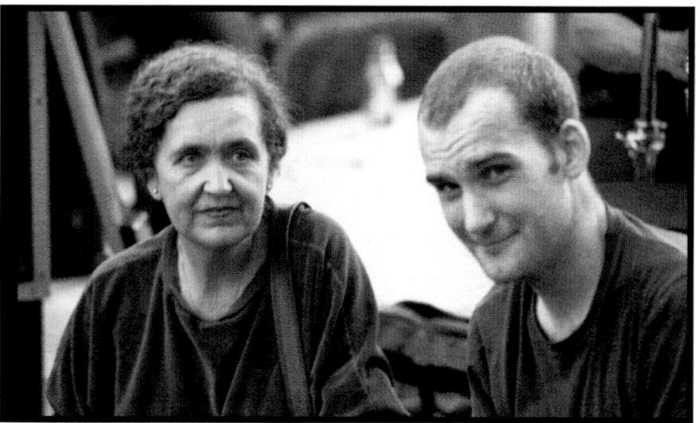

Ginger MacKaye

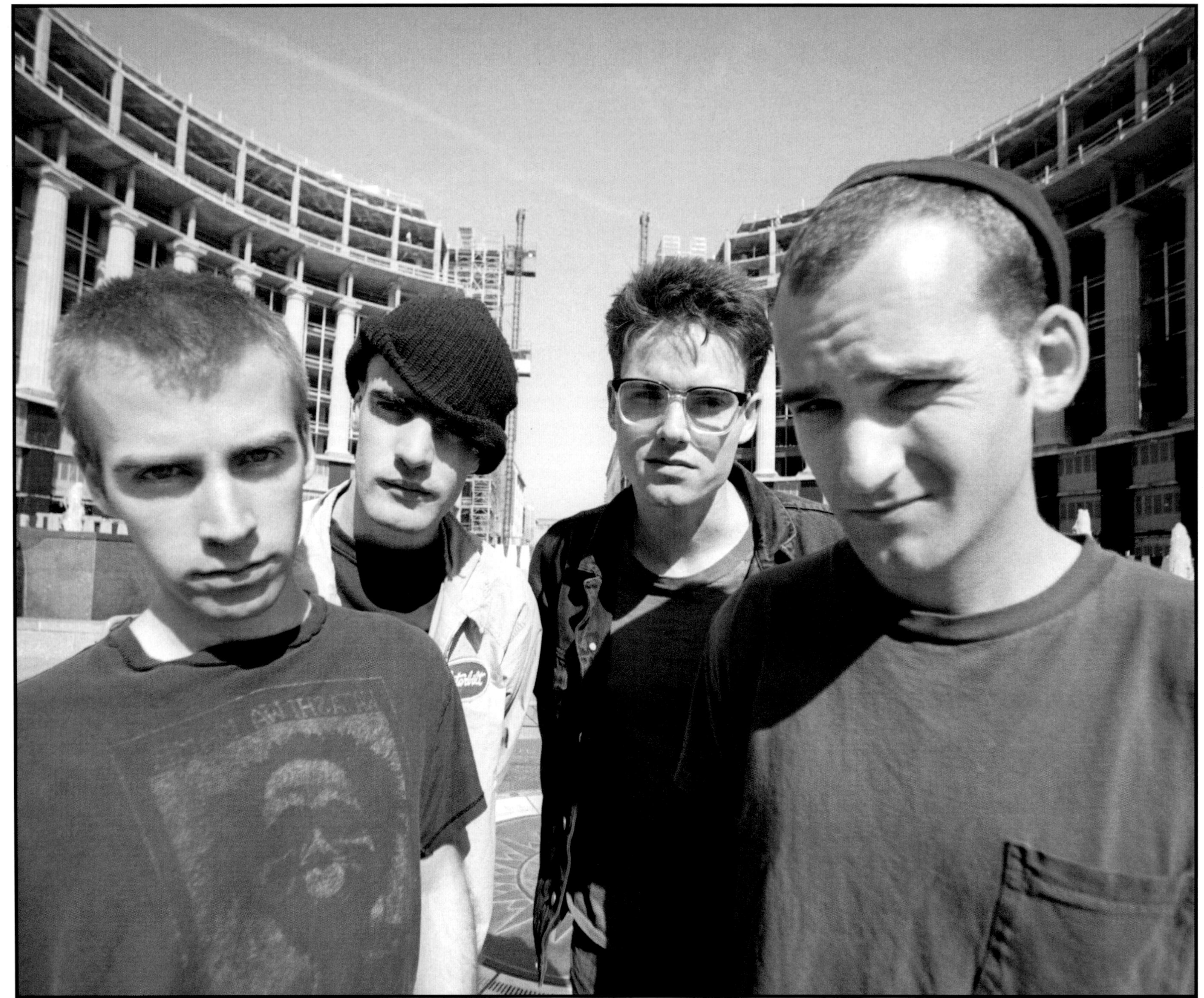

DC, 1992

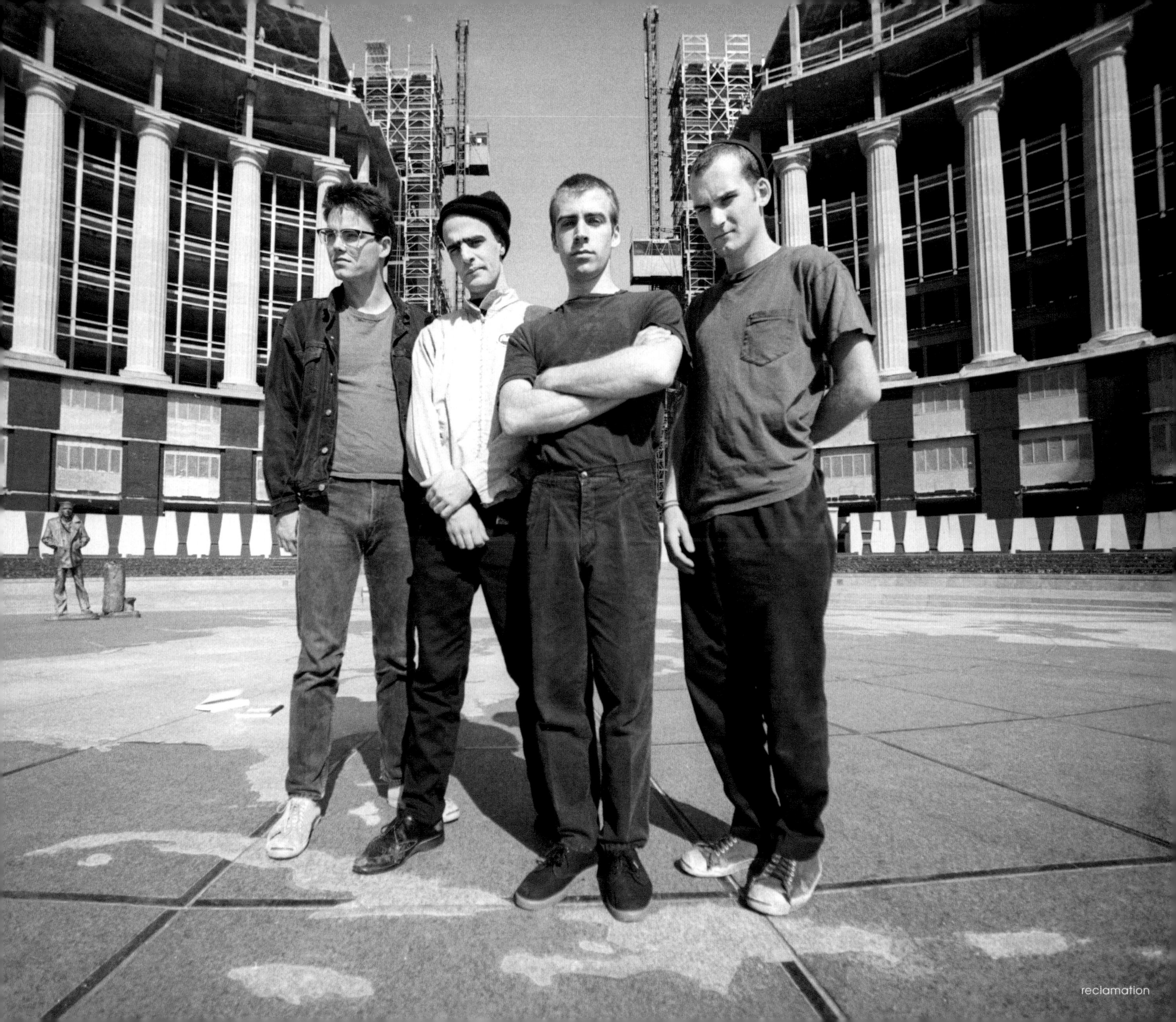

reclamation

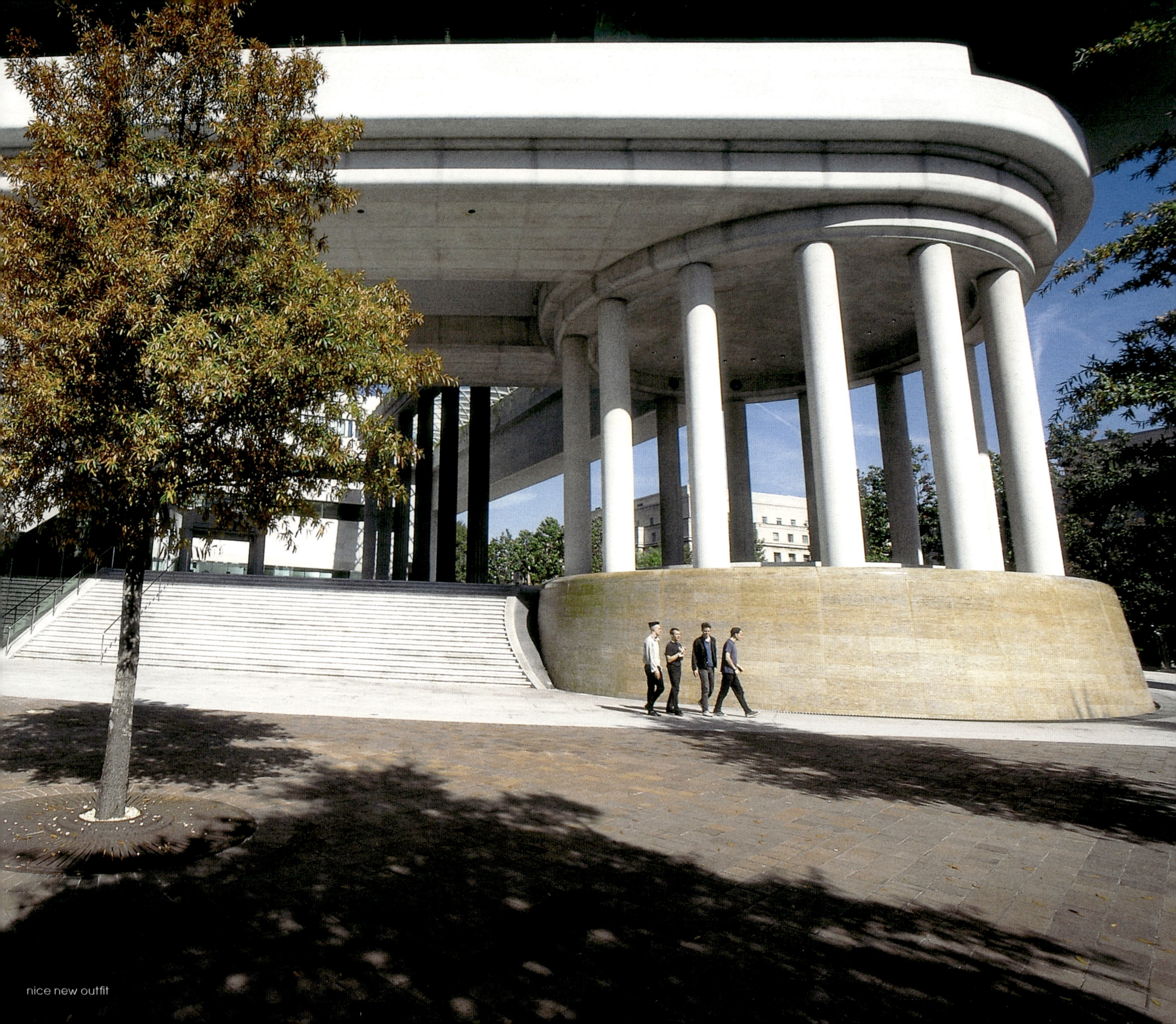

nice new outfit

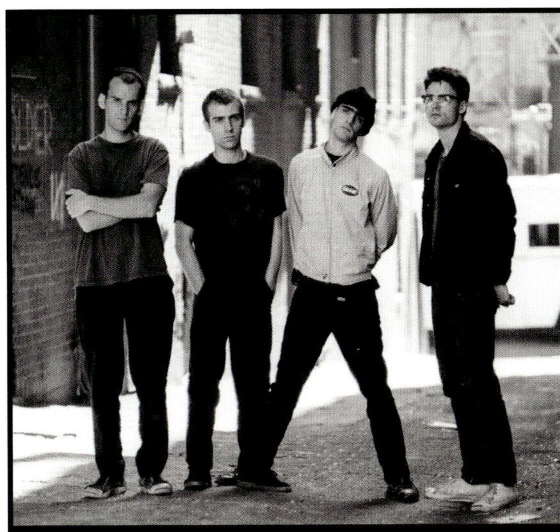

Walking around town before the show looking for cool locations.

As you can see on the first page of the book, the common DC landmarks were something to be avoided at almost all costs if I wanted a comfortable-looking shot.

Although the iconic landmarks represent DC to most outsiders, myself included, for many of the real residents, Washington, DC, is a place far from what the big monuments represent.

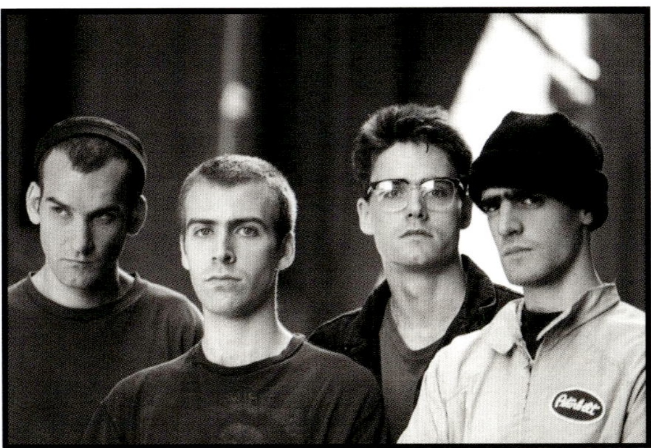

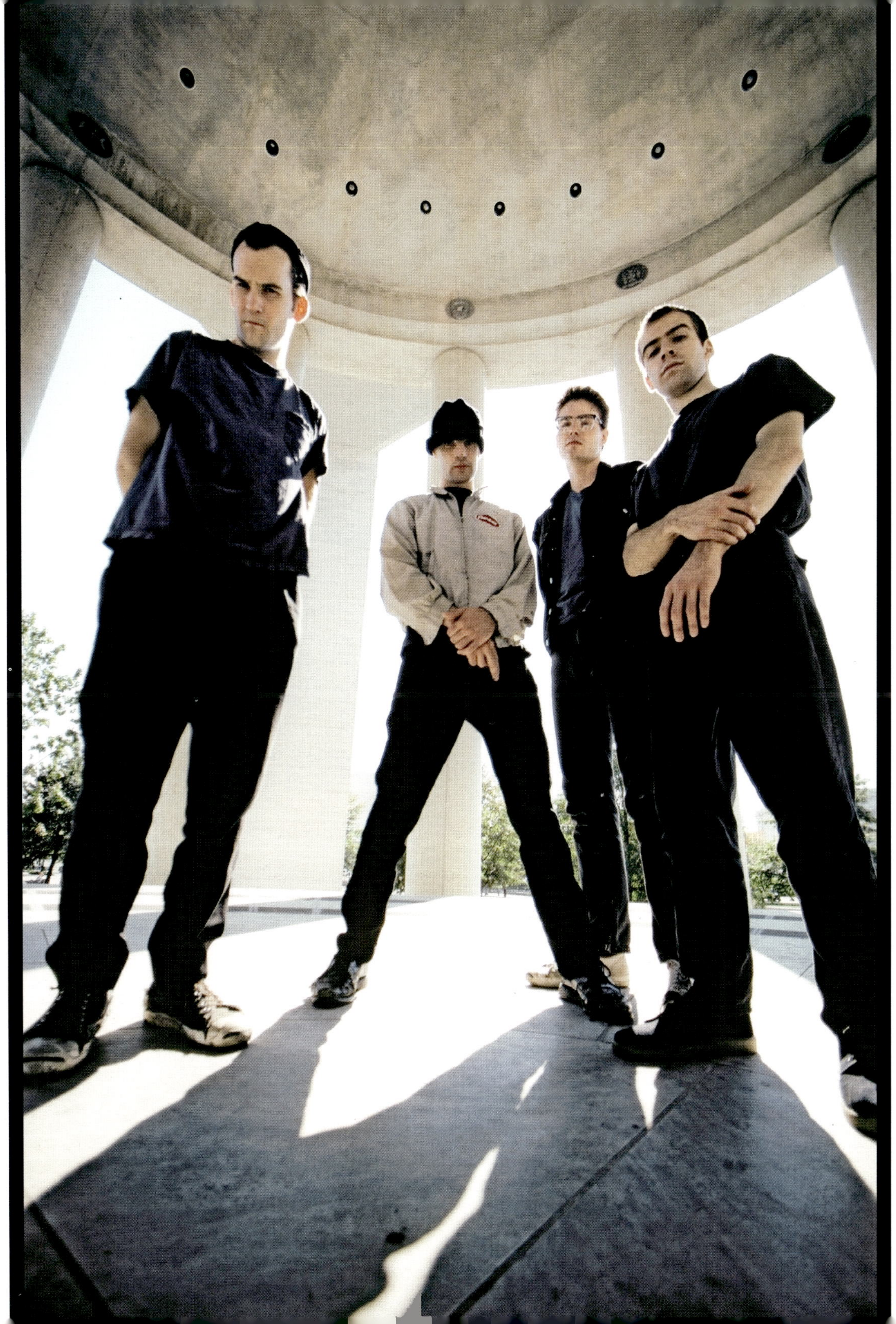

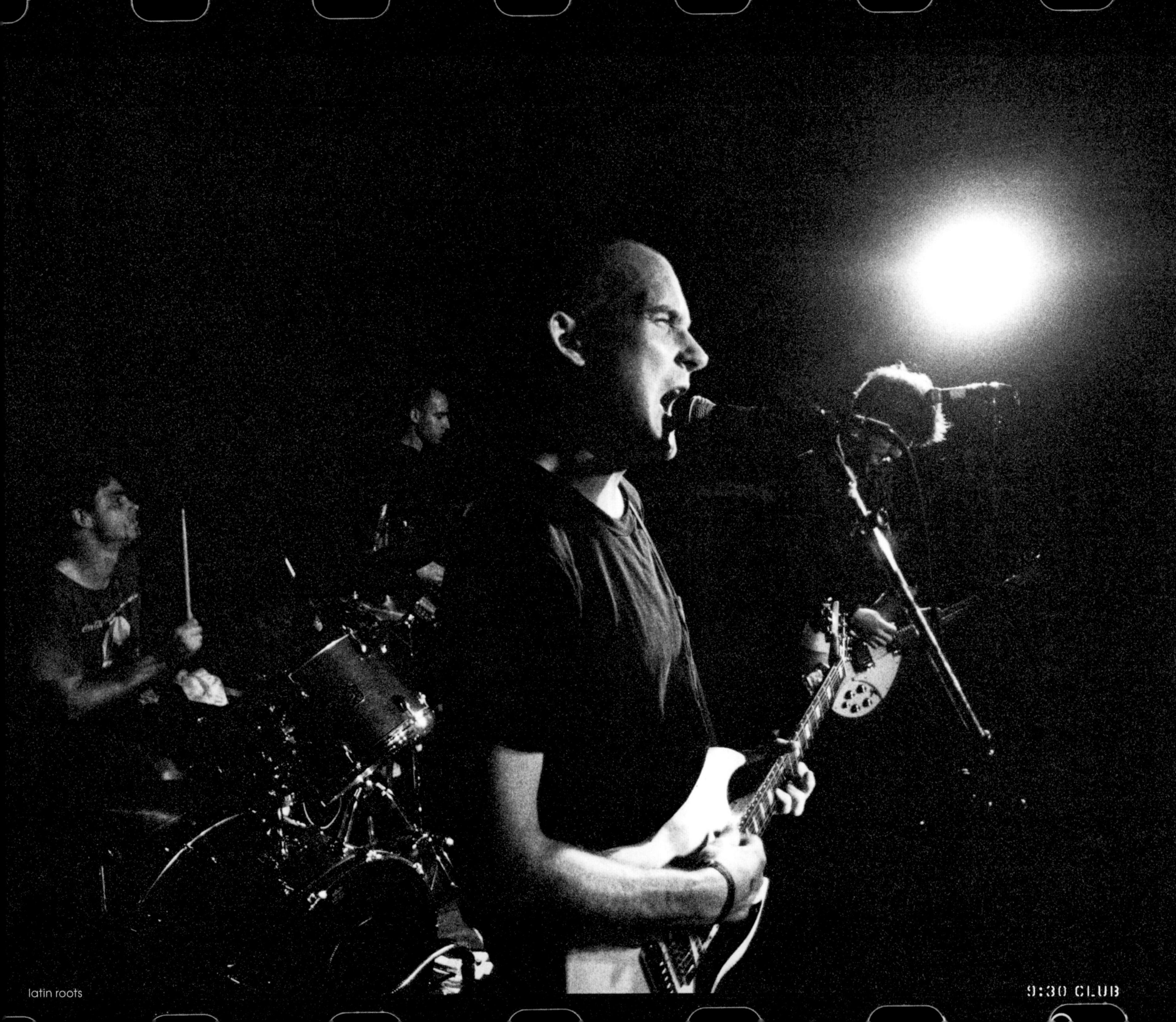
latin roots

9:30 CLUB

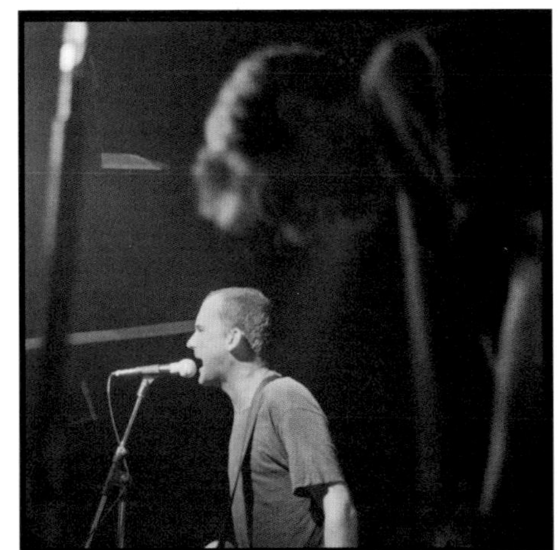

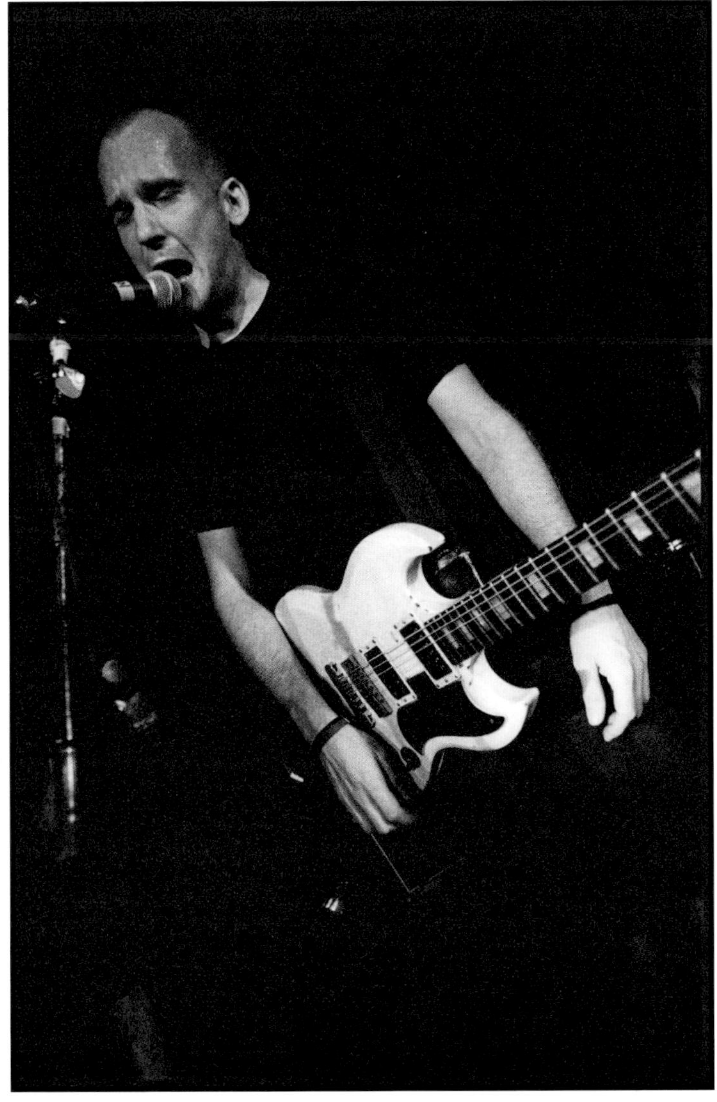

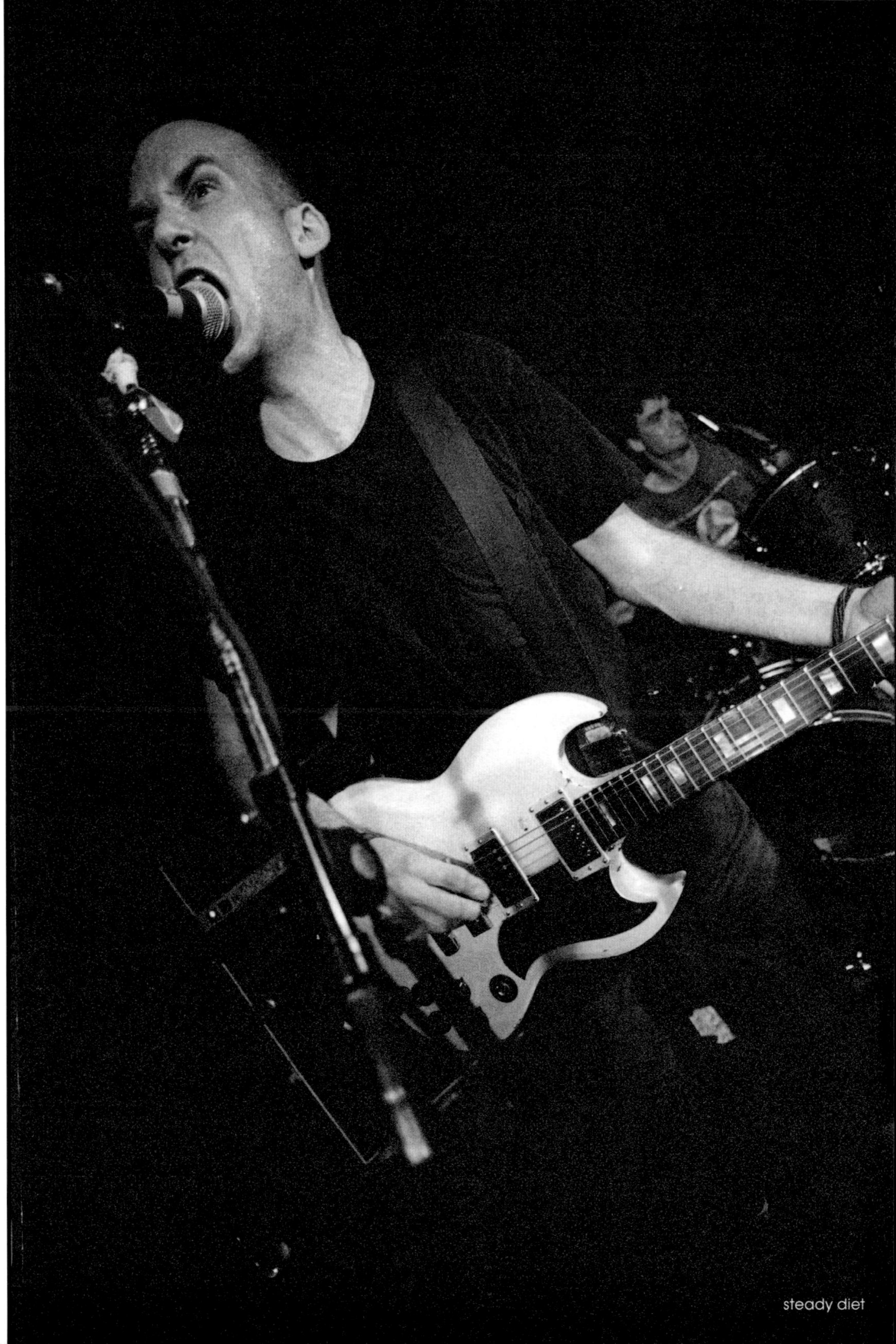

steady diet

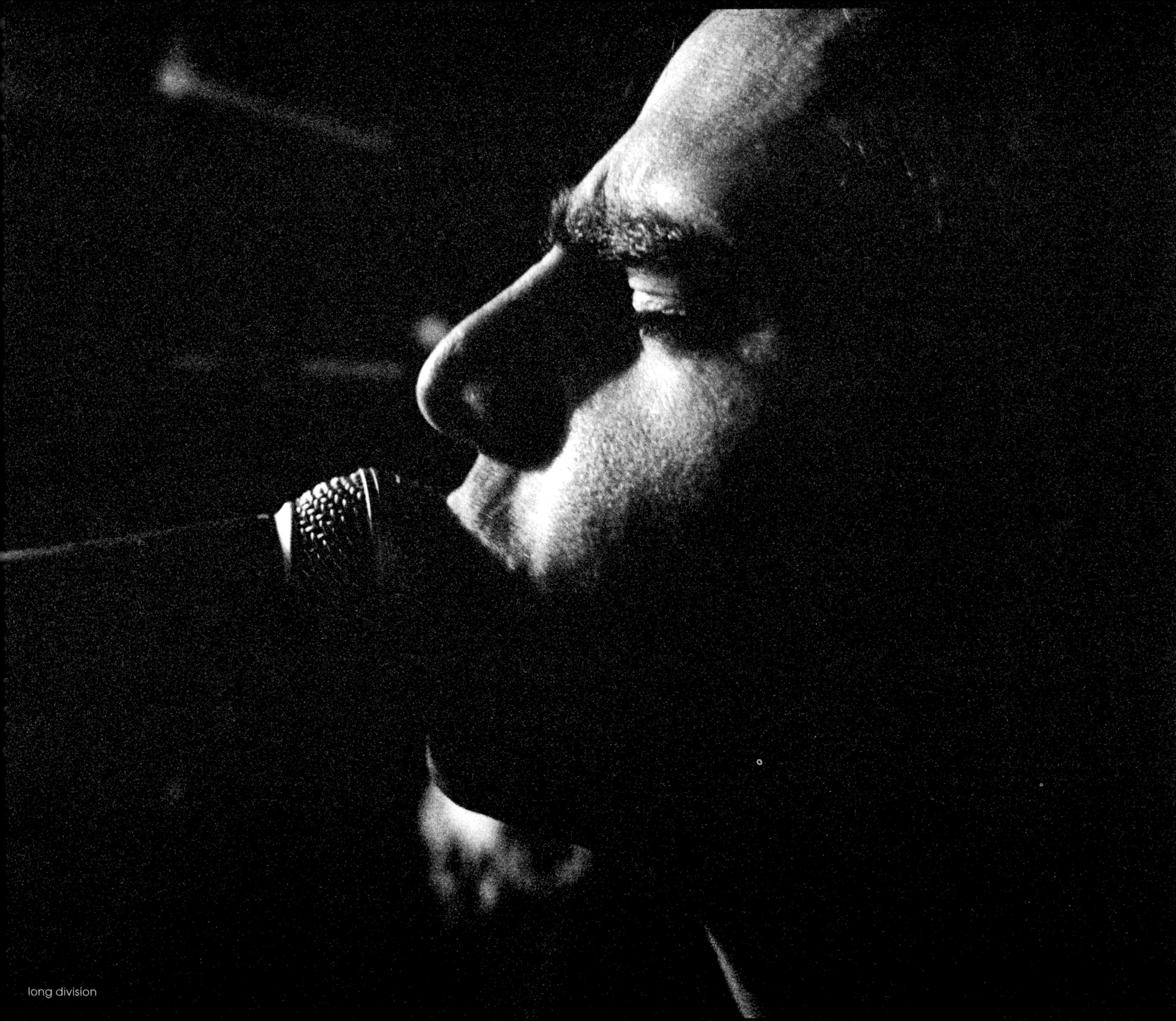

long division

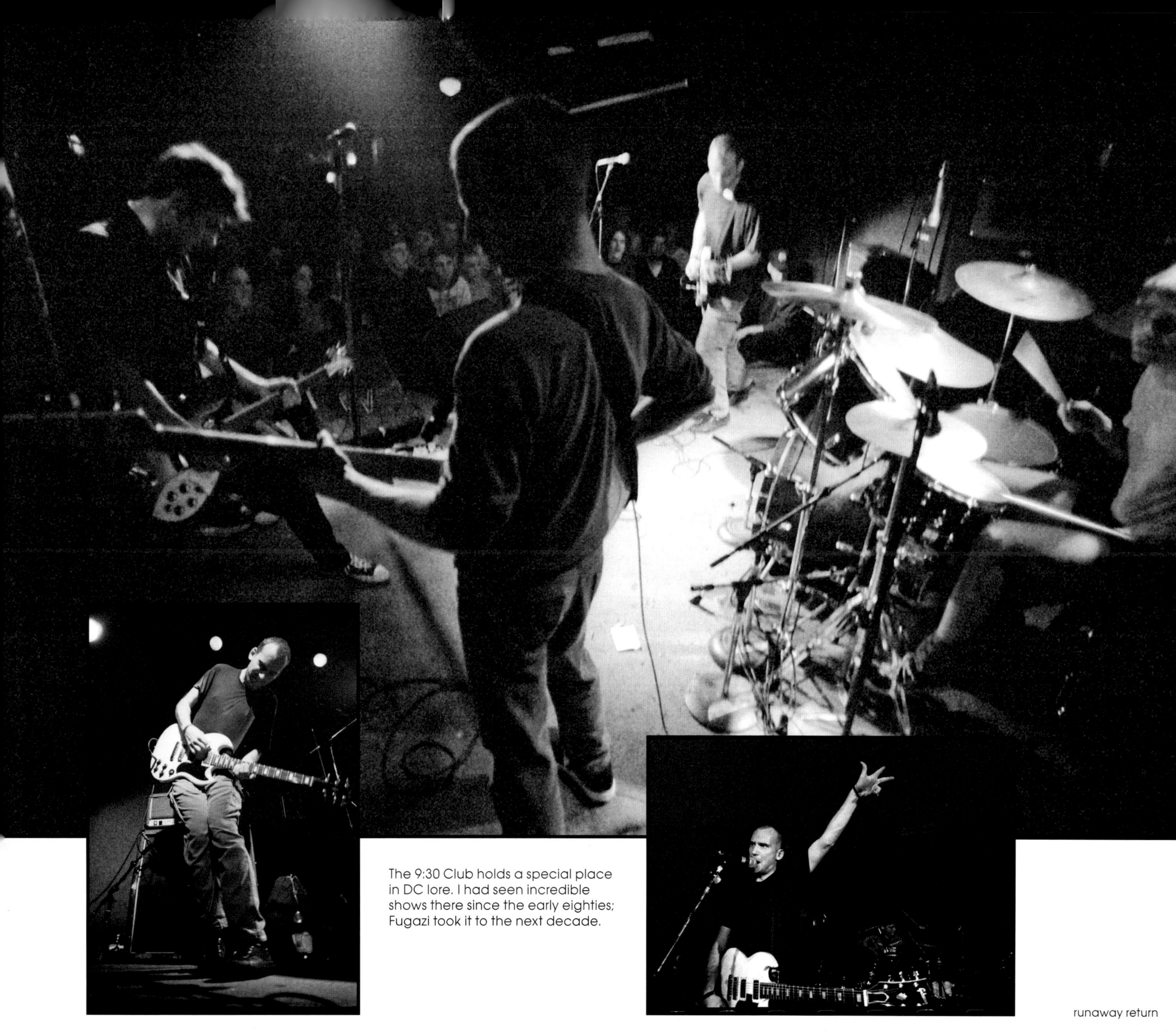

The 9:30 Club holds a special place in DC lore. I had seen incredible shows there since the early eighties; Fugazi took it to the next decade.

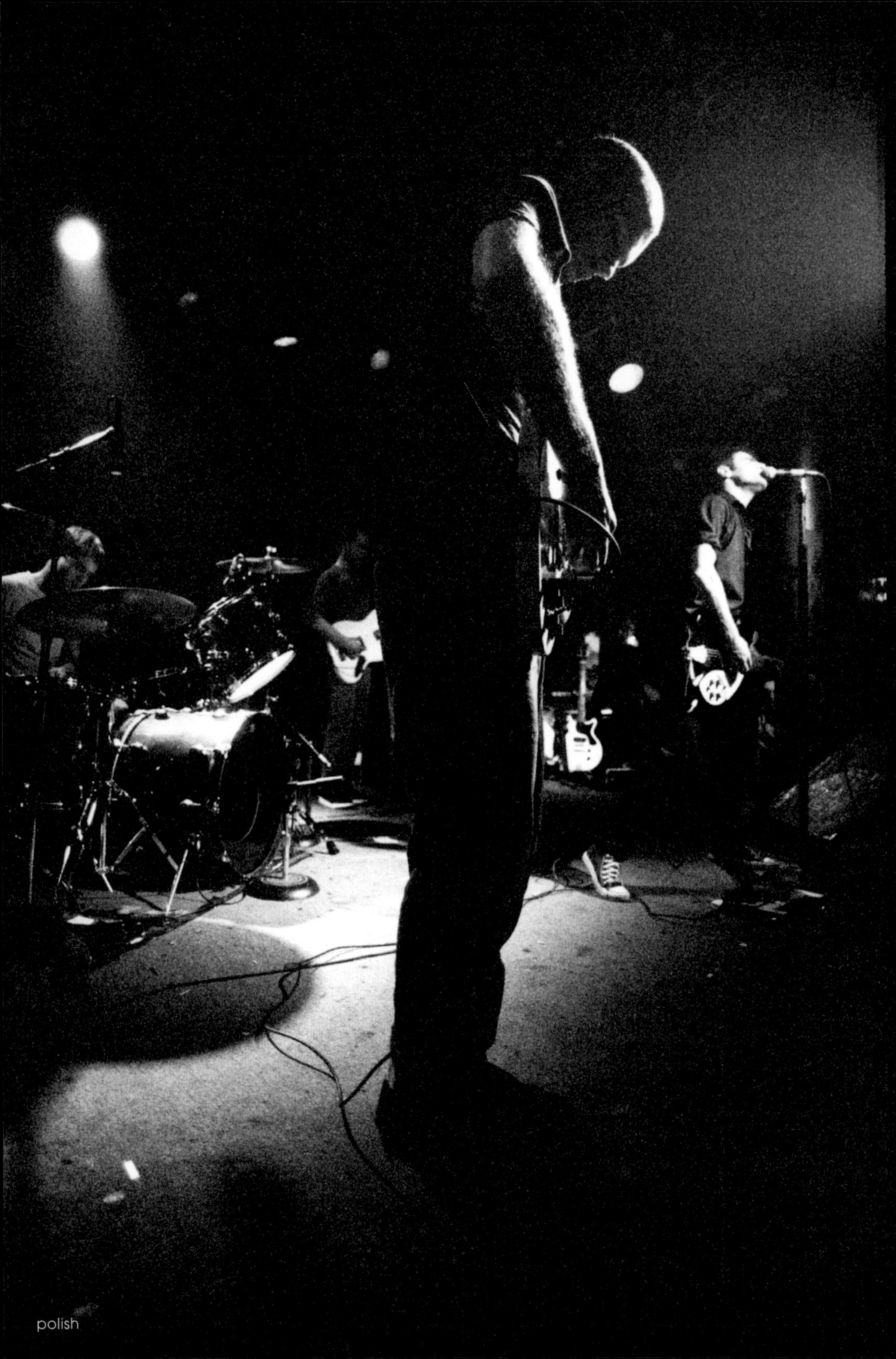

polish

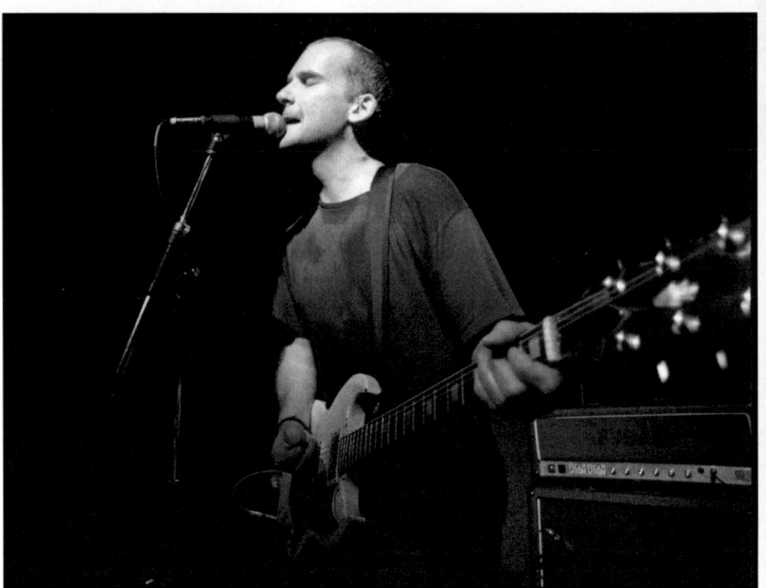

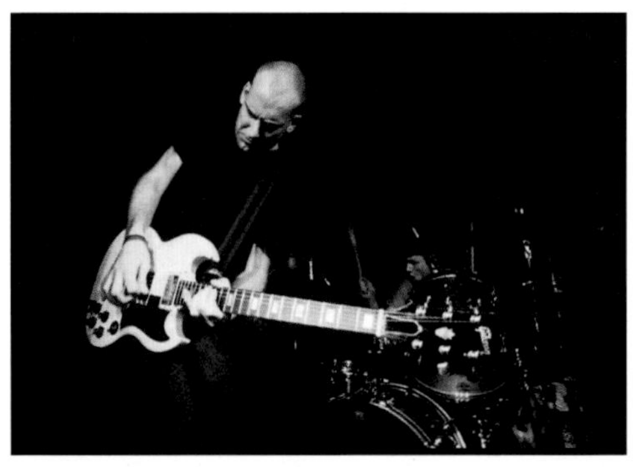

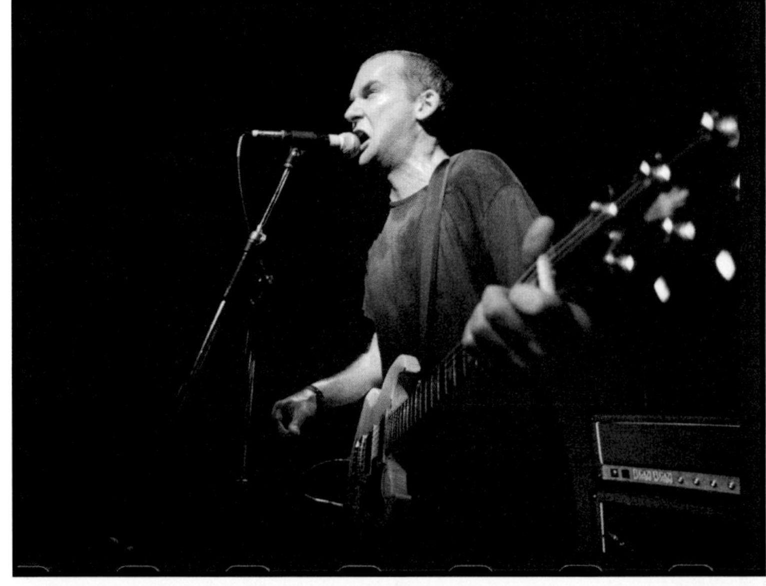

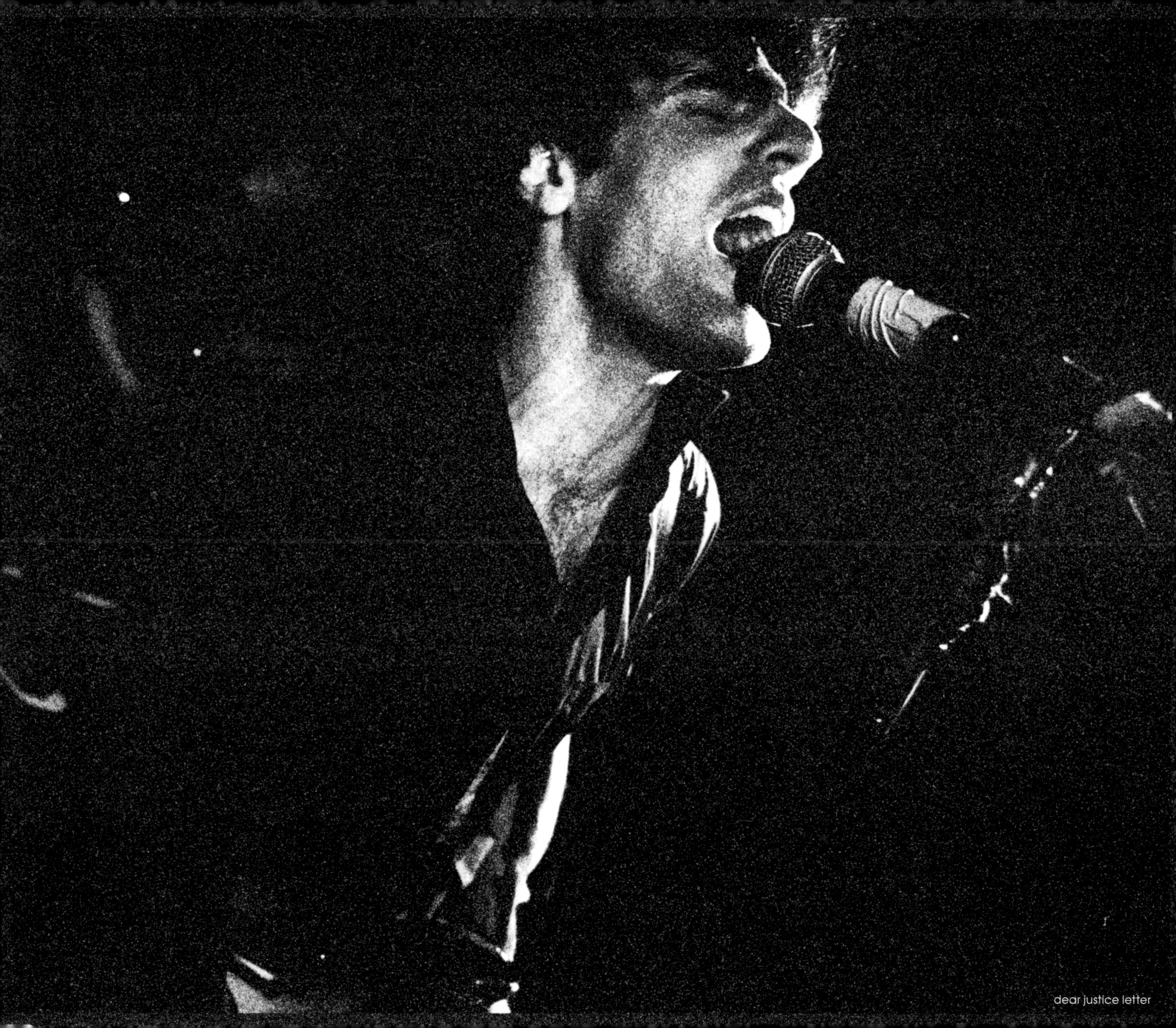
dear justice letter

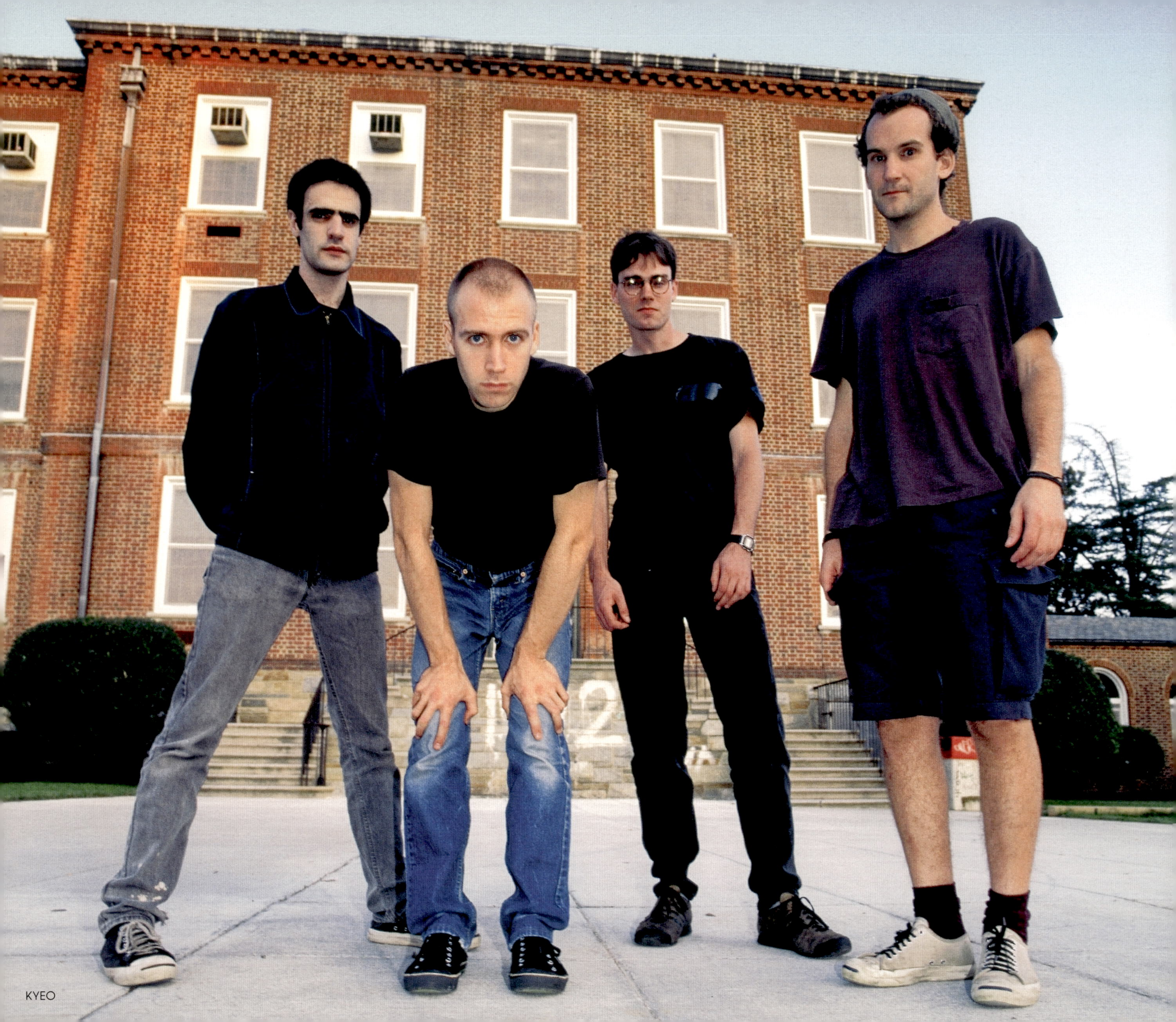

KYEO

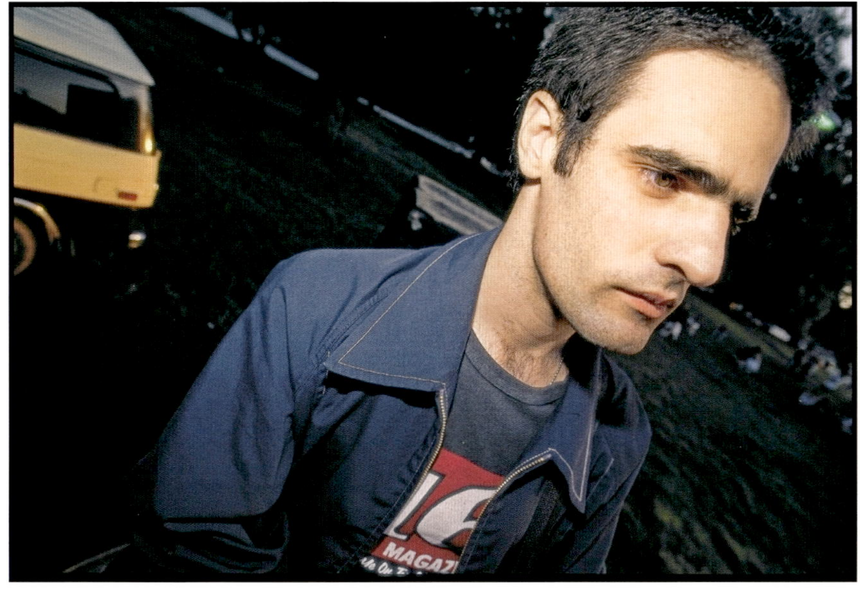

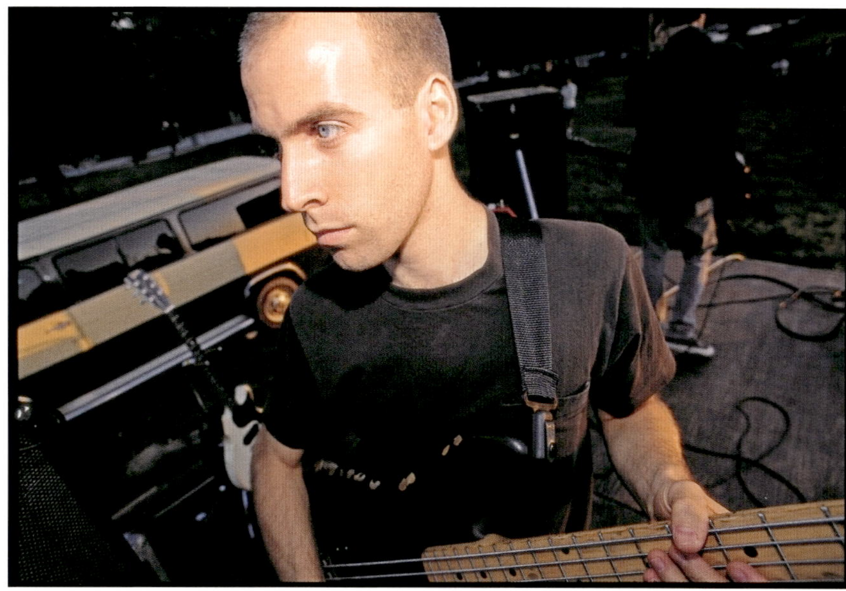

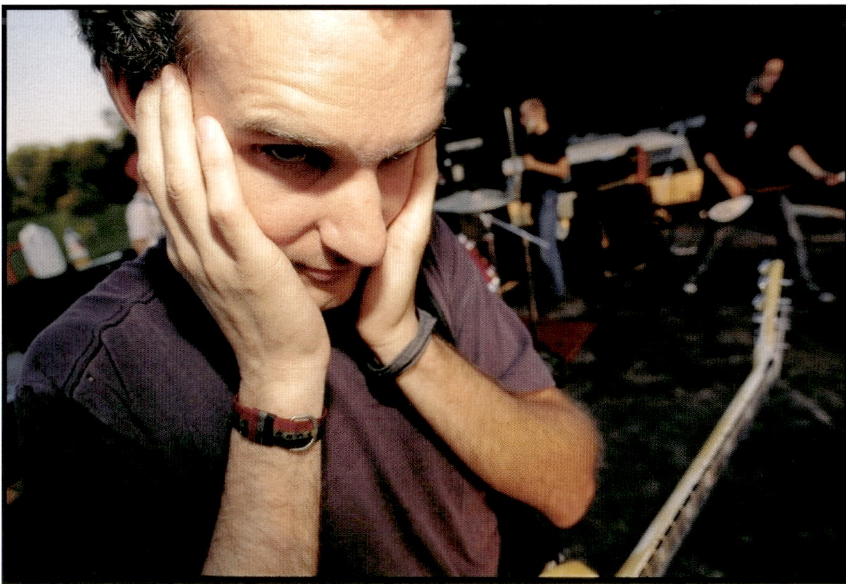

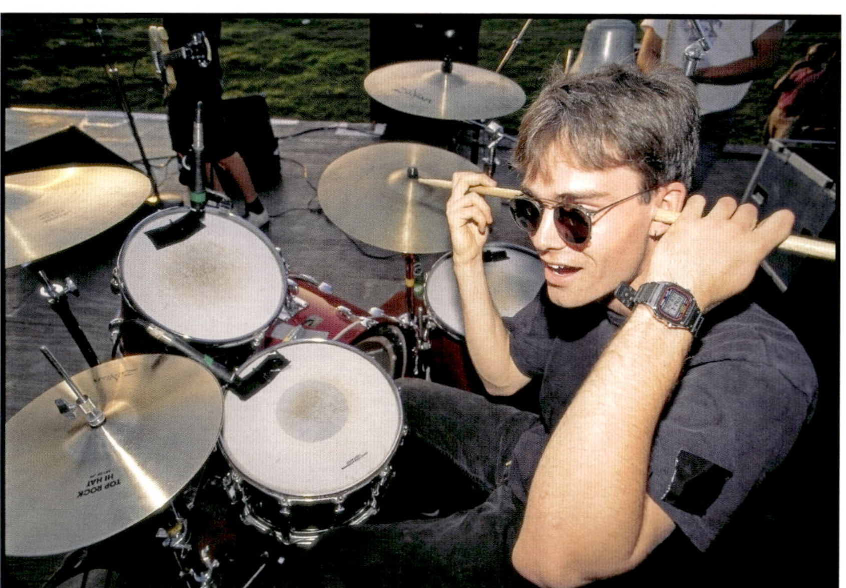

Wilson High School just accross the street from Fort Reno (left). Sound check portraits (above). In the field at Fort Reno (next page).

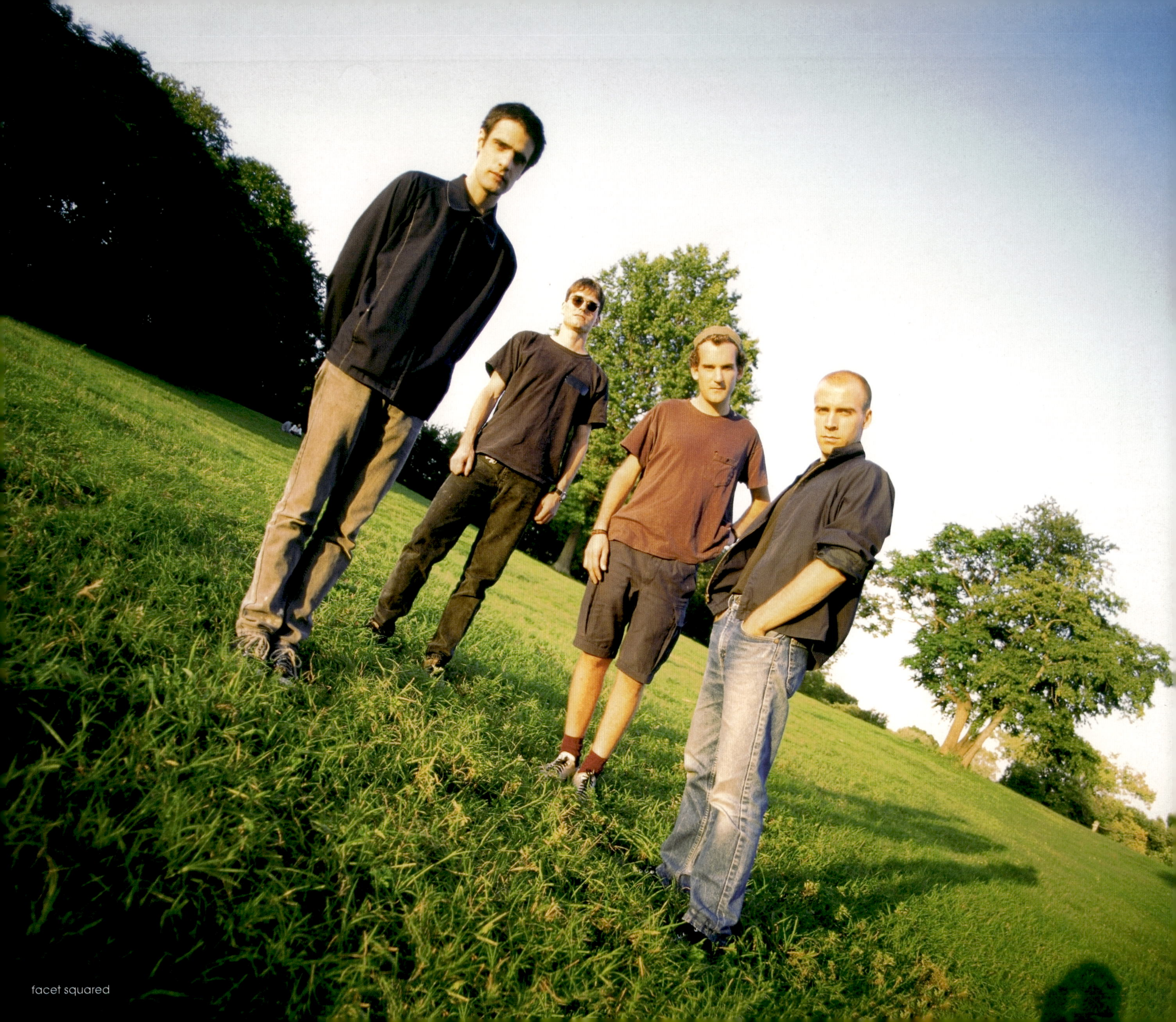

facet squared

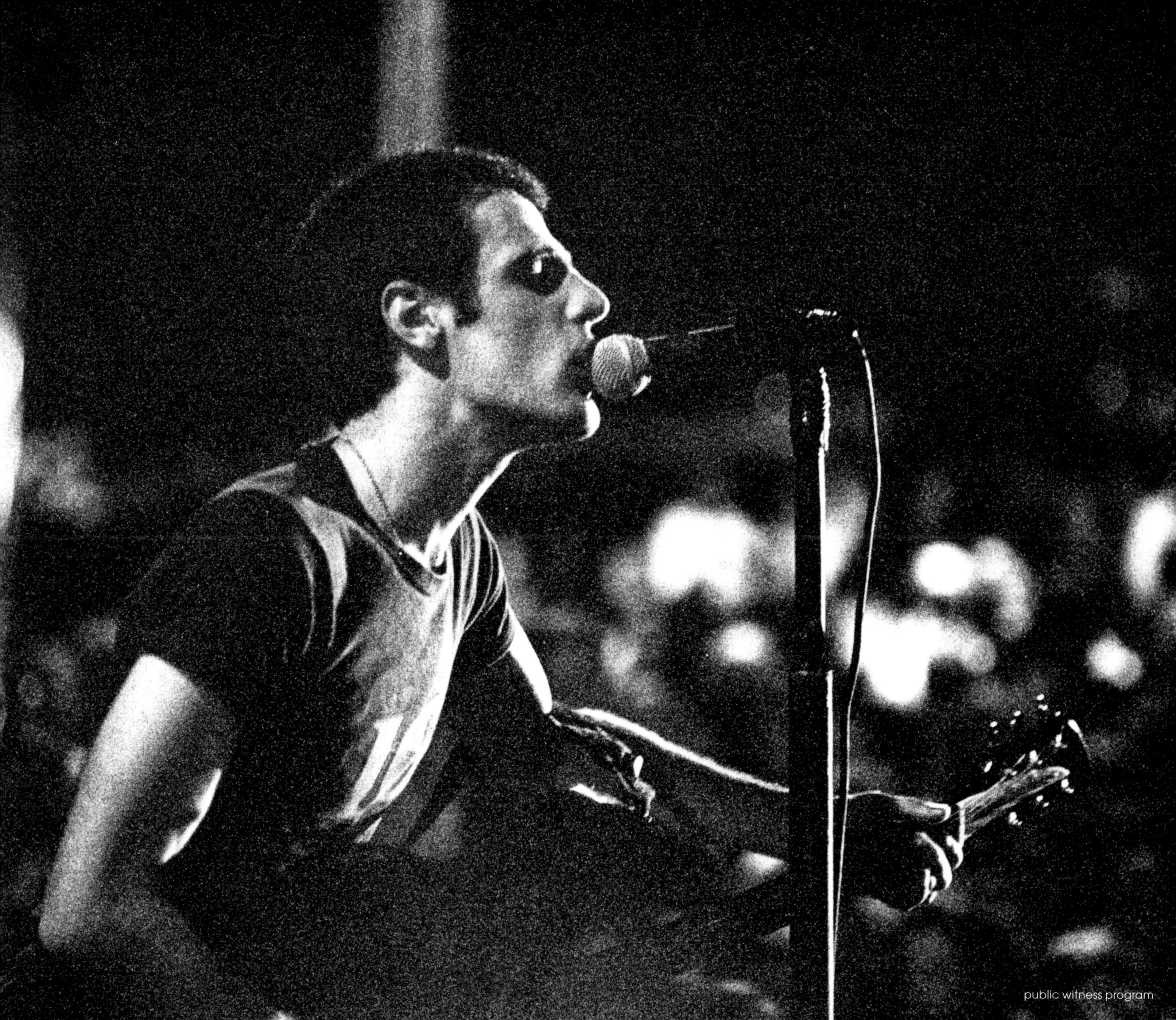
public witness program

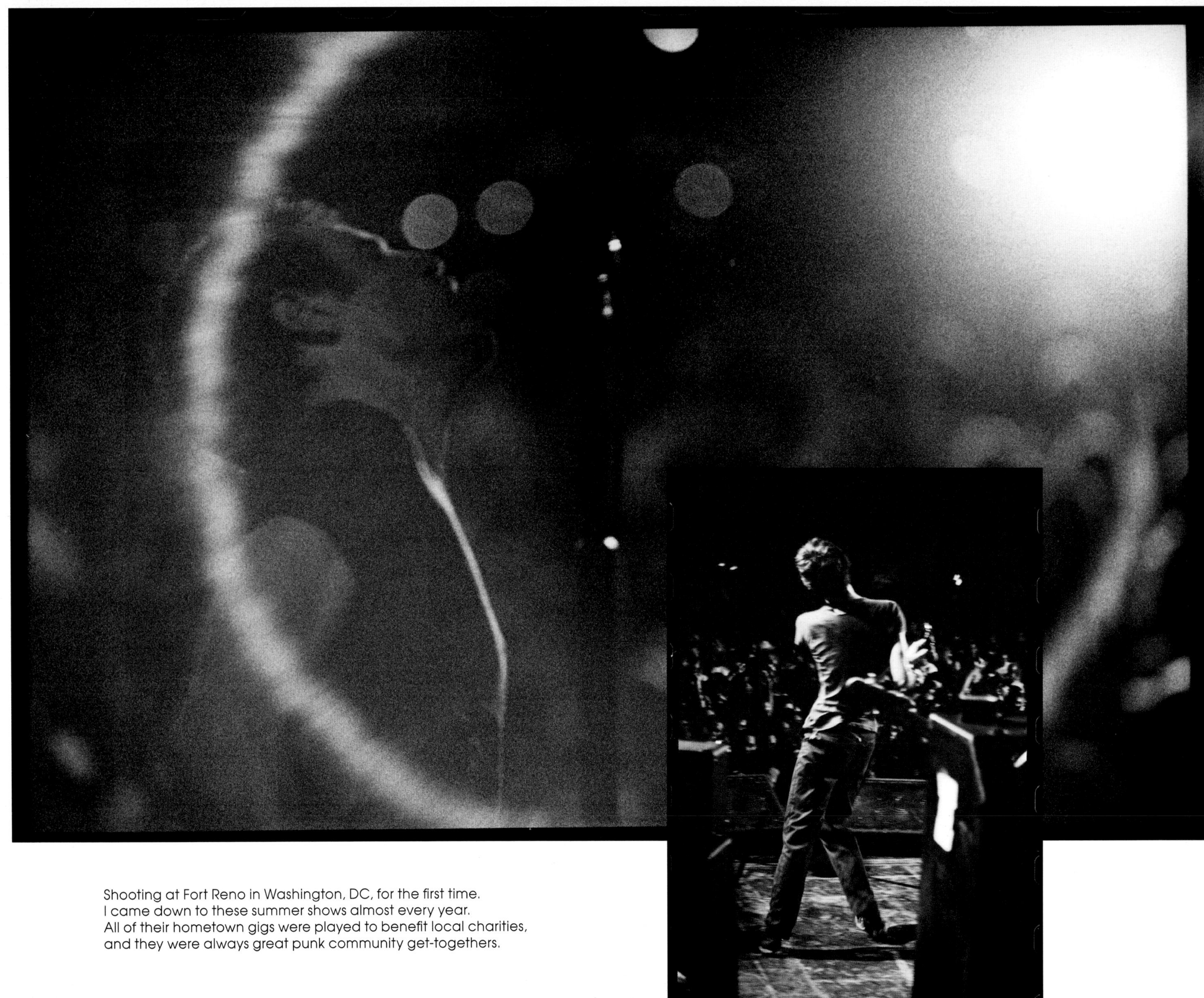

Shooting at Fort Reno in Washington, DC, for the first time.
I came down to these summer shows almost every year.
All of their hometown gigs were played to benefit local charities,
and they were always great punk community get-togethers.

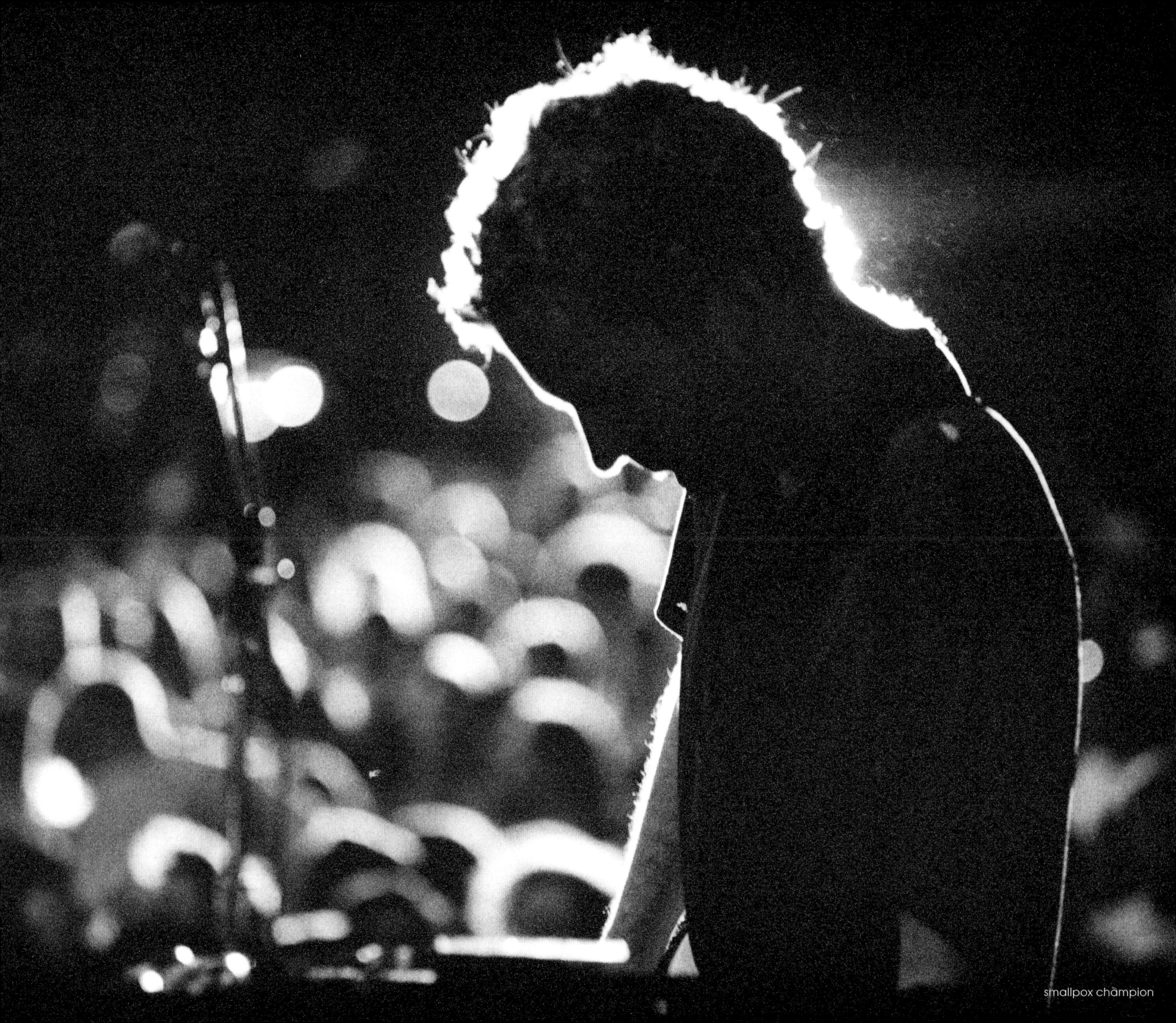
smallpox champion

NYC, SEPTEMBER 1993

ROSELAND

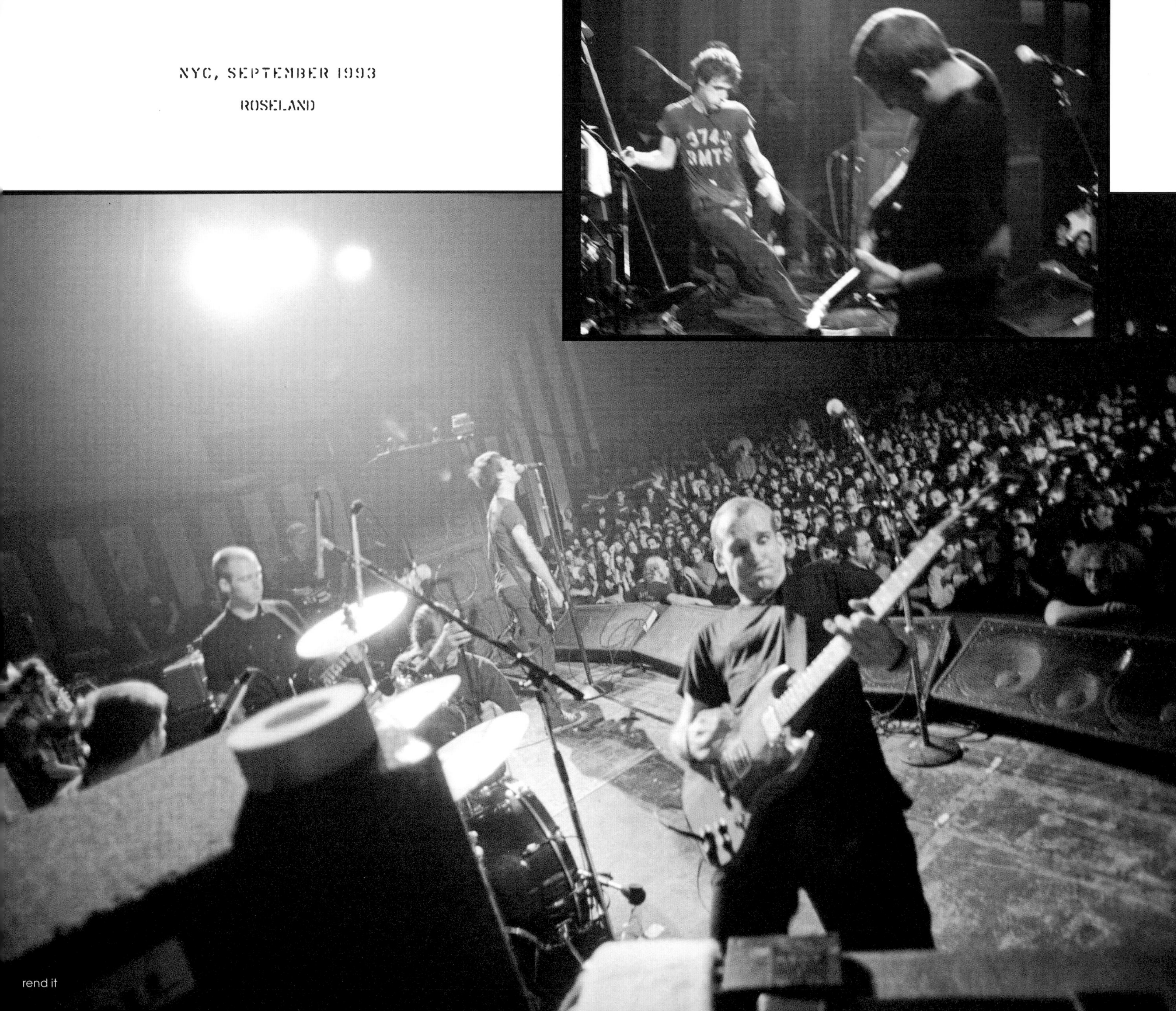

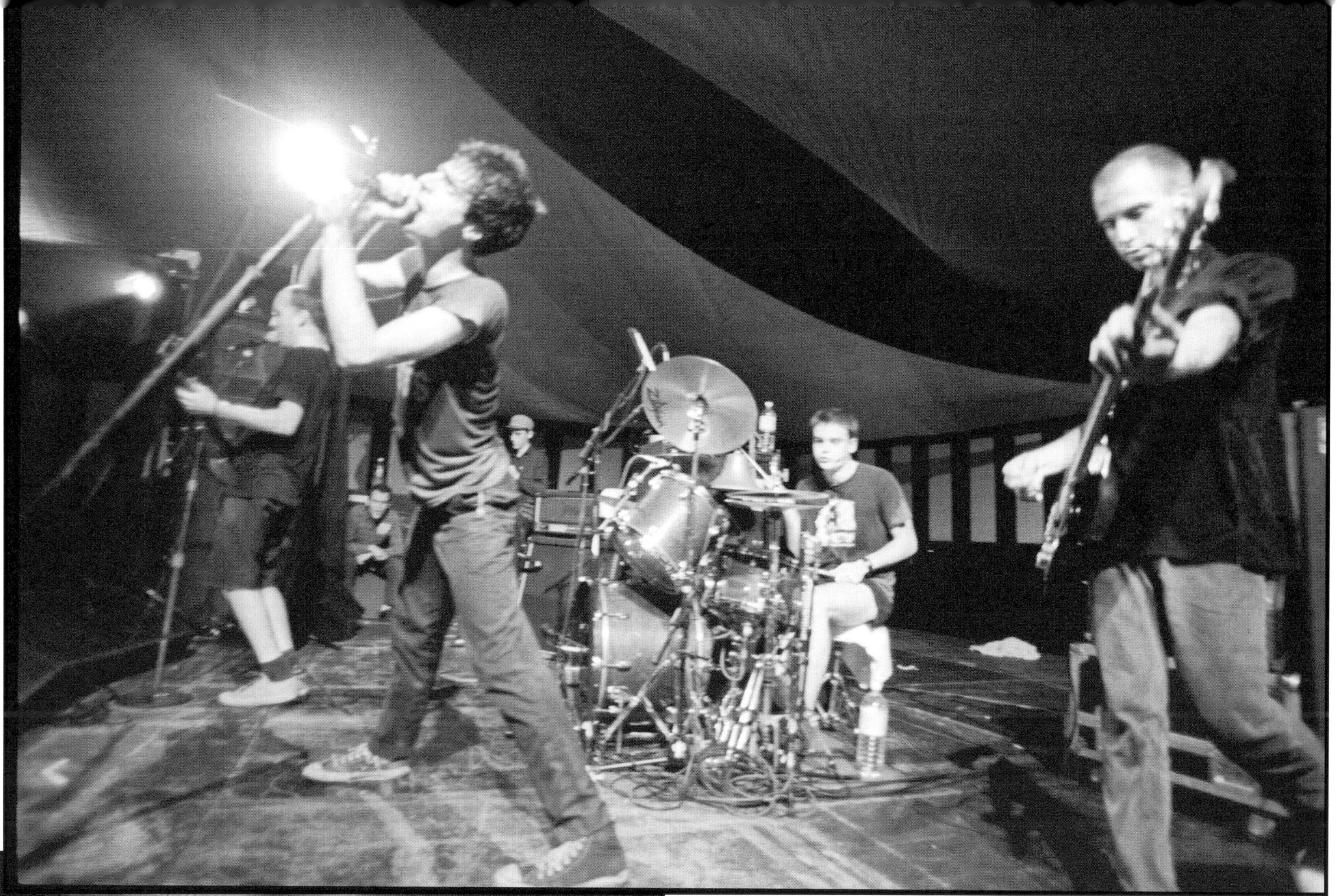

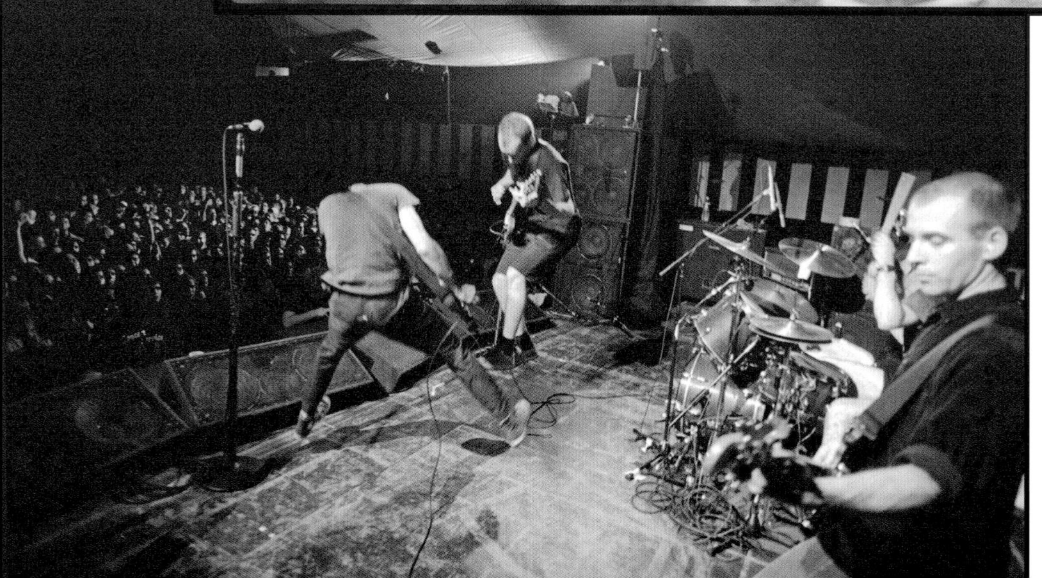

If my memory serves me, this was the show where I witnessed the legendary music mogul Ahmet Ertegün coming backstage to try to get this "unsignable" (really uninterested) group to sign with him. He offered them "anything you want" and said, "Last time I did this was when I offered the Rolling Stones their own record label and ten million dollars." Of course Fugazi politely declined, and Ian then changed the subject and continued to talk to Ertegün about their shared love of Washington, DC.

This series of shows at Roseland was phenomenal, with great crowds and great light for pictures, since Jem Cohen (seen in the background in a few of these shots) was there with a crew filming live segments for the Fugazi film *Instrument*.

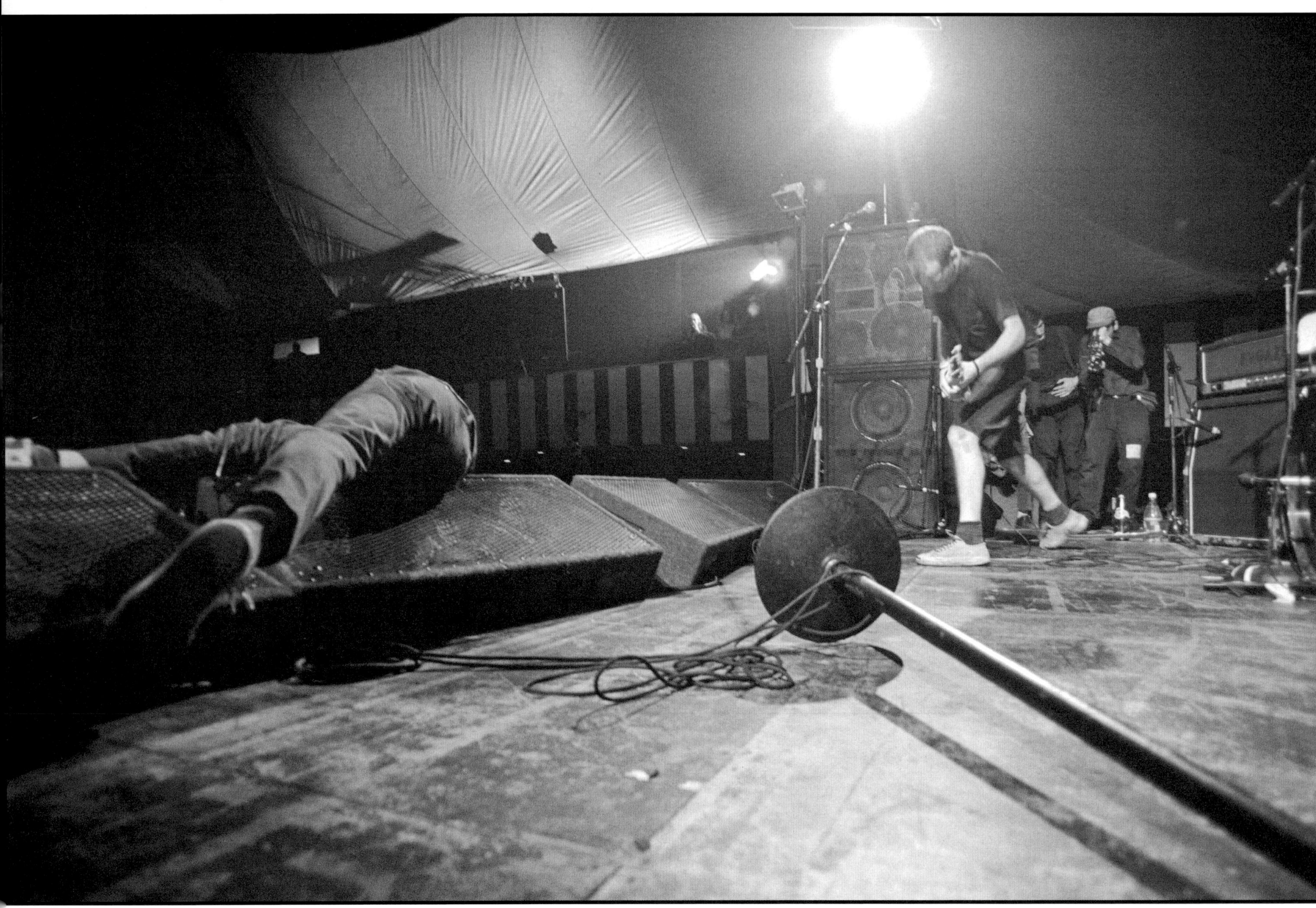

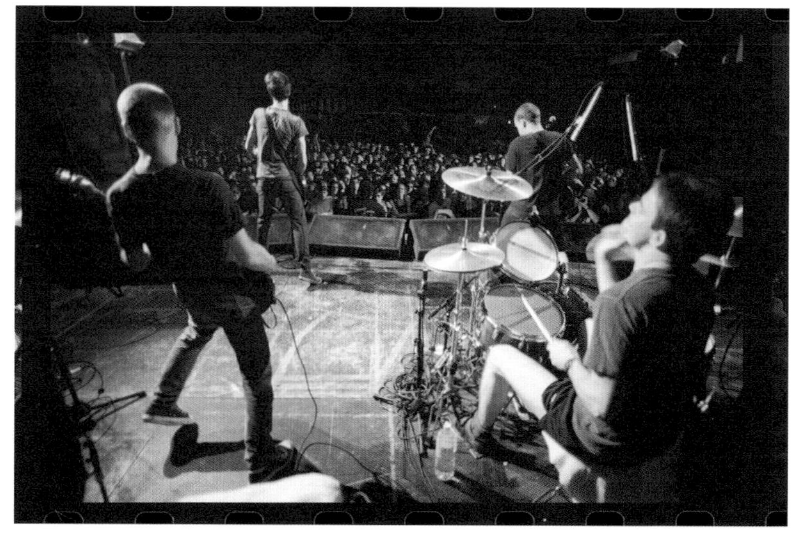

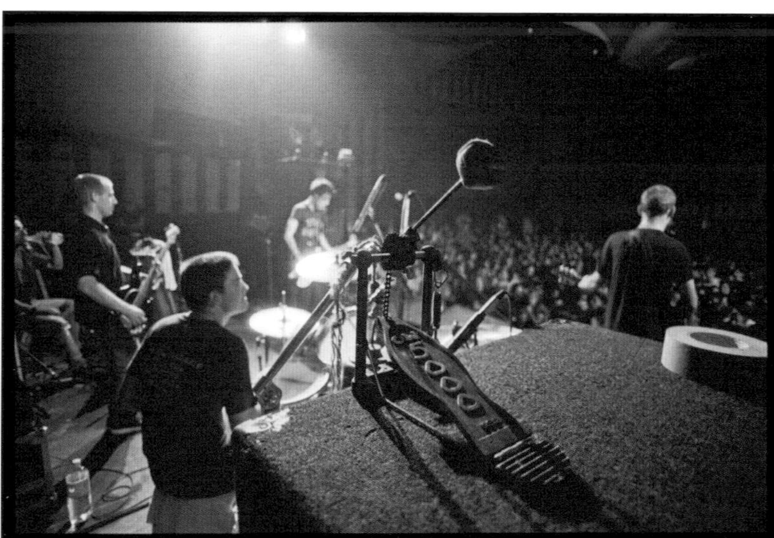

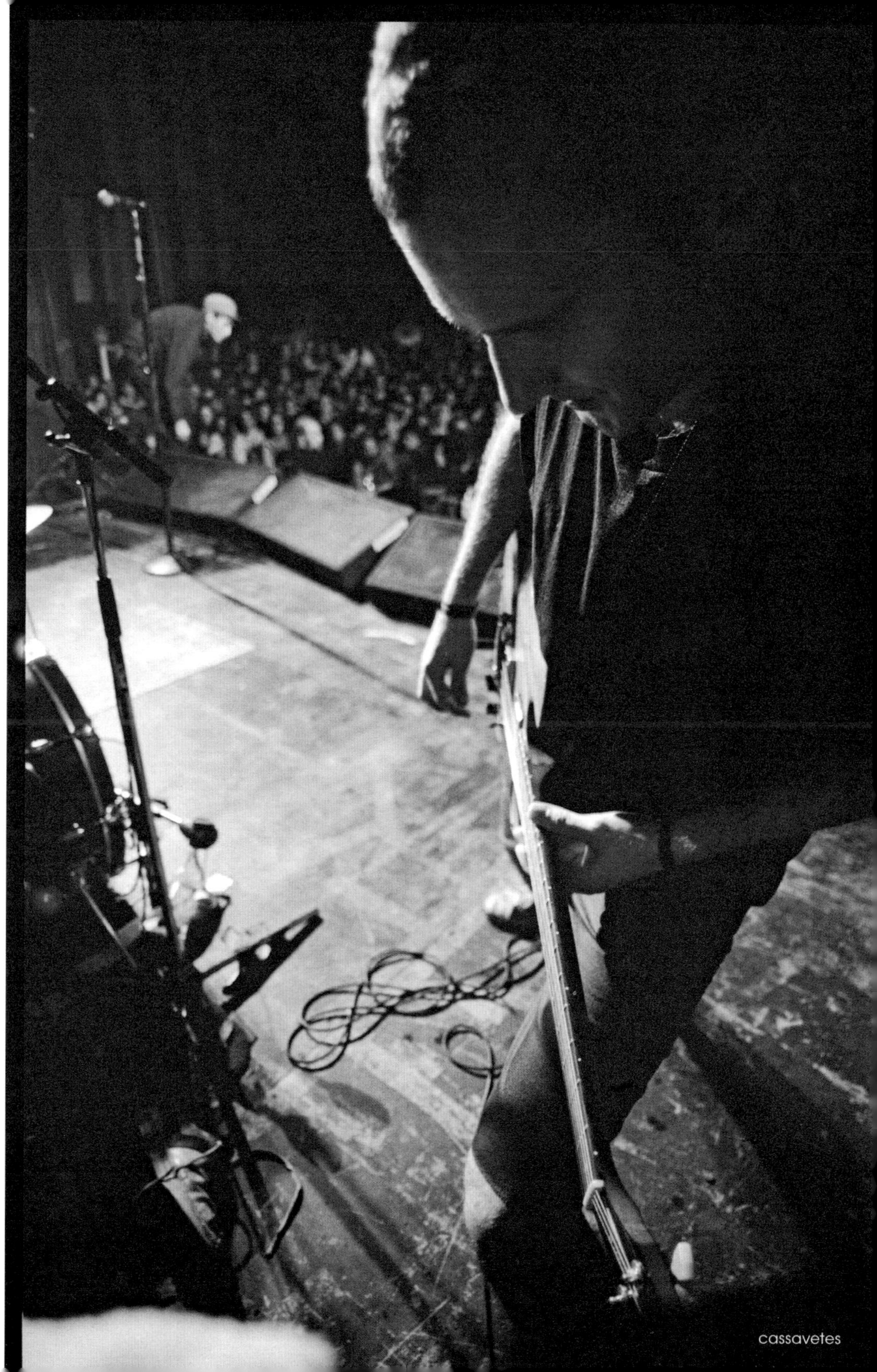

cassavetes

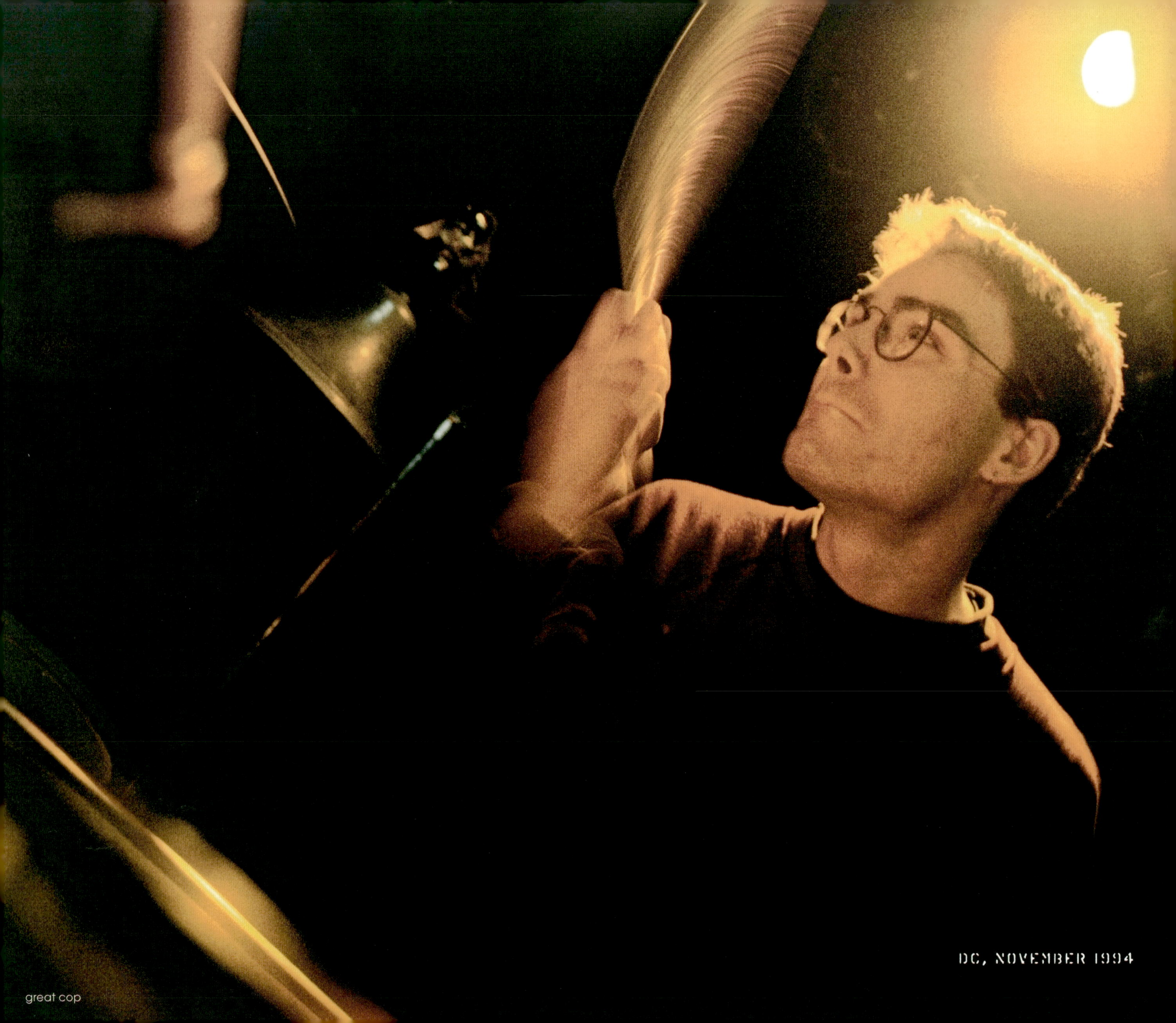

DC, NOVEMBER 1994

great cop

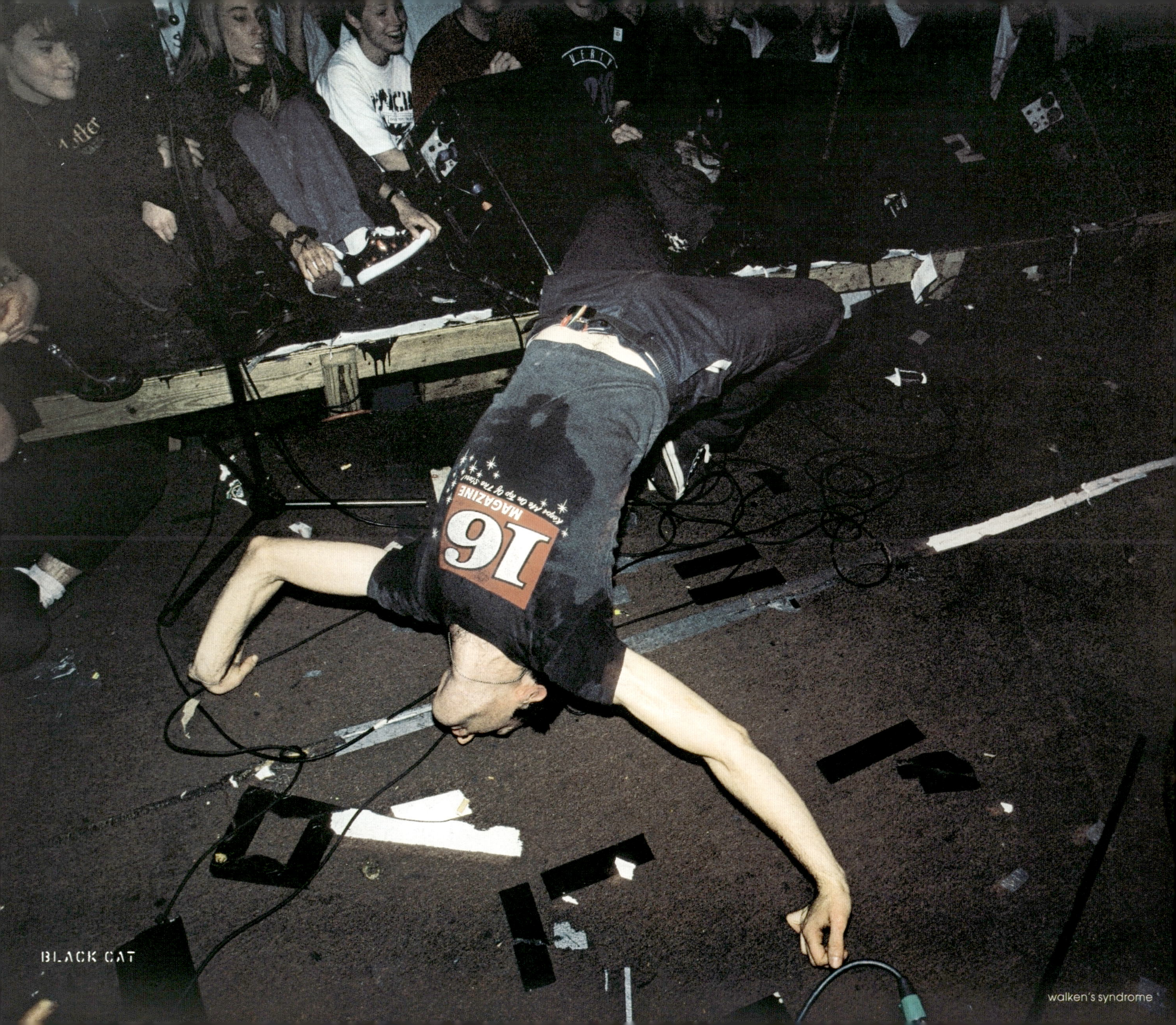

BLACK CAT

walken's syndrome

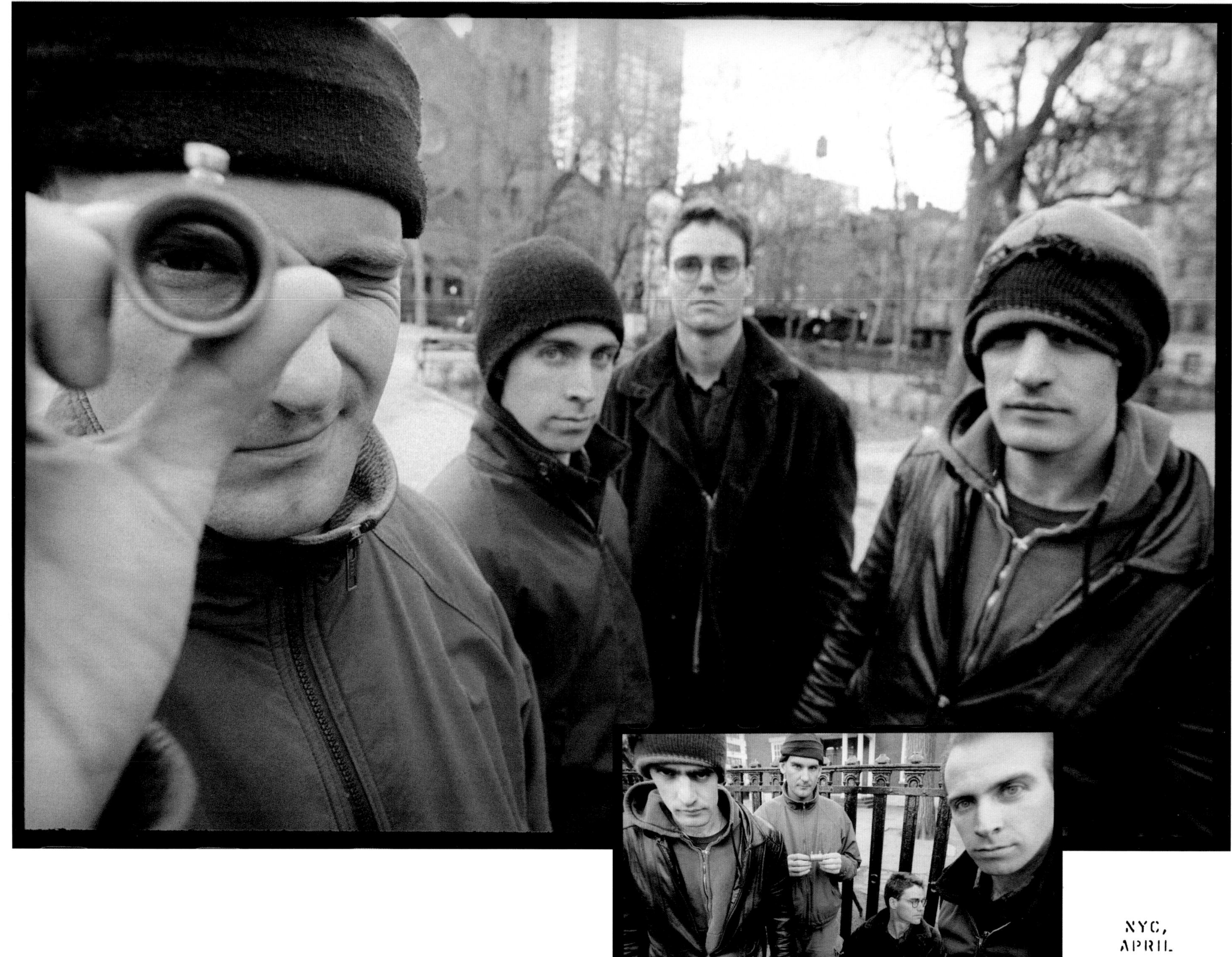

NYC,
APRIL
1995

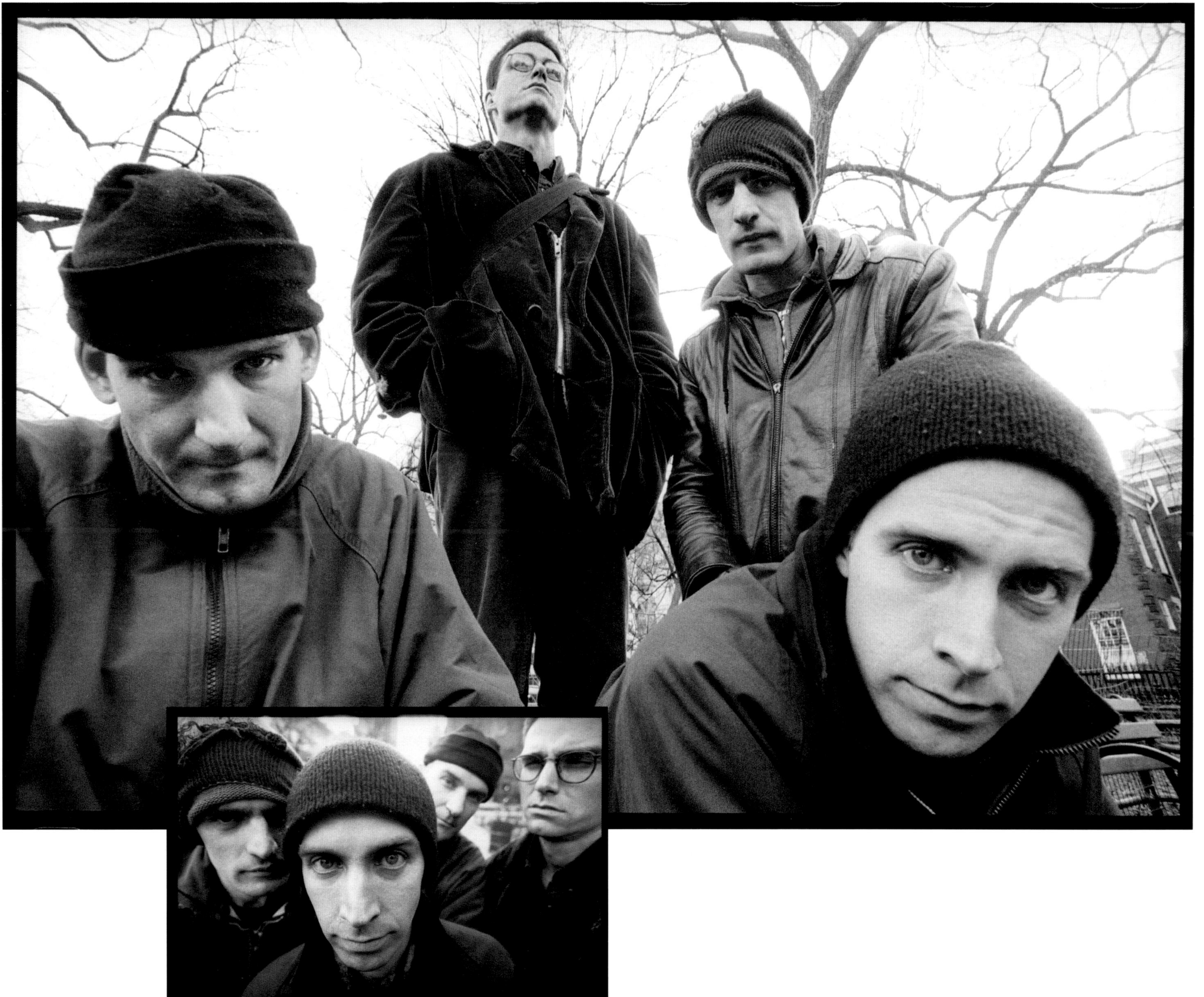

last chance for a slow dance

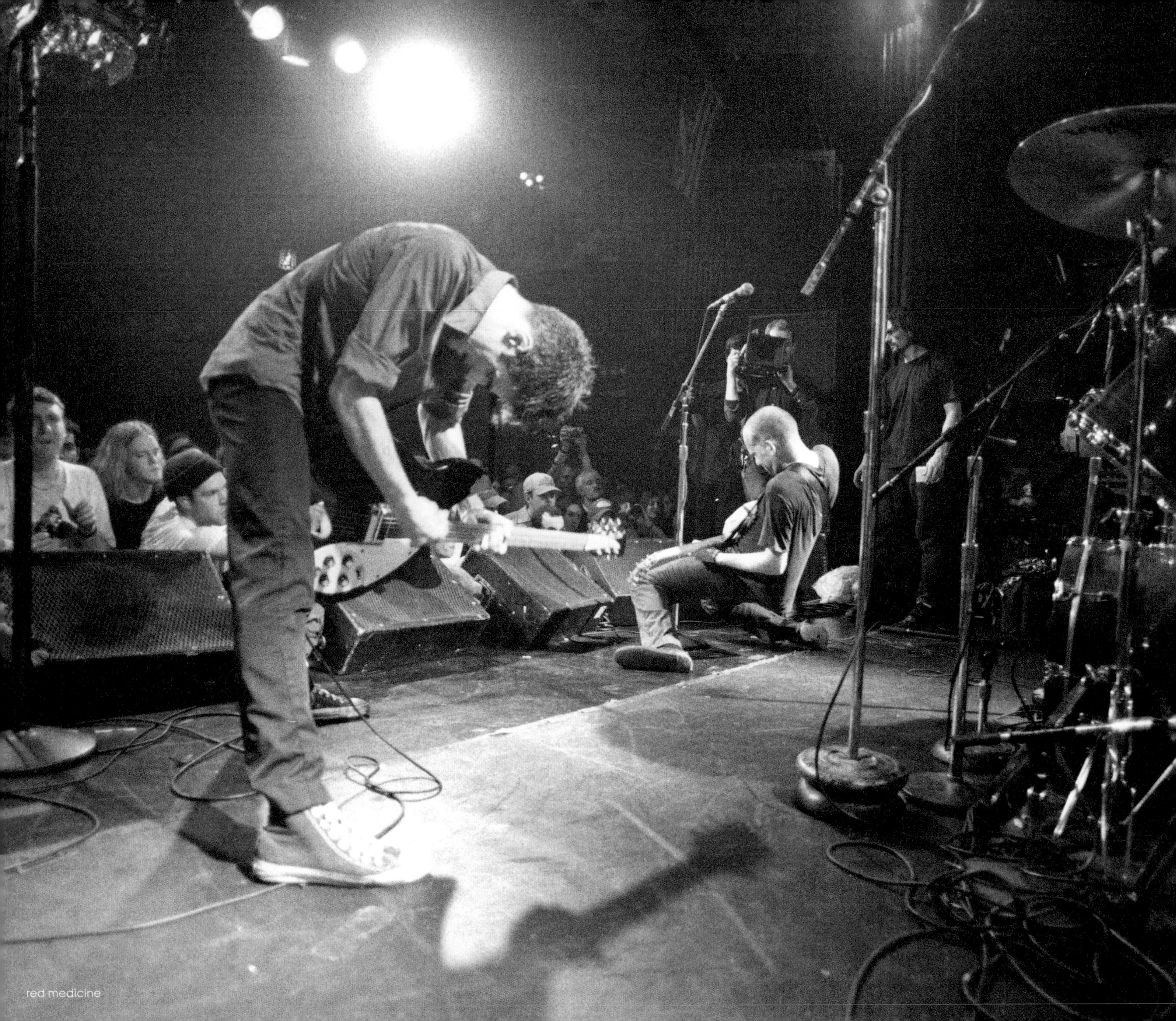

red medicine

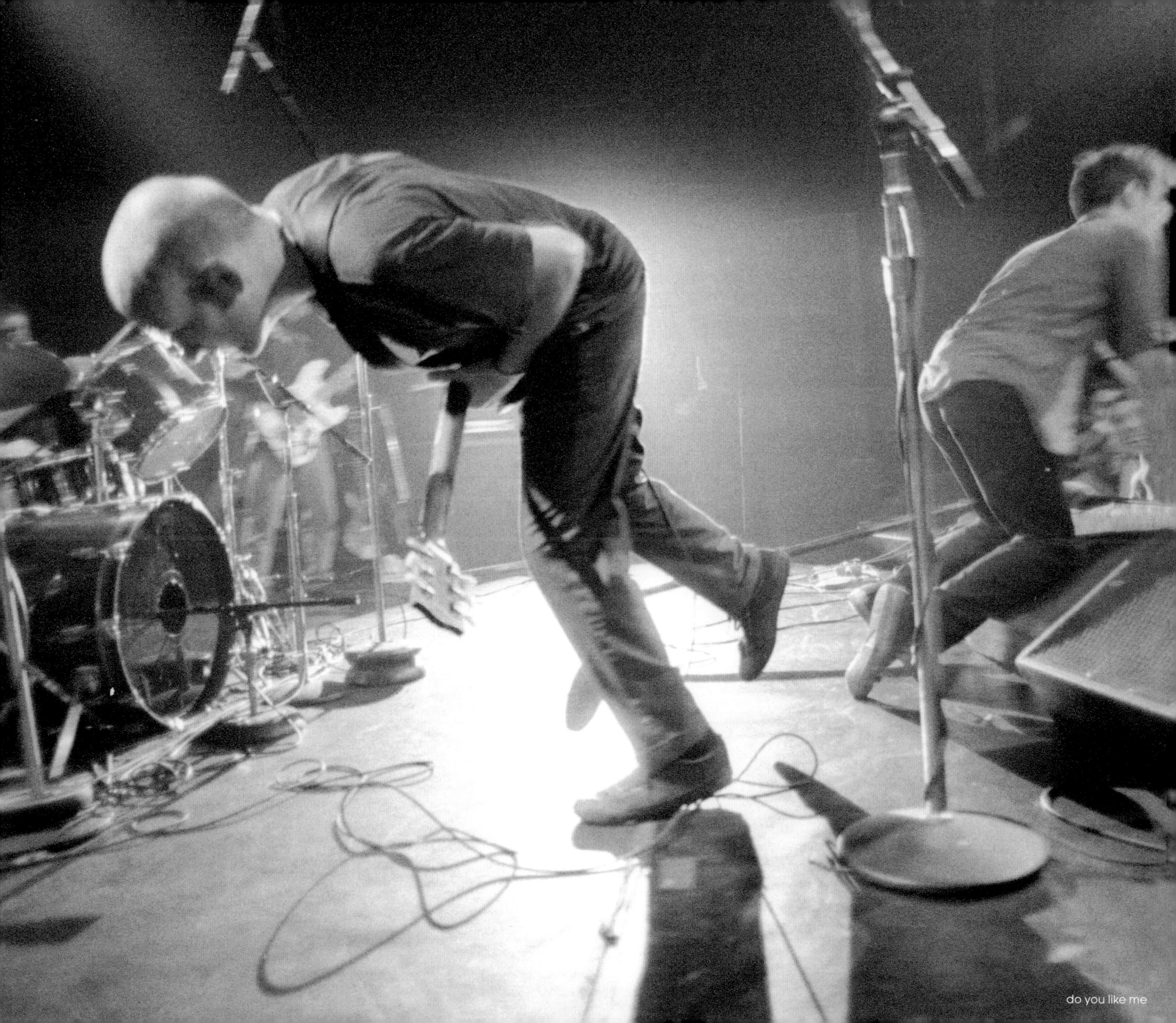

do you like me

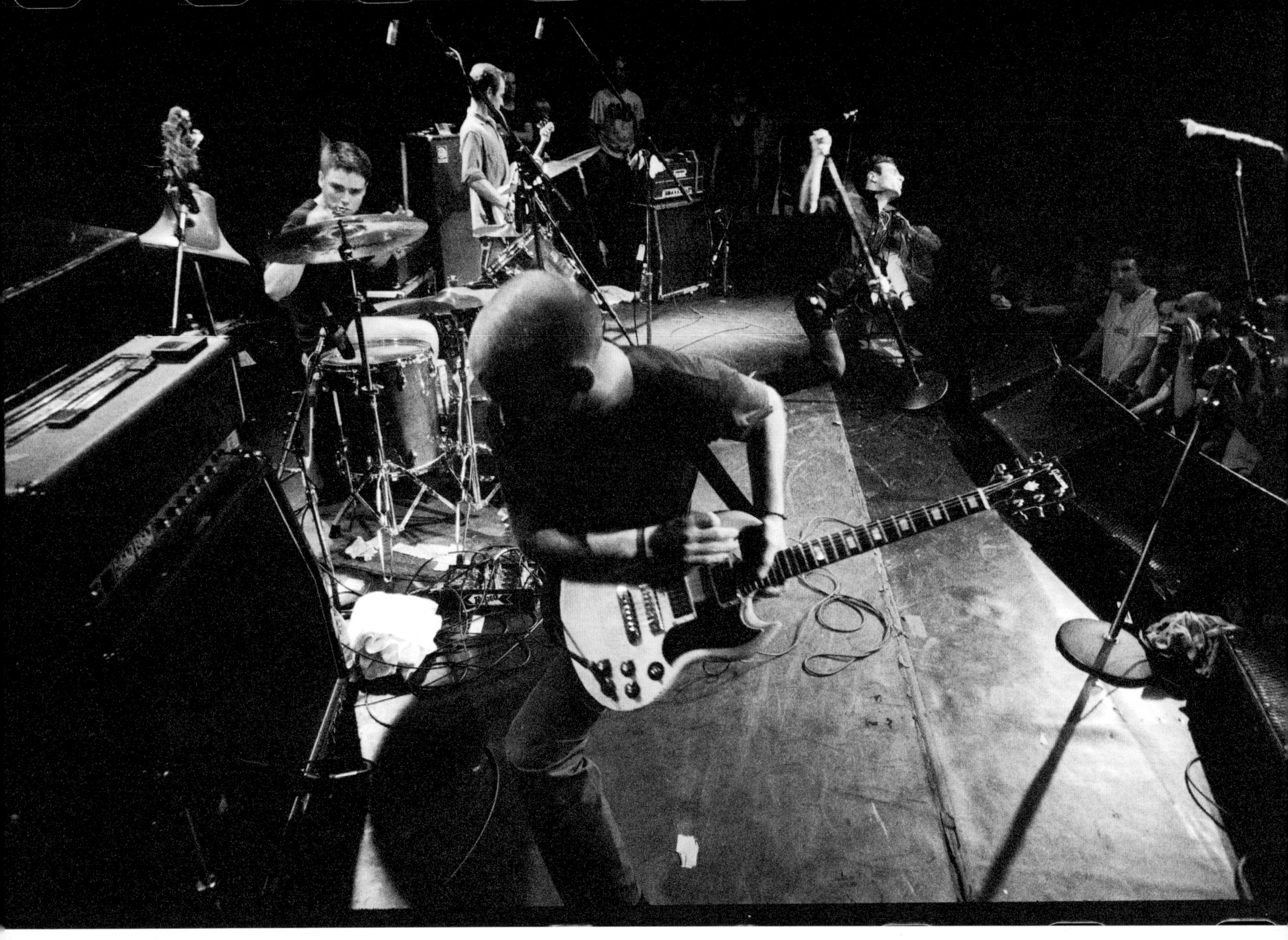

IRVING PLAZA

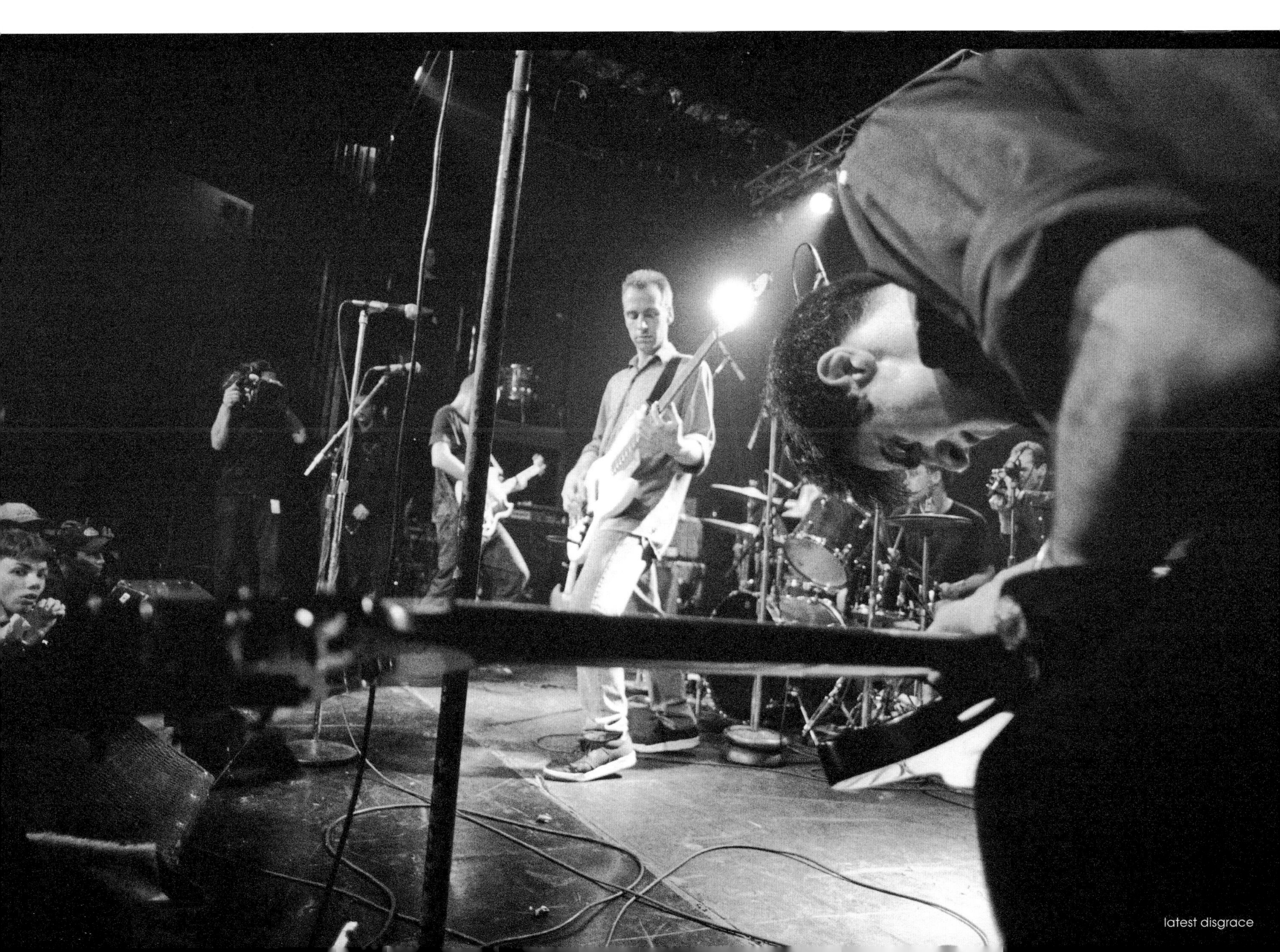

latest disgrace

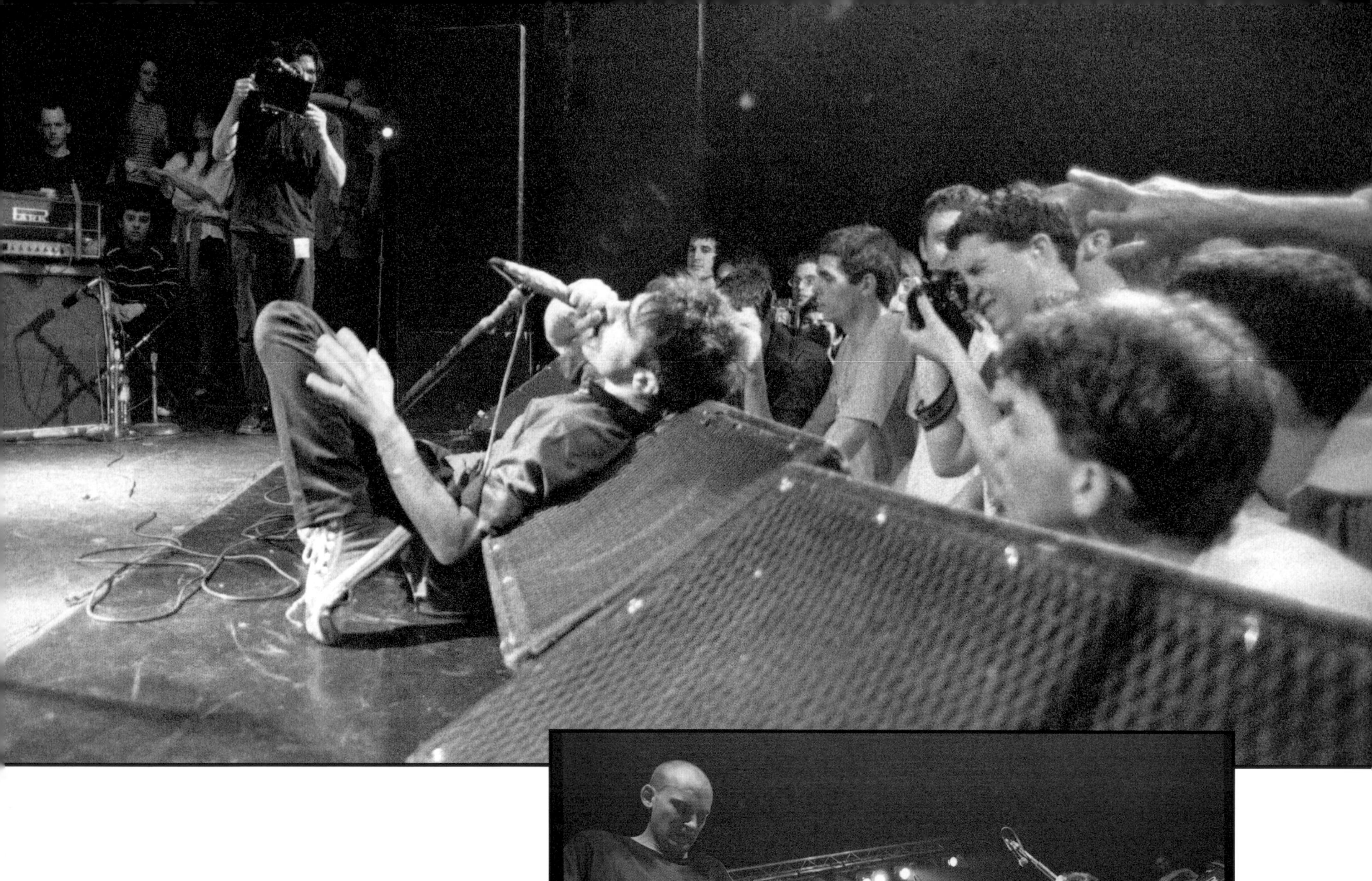

birthday pony

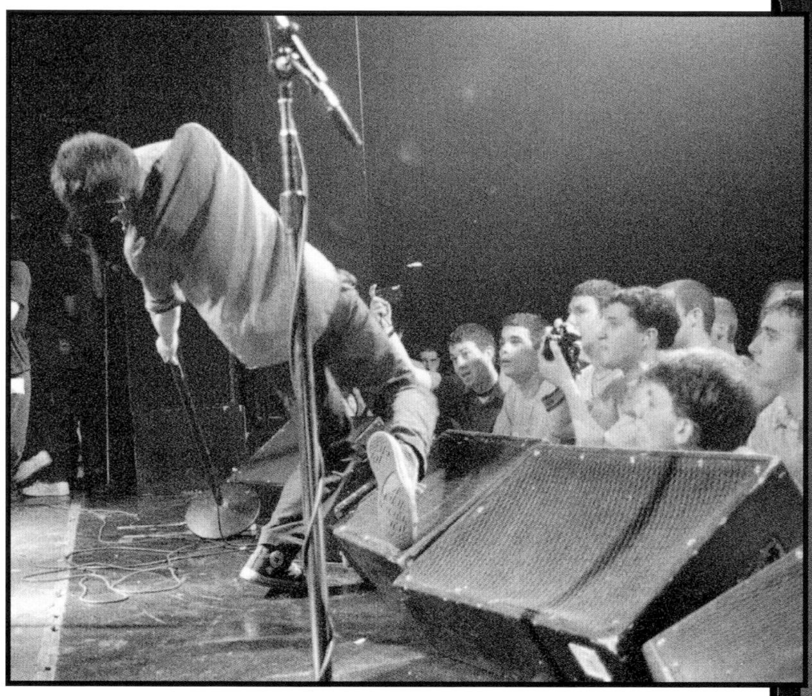

Another incredible series of shows on three consecutive nights in New York City.

We shot band portraits twice during these few days.

These were really great performances and fun times: perhaps the most comfortable band portraits we ever took came on these days.

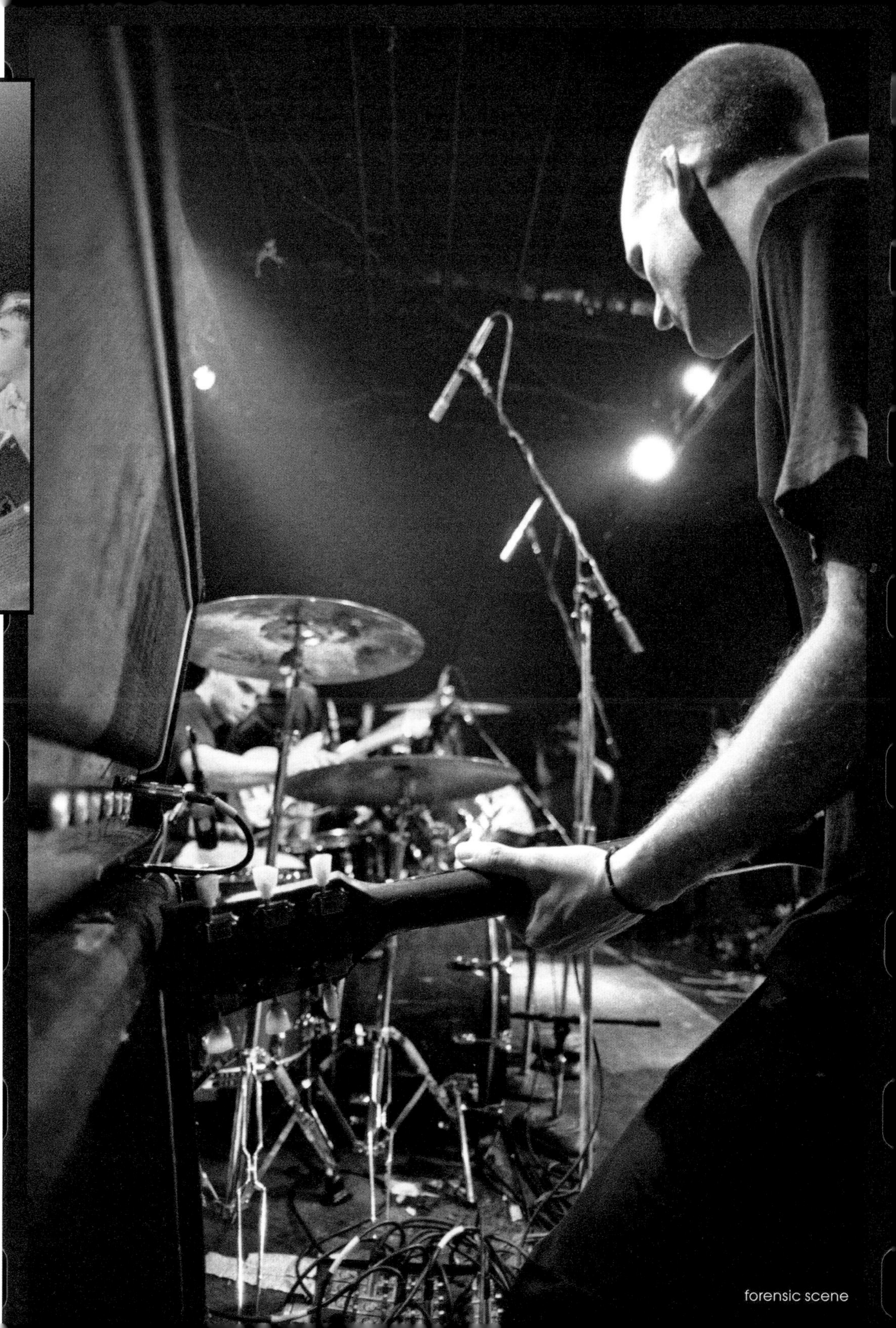

forensic scene

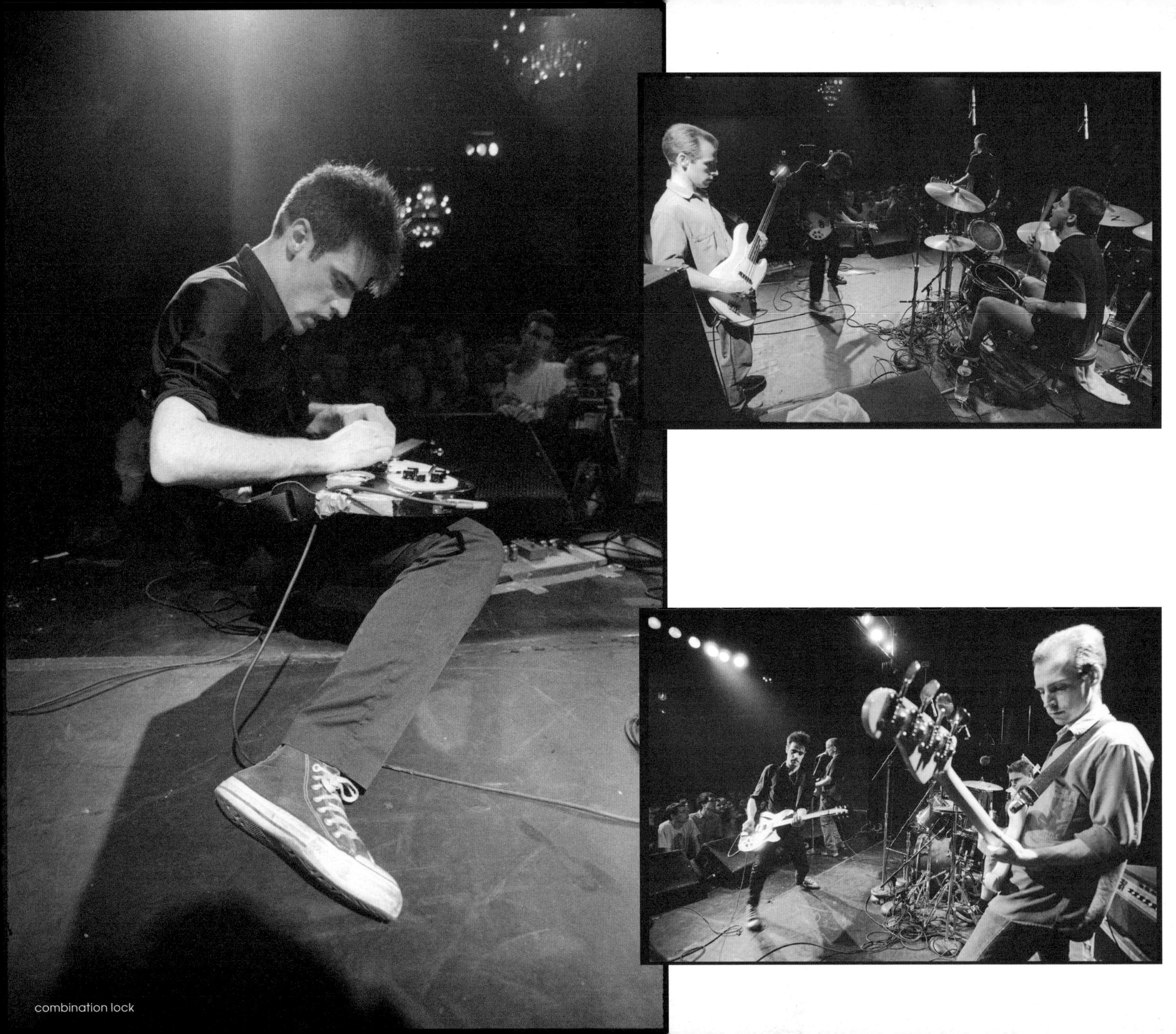

combination lock

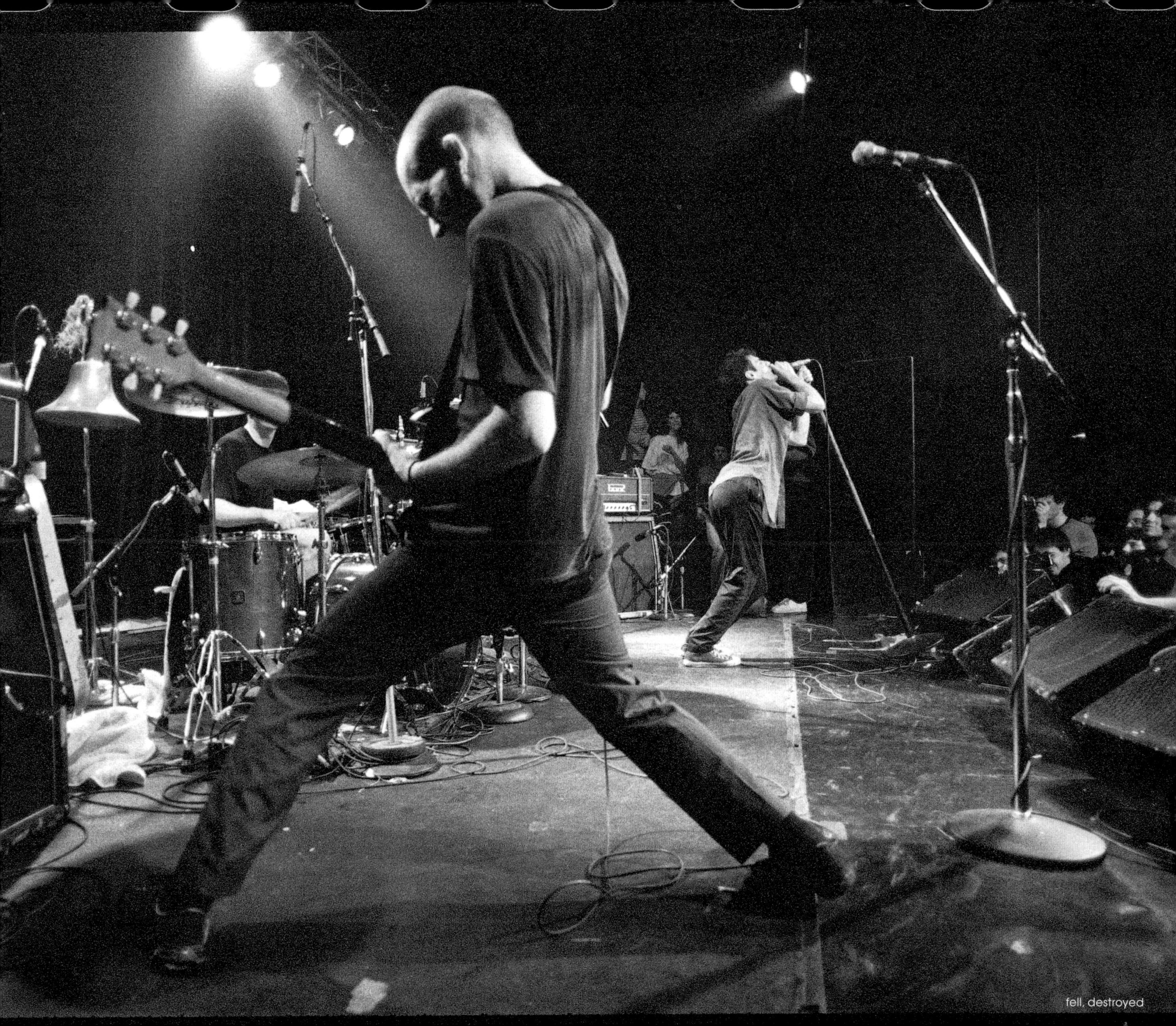

fell, destroyed

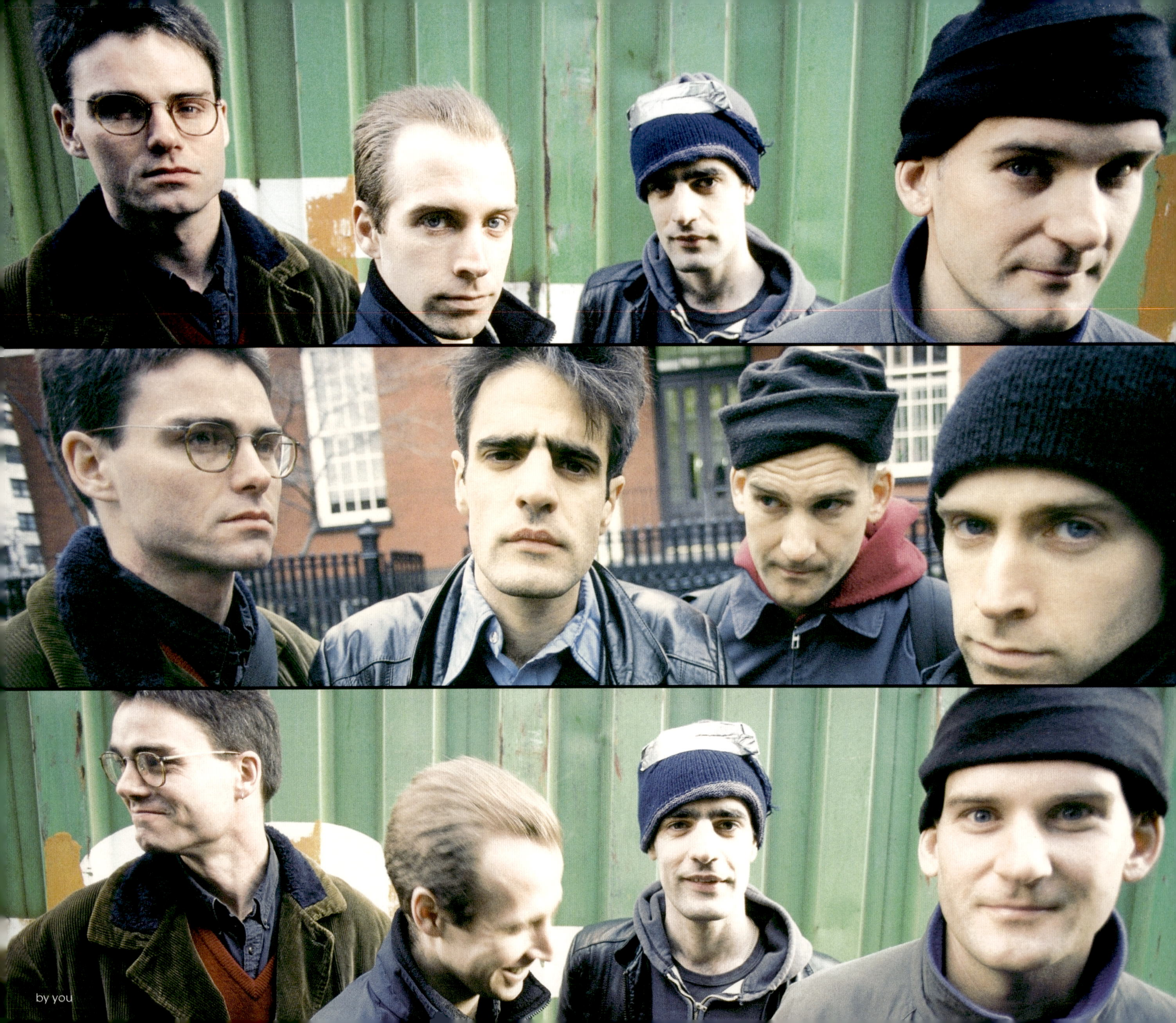

by you

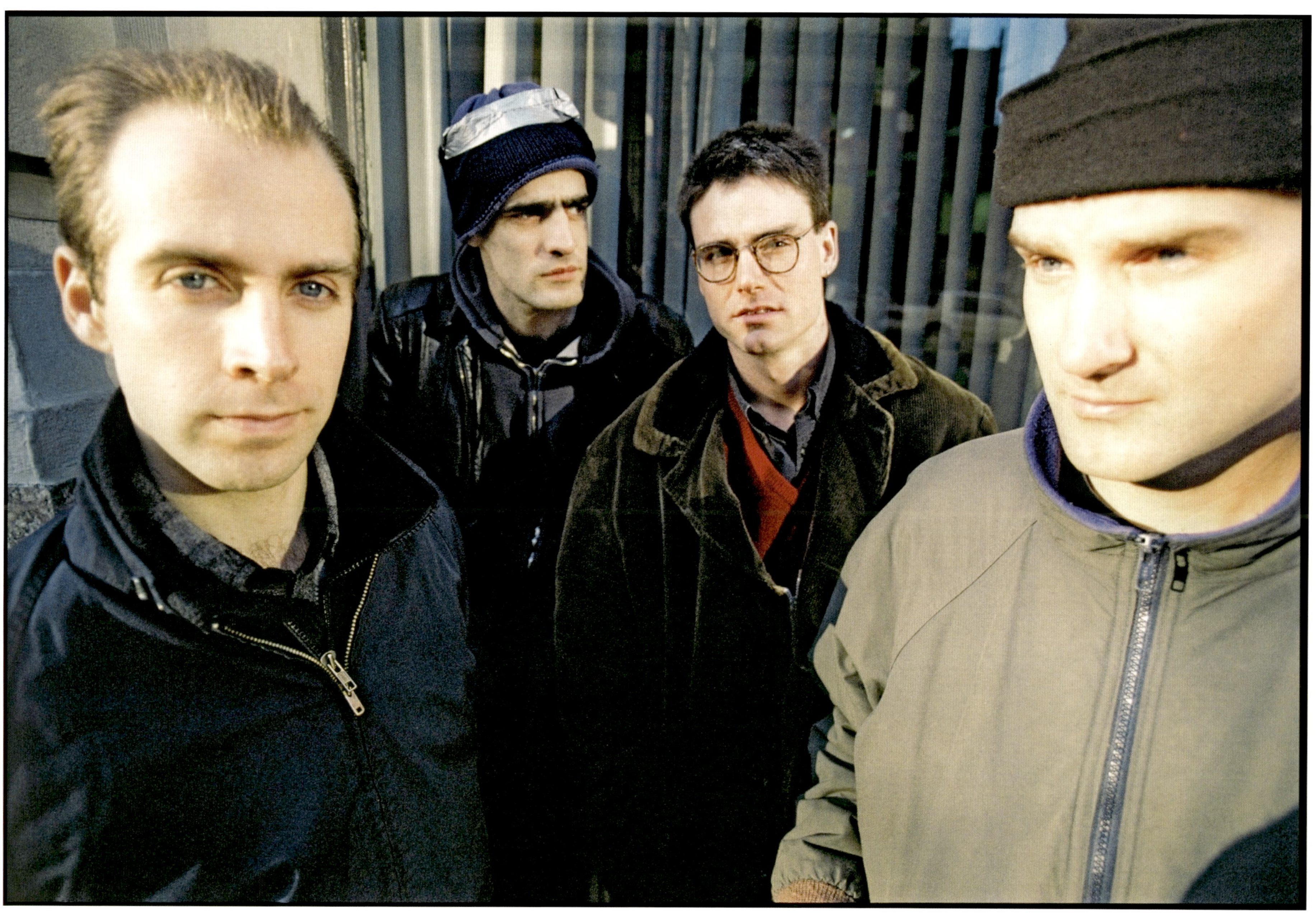

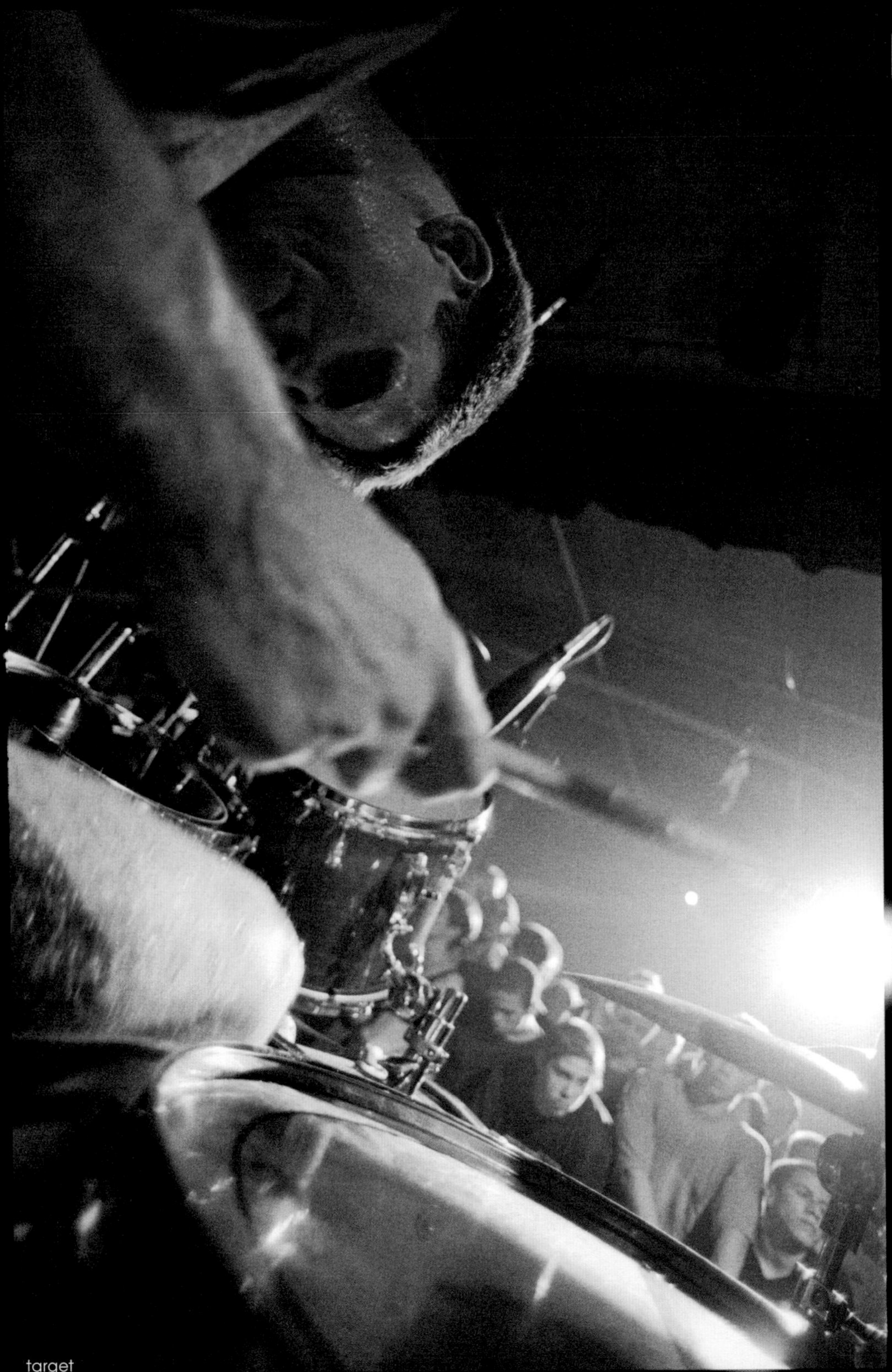

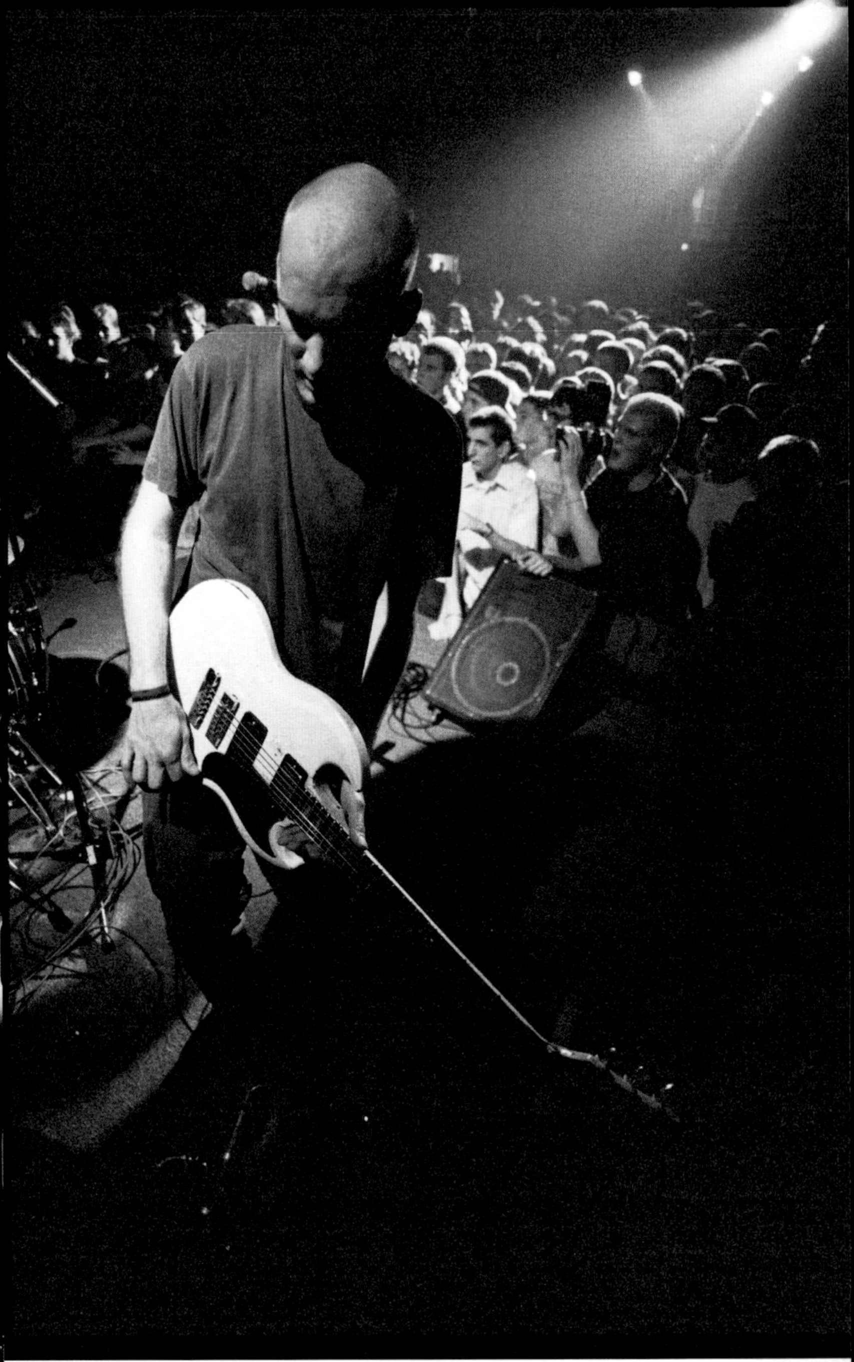

LONG ISLAND, NY, SEPTEMBER 1995

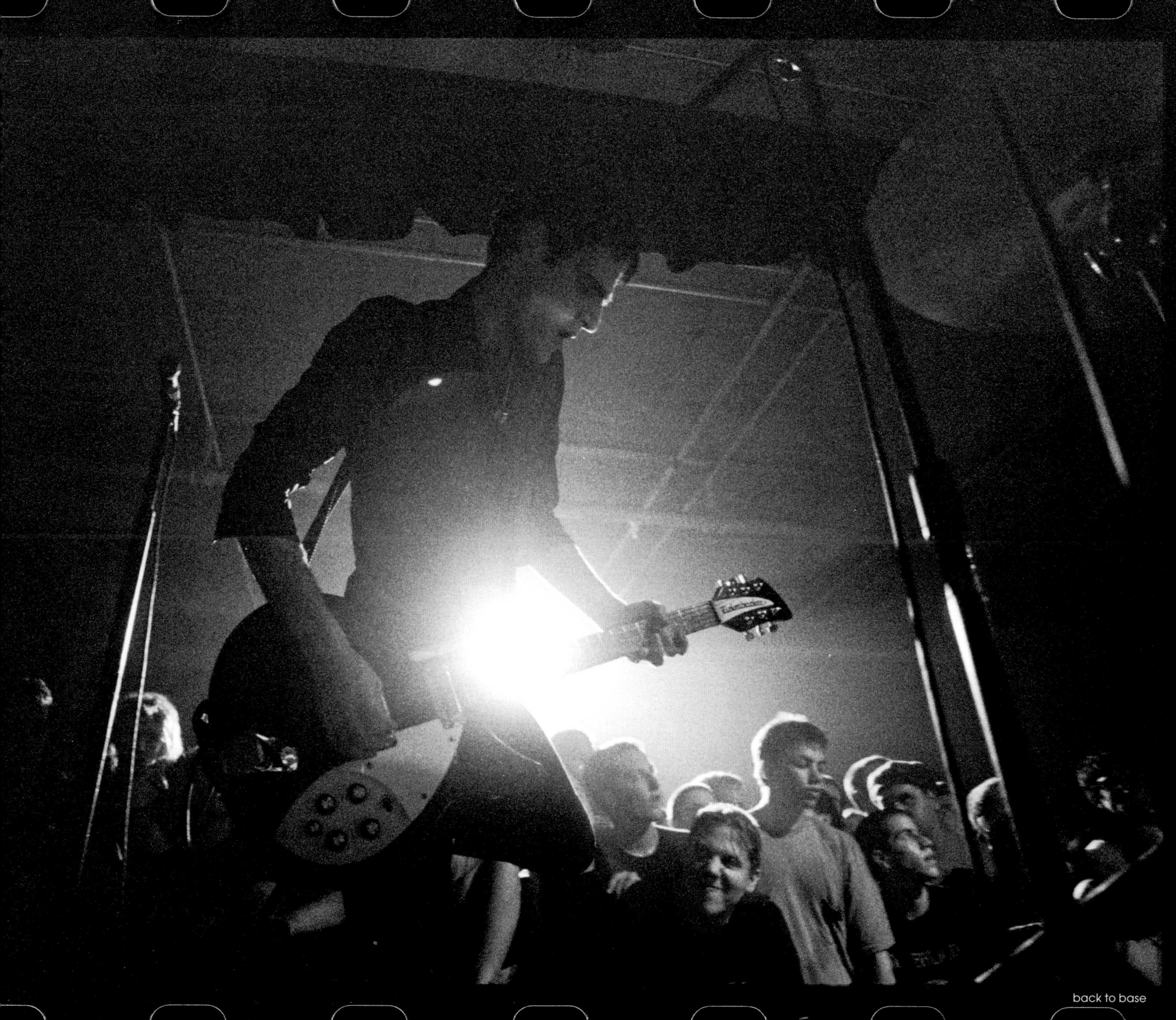

back to base

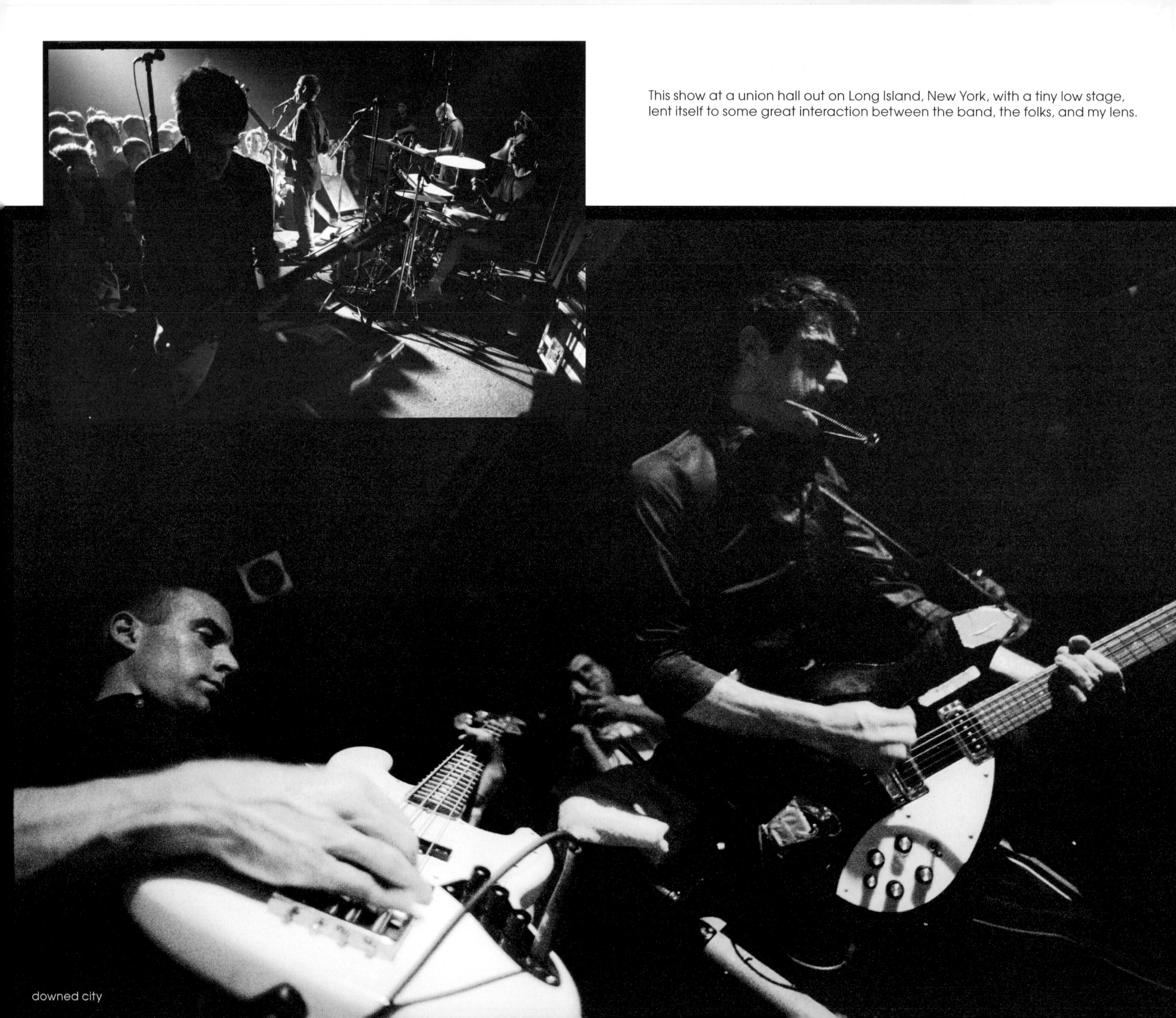

This show at a union hall out on Long Island, New York, with a tiny low stage, lent itself to some great interaction between the band, the folks, and my lens.

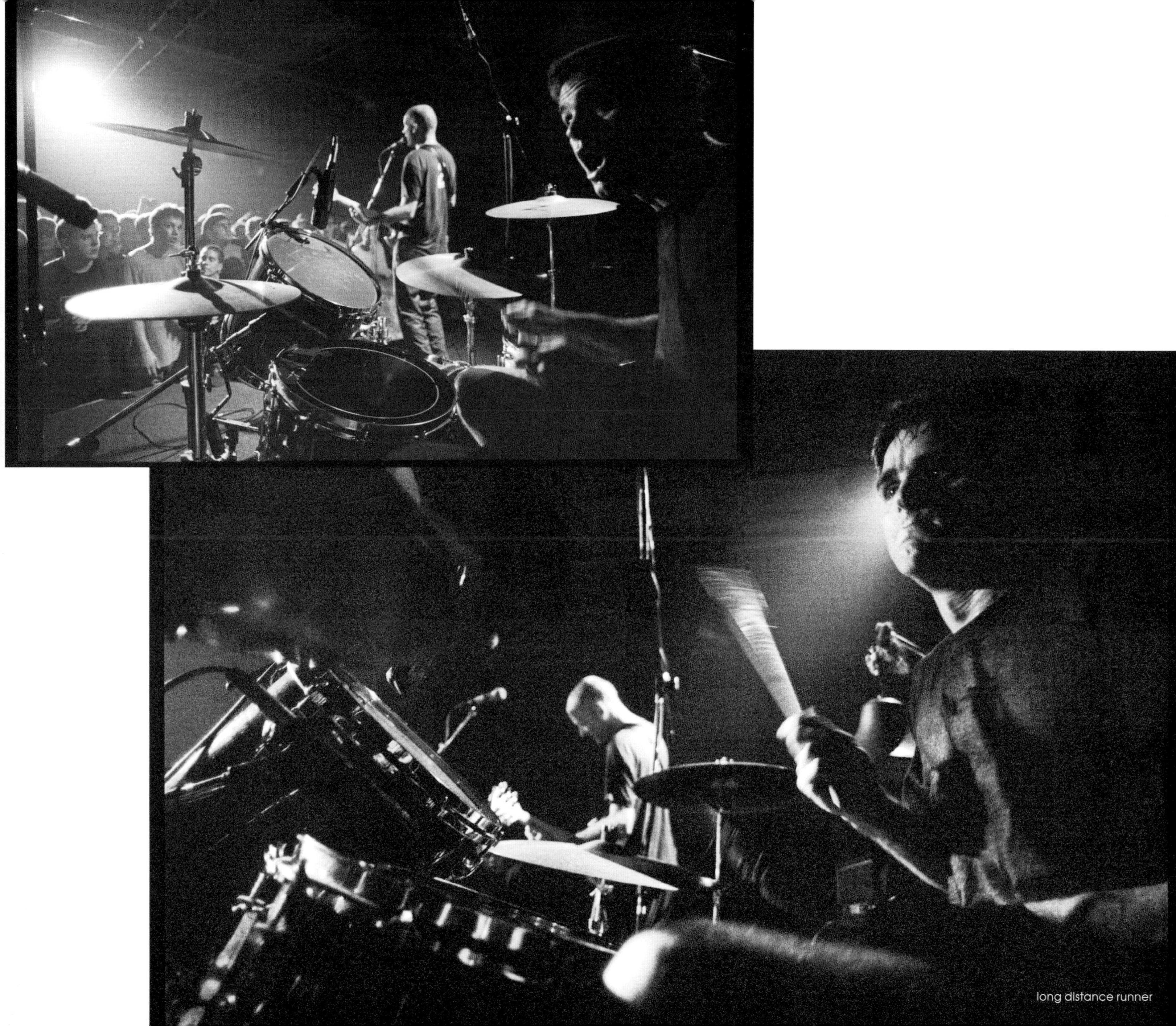

long distance runner

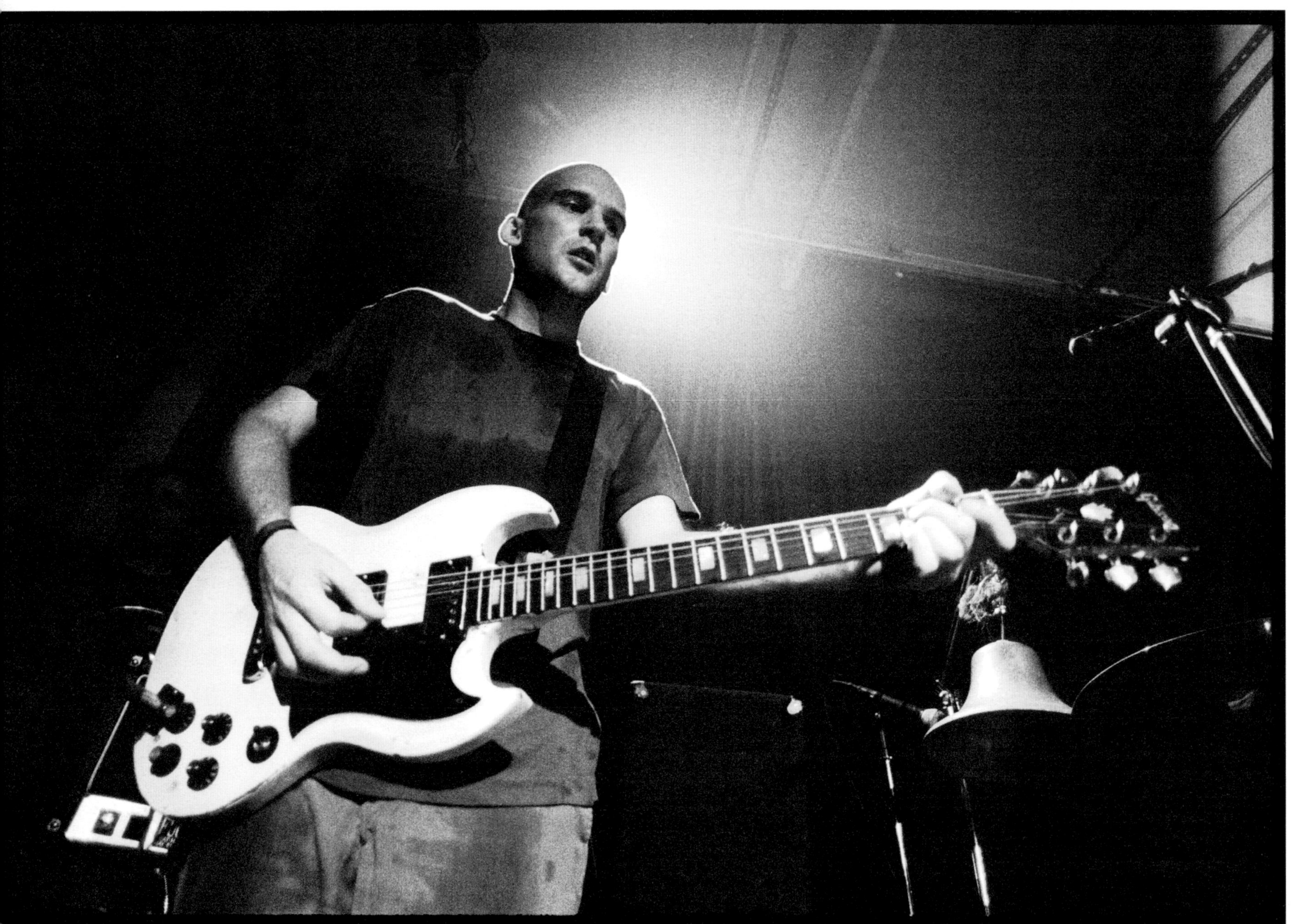

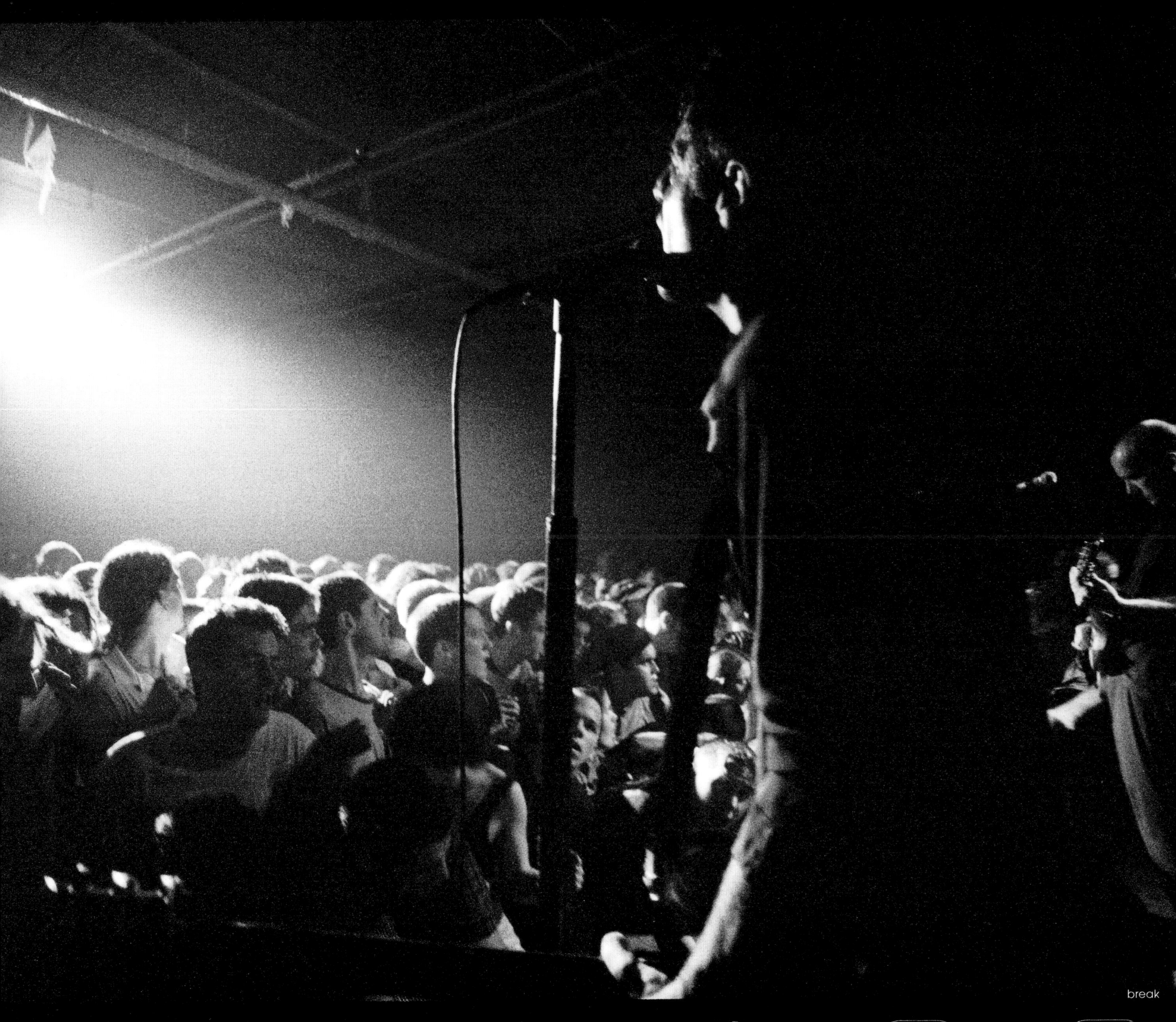

break

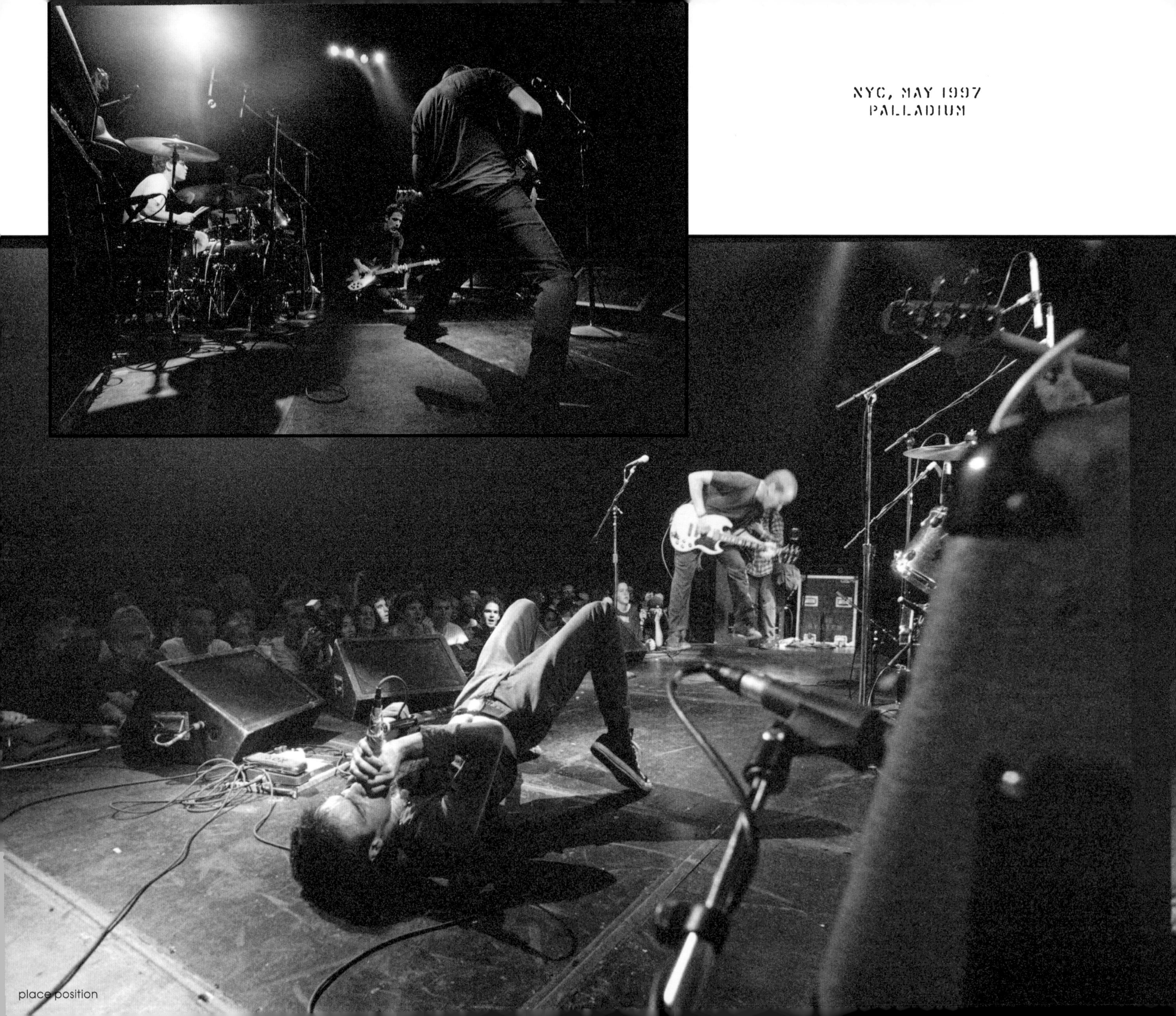

NYC, MAY 1997
PALLADIUM

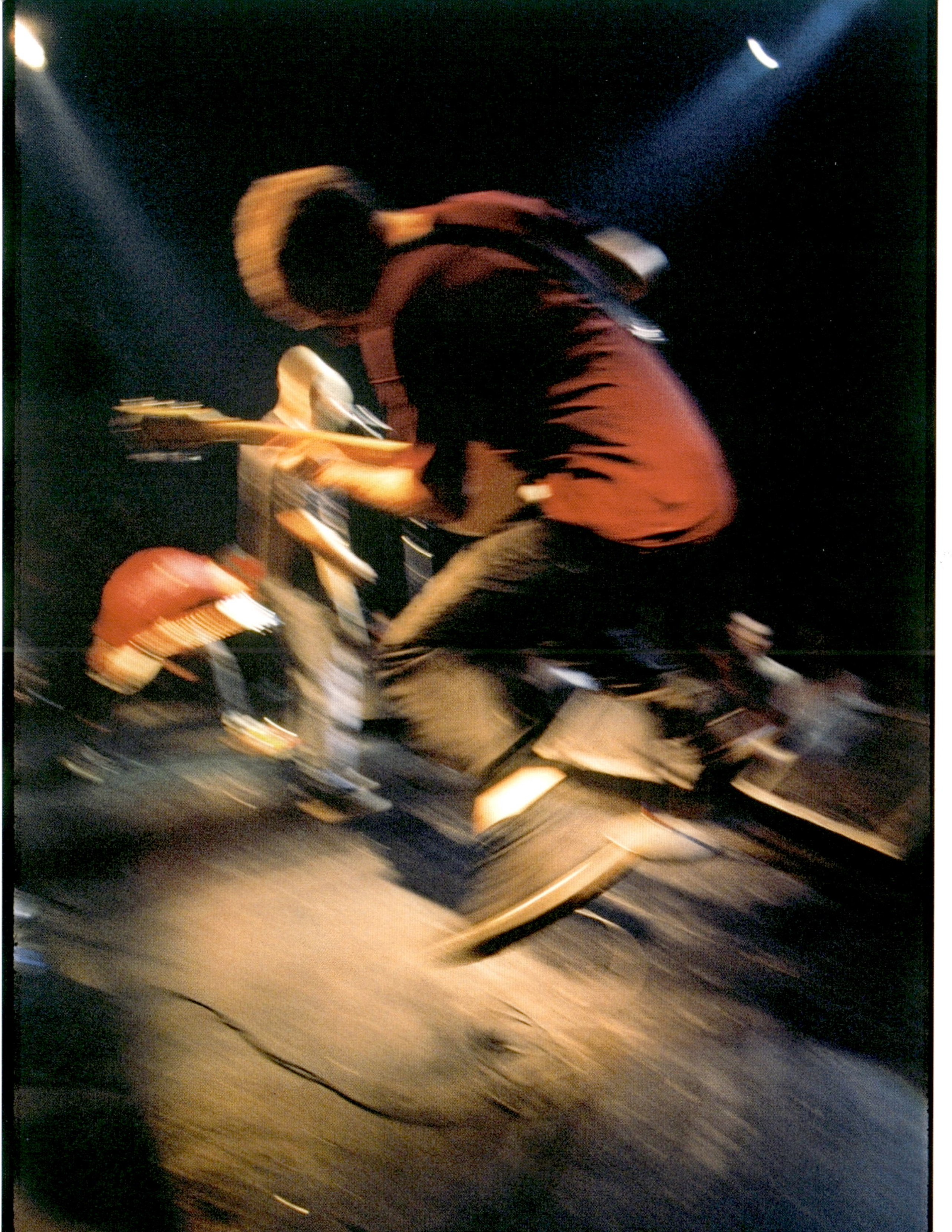

recap modotti

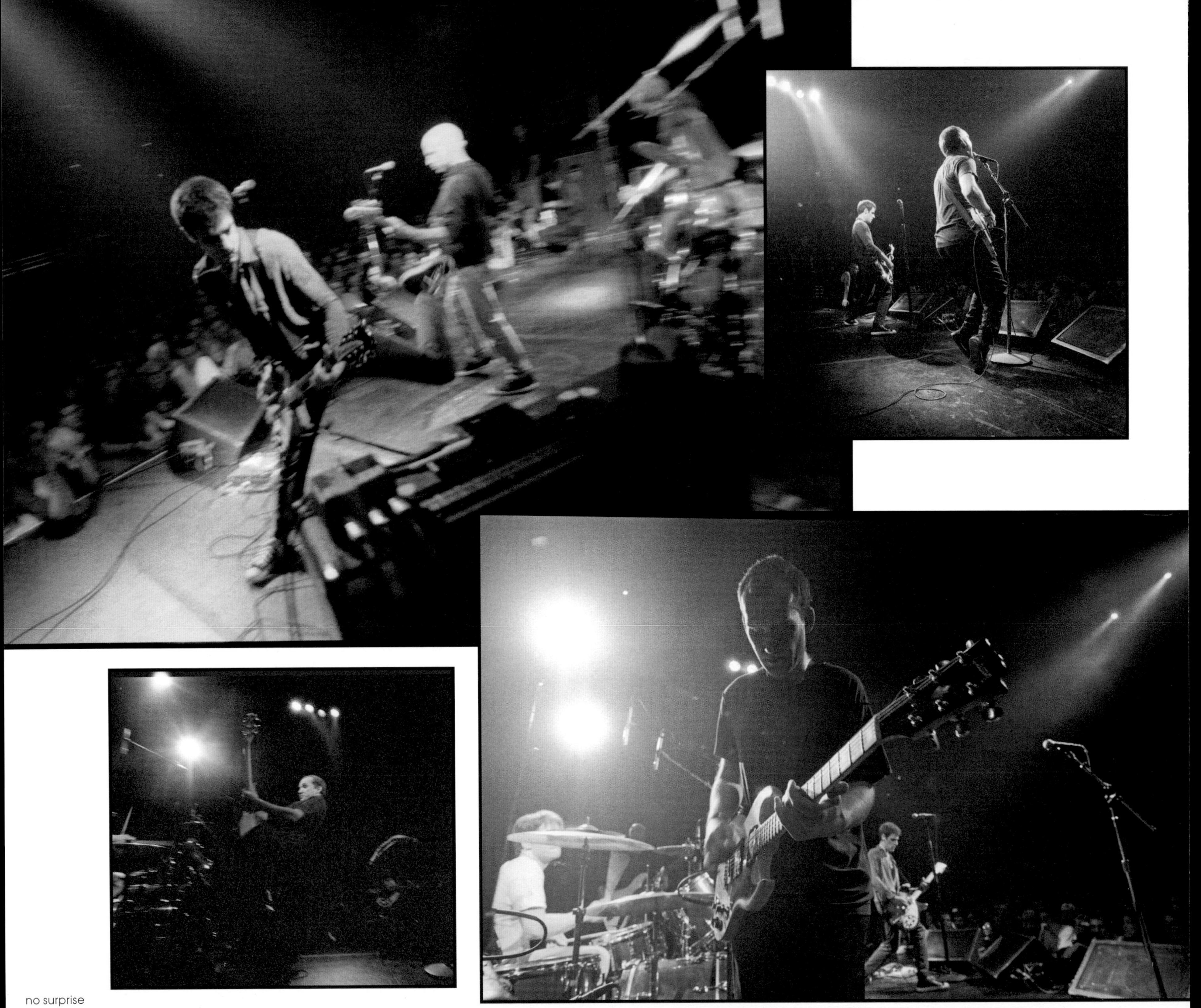

no surprise

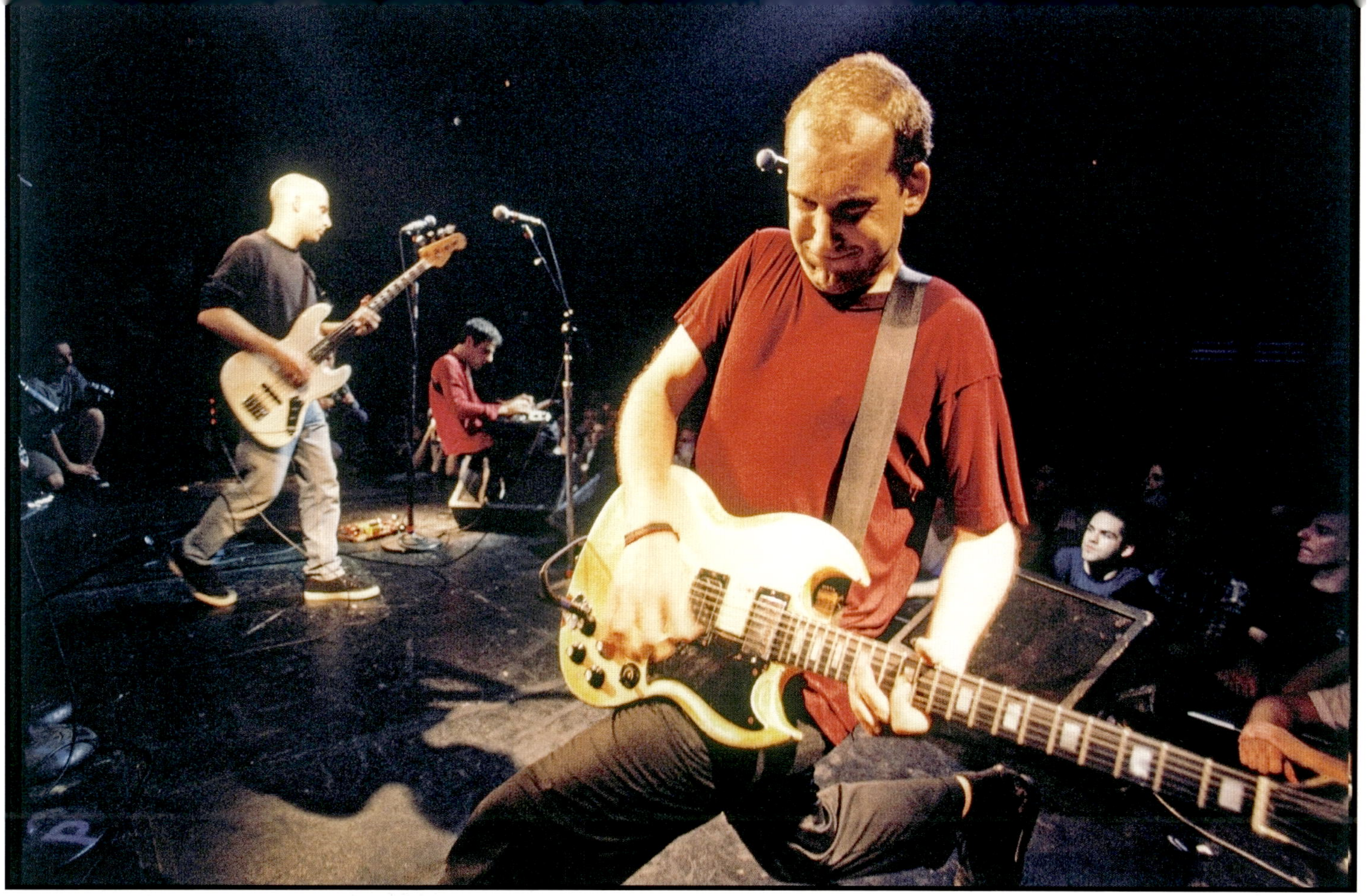

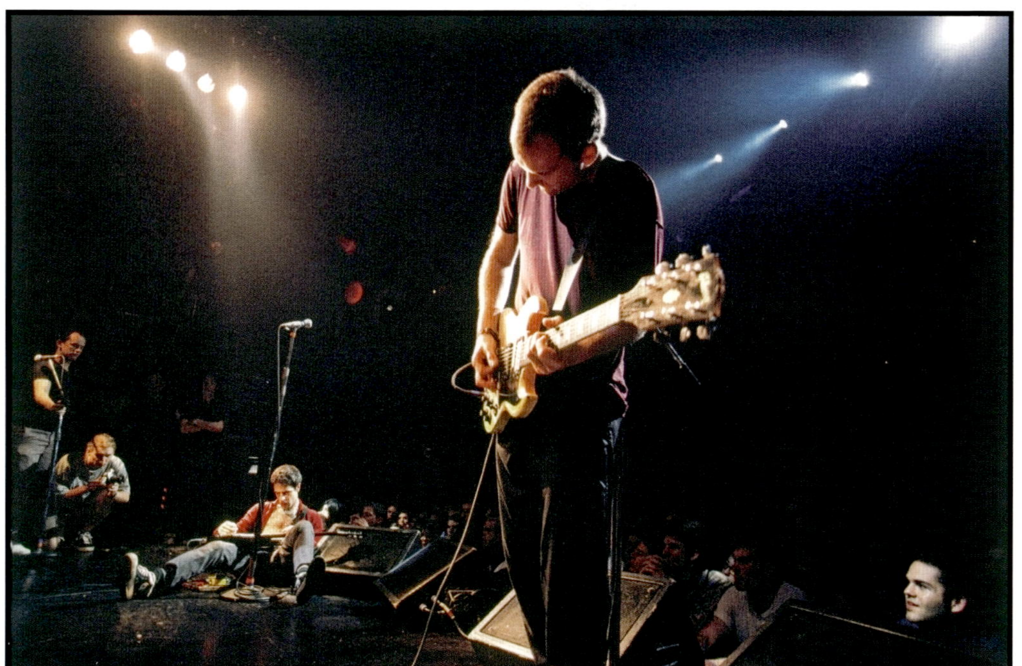

Seeing Fugazi at the Palladium was an incredible event: besides the fact that I had seen fantastic shows there since the late seventies, this was to be the last live show ever at the legendary venue. The promoter actually claimed he lost money even though the show was sold out (obviously due in part to Fugazi still insisting on a low ticket price); he did it just to be able to claim that he put on a Fugazi show!

At this time they were too popular for any other (non-arena) venue in New York City, and in fact played a less-publicized show the following night just a few blocks away.

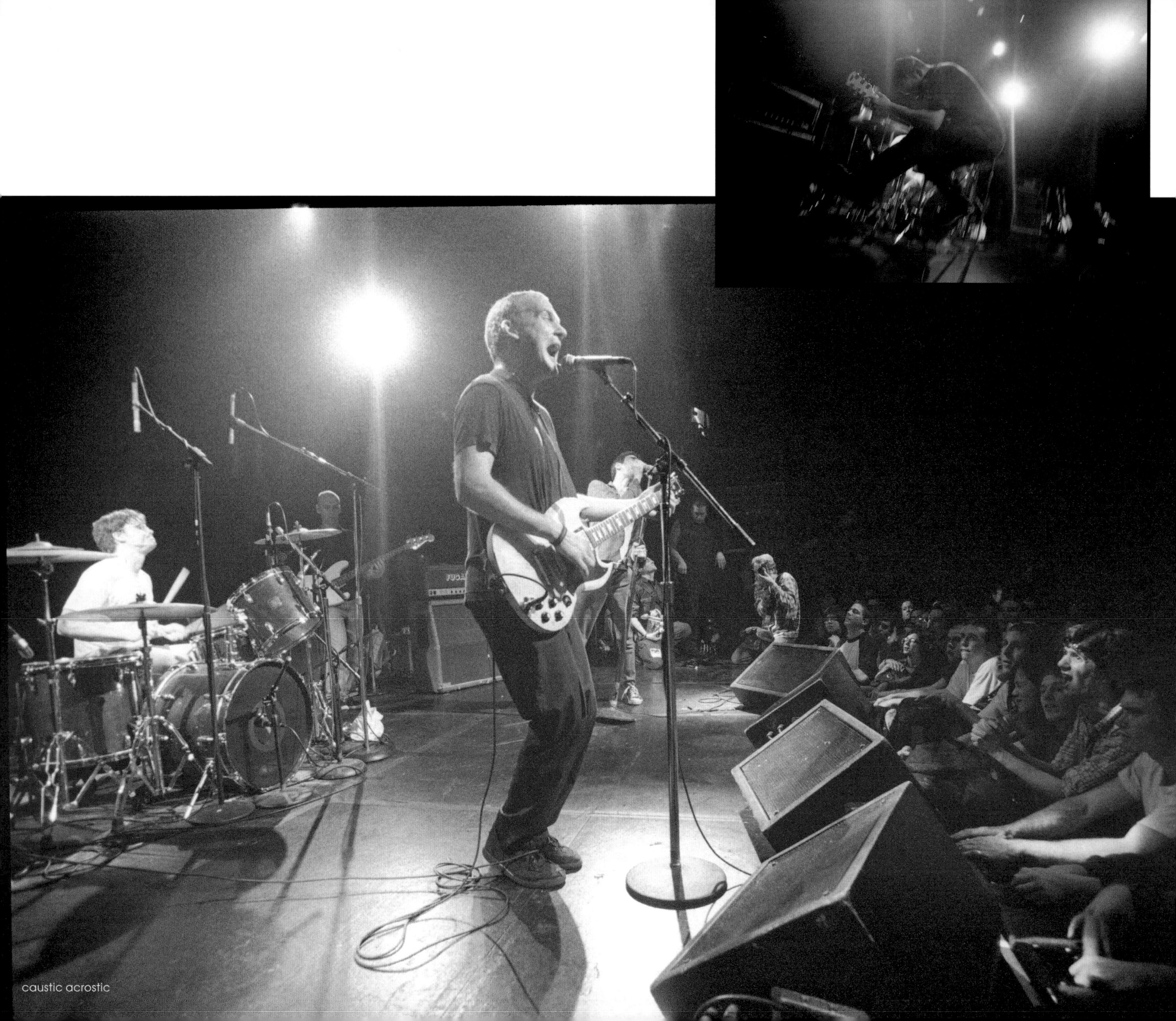

caustic acrostic

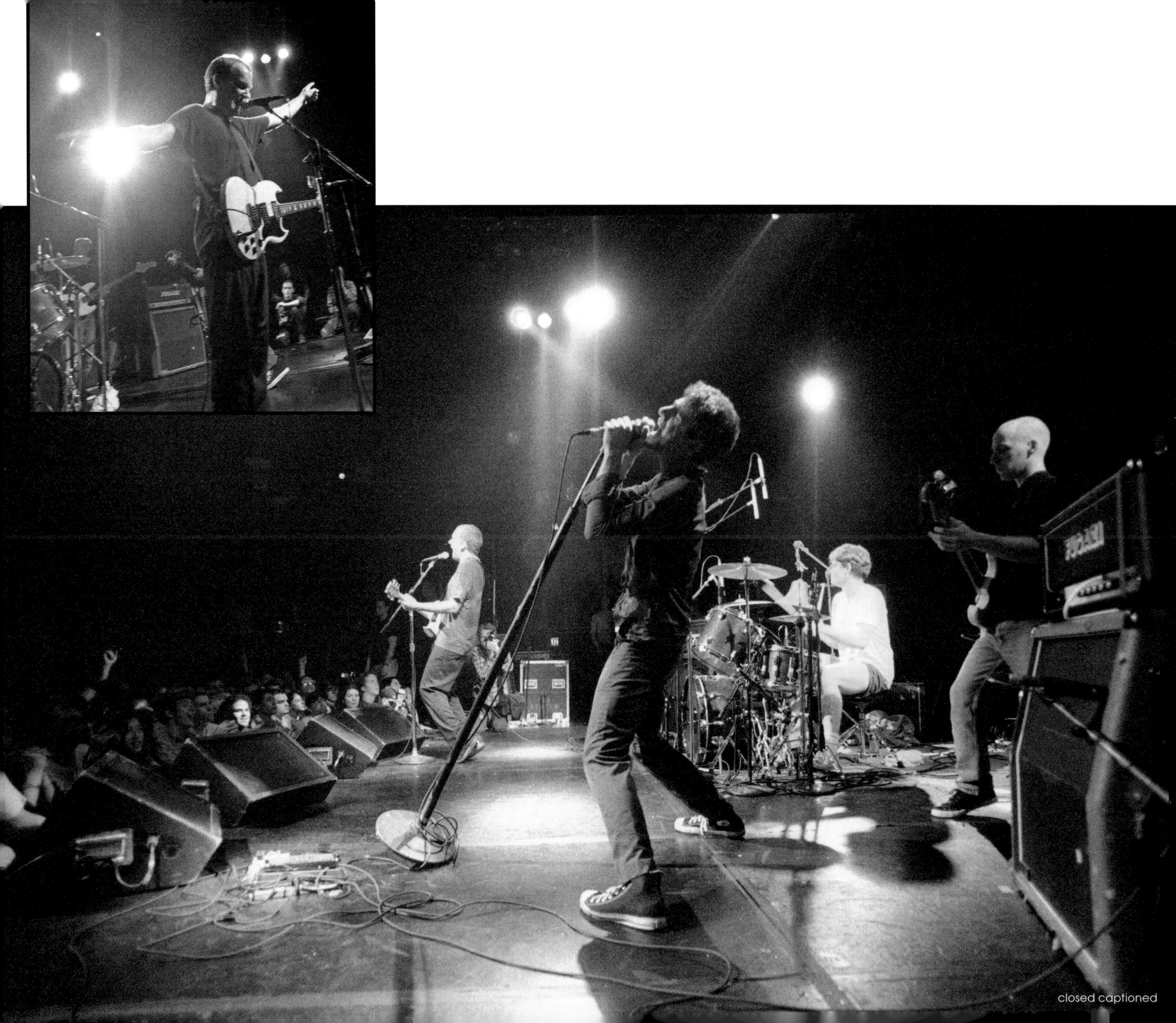

closed captioned

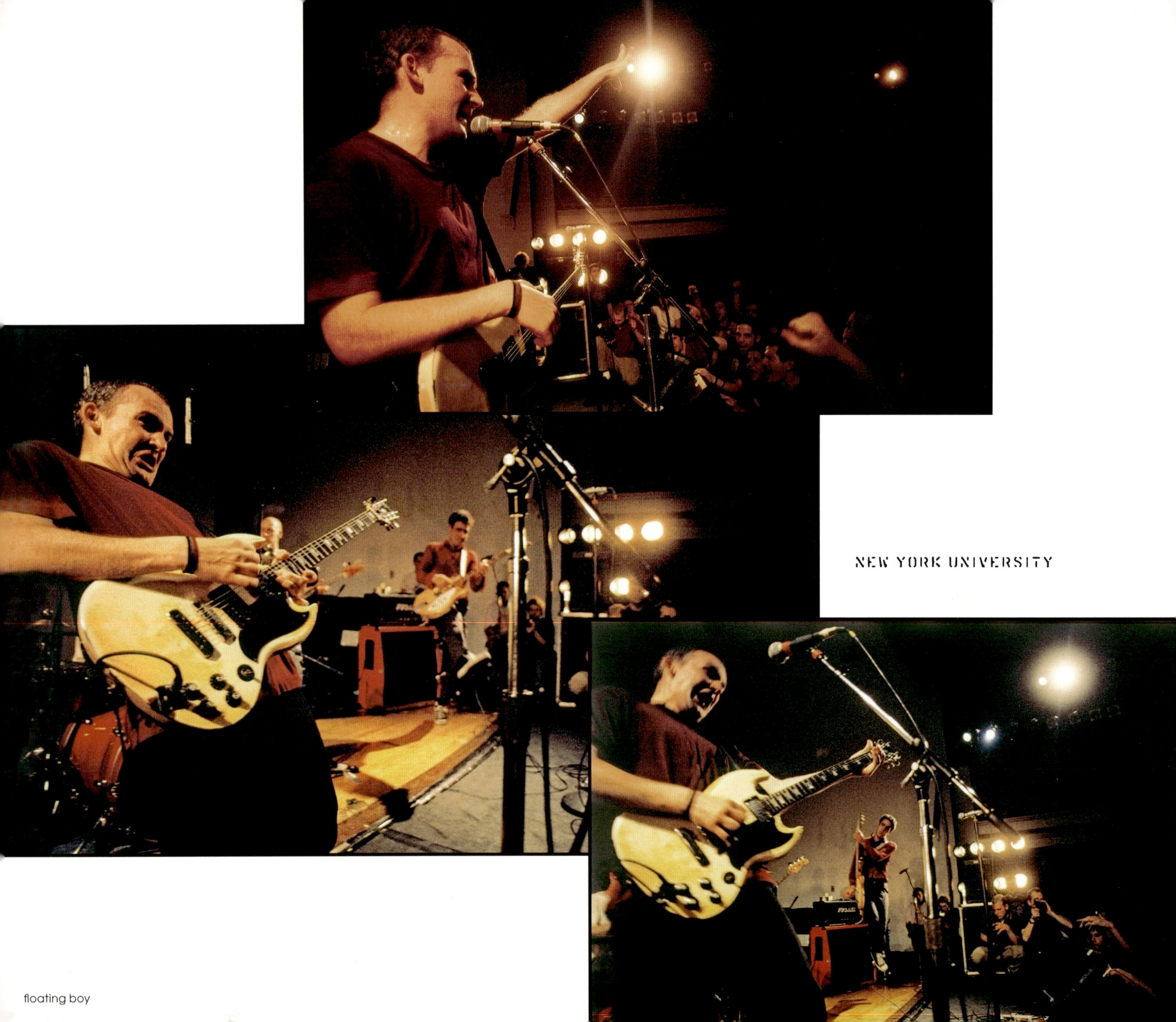

NEW YORK UNIVERSITY

floating boy

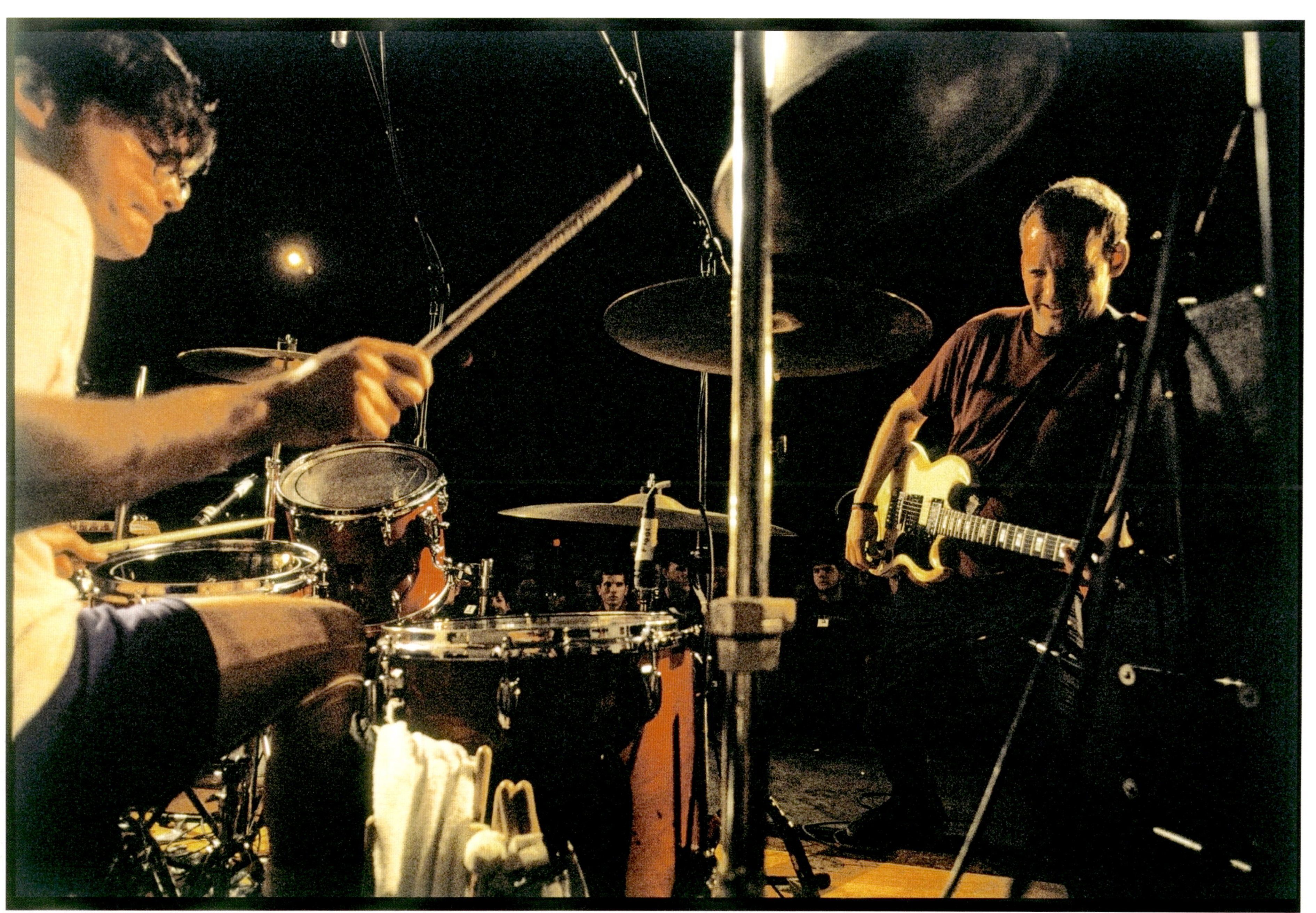

Loeb Student Center at NYU: another building gone to the wrecking ball, just like the Palladium before it.

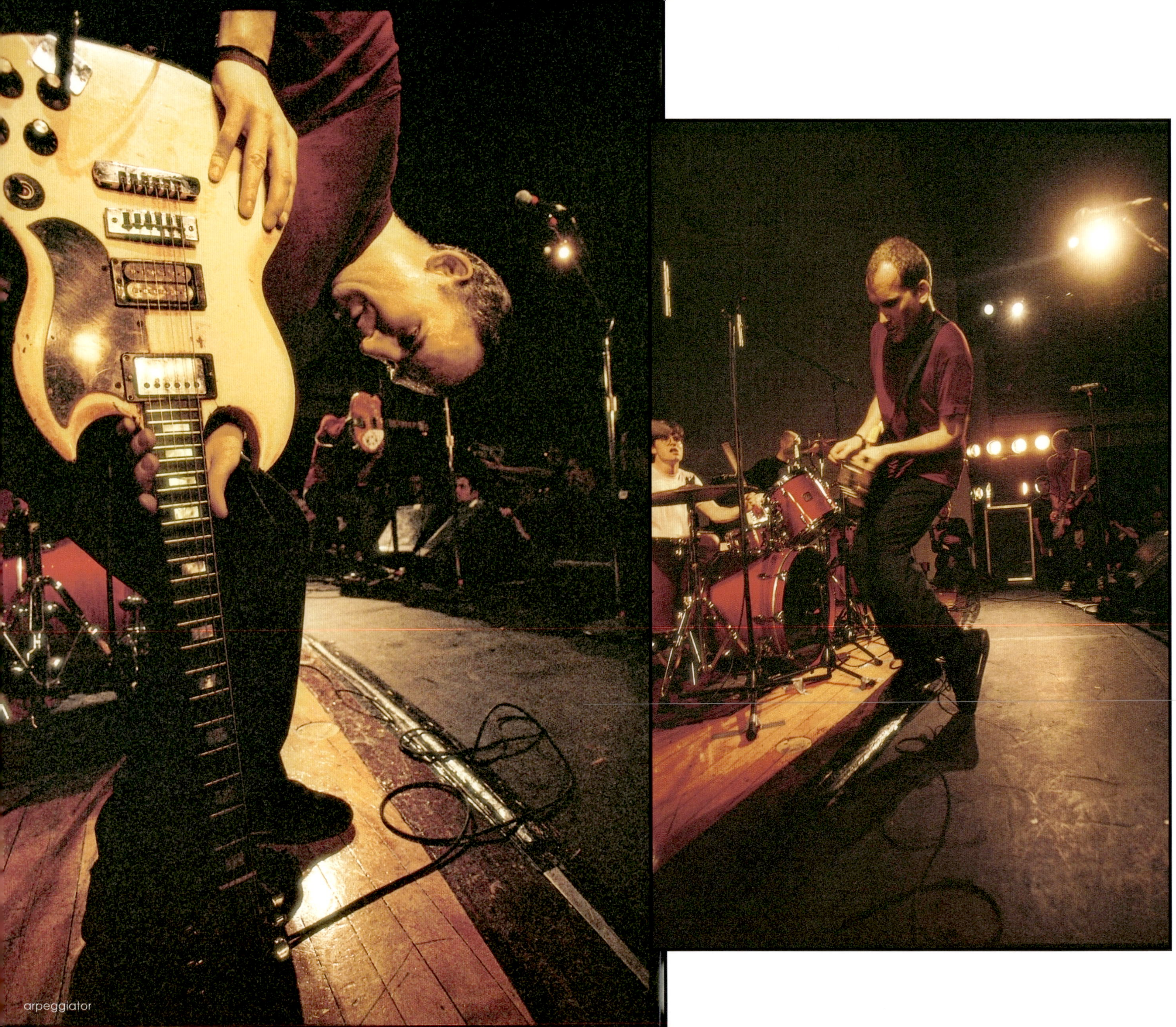

arpeggiator

MAY 1997

guilford fall

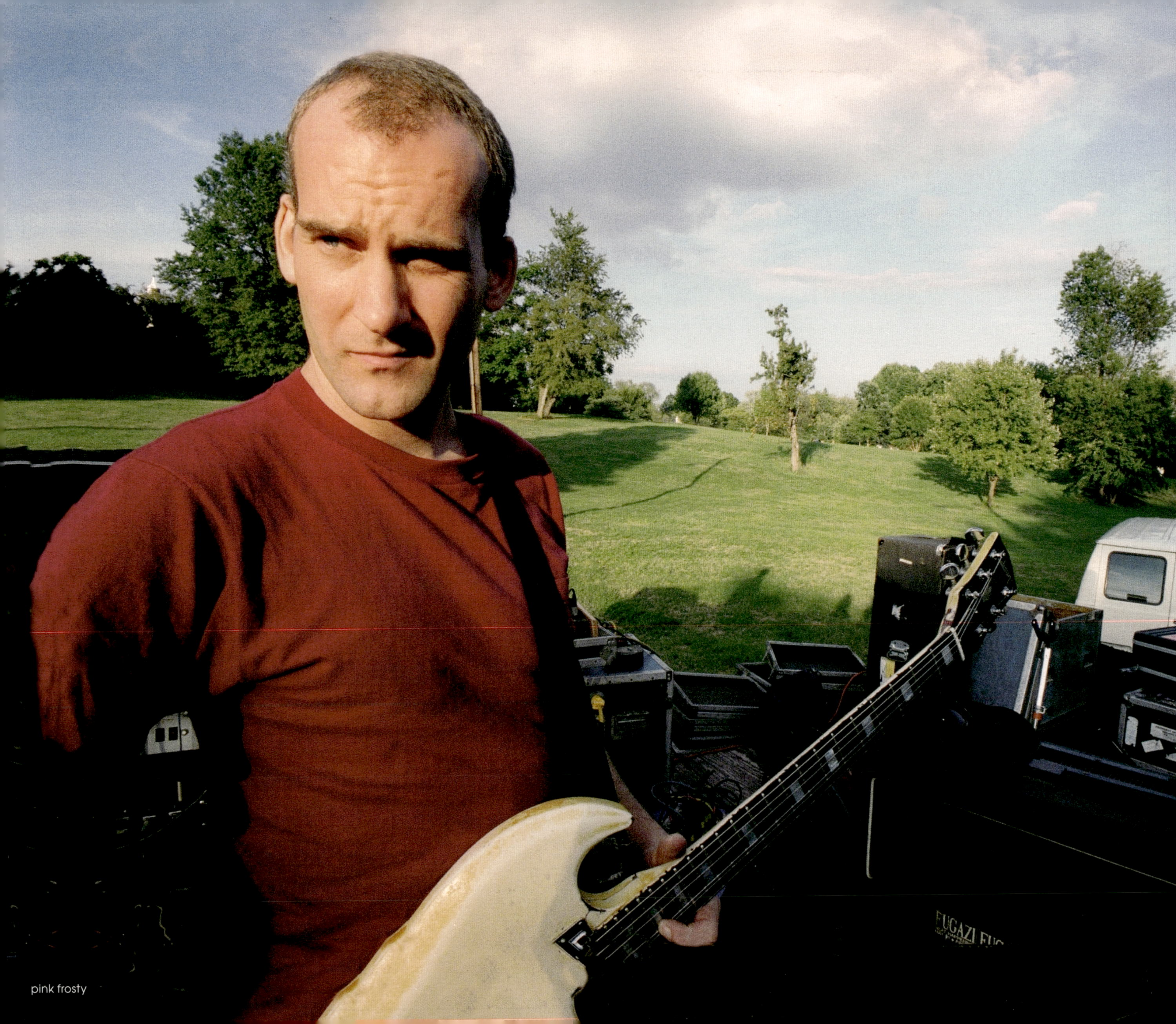

pink frosty

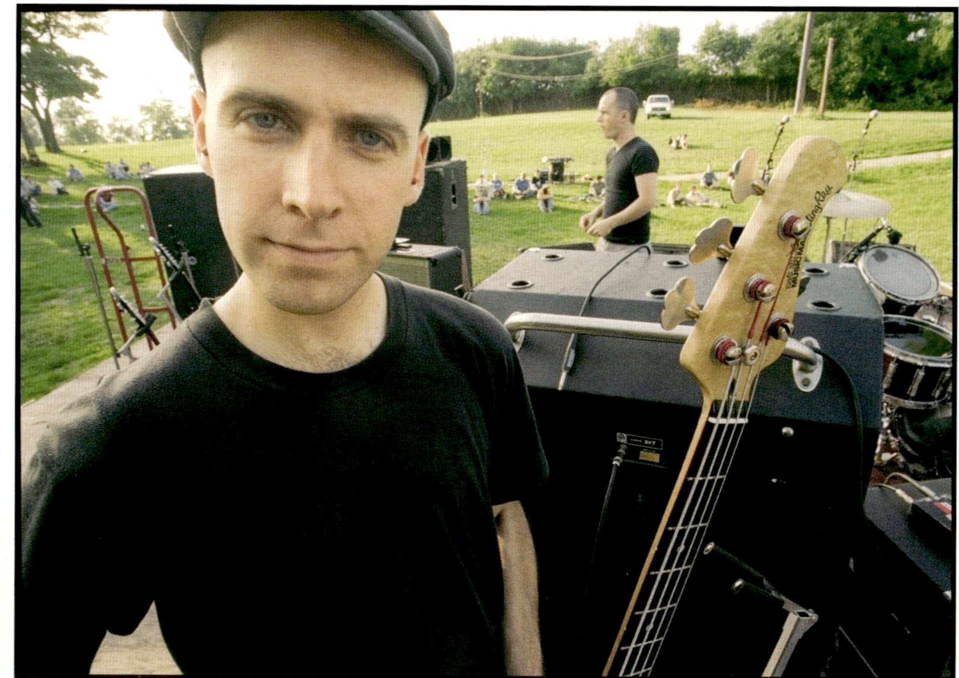

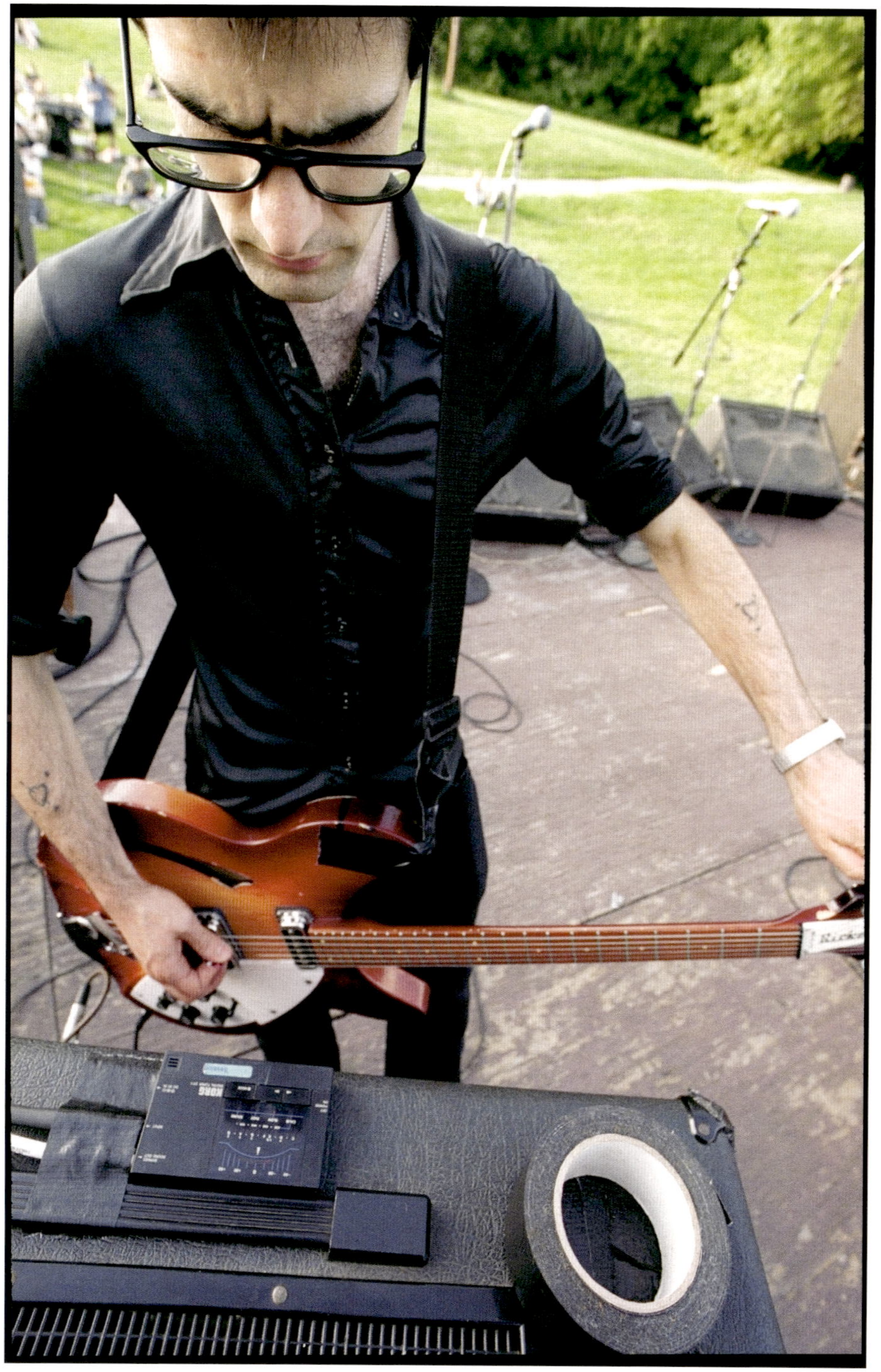

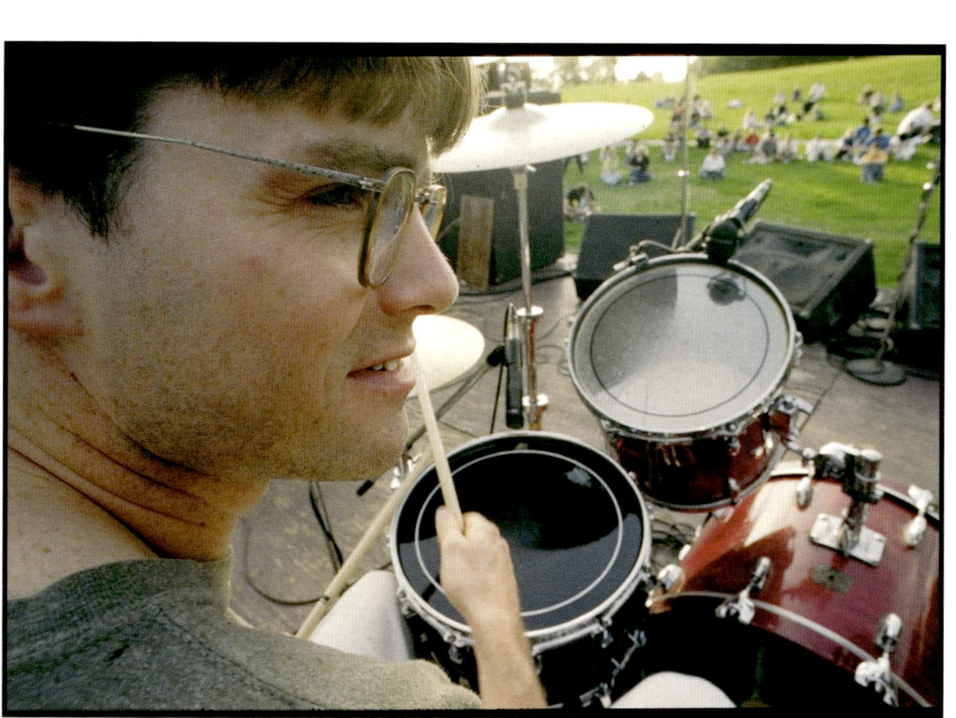

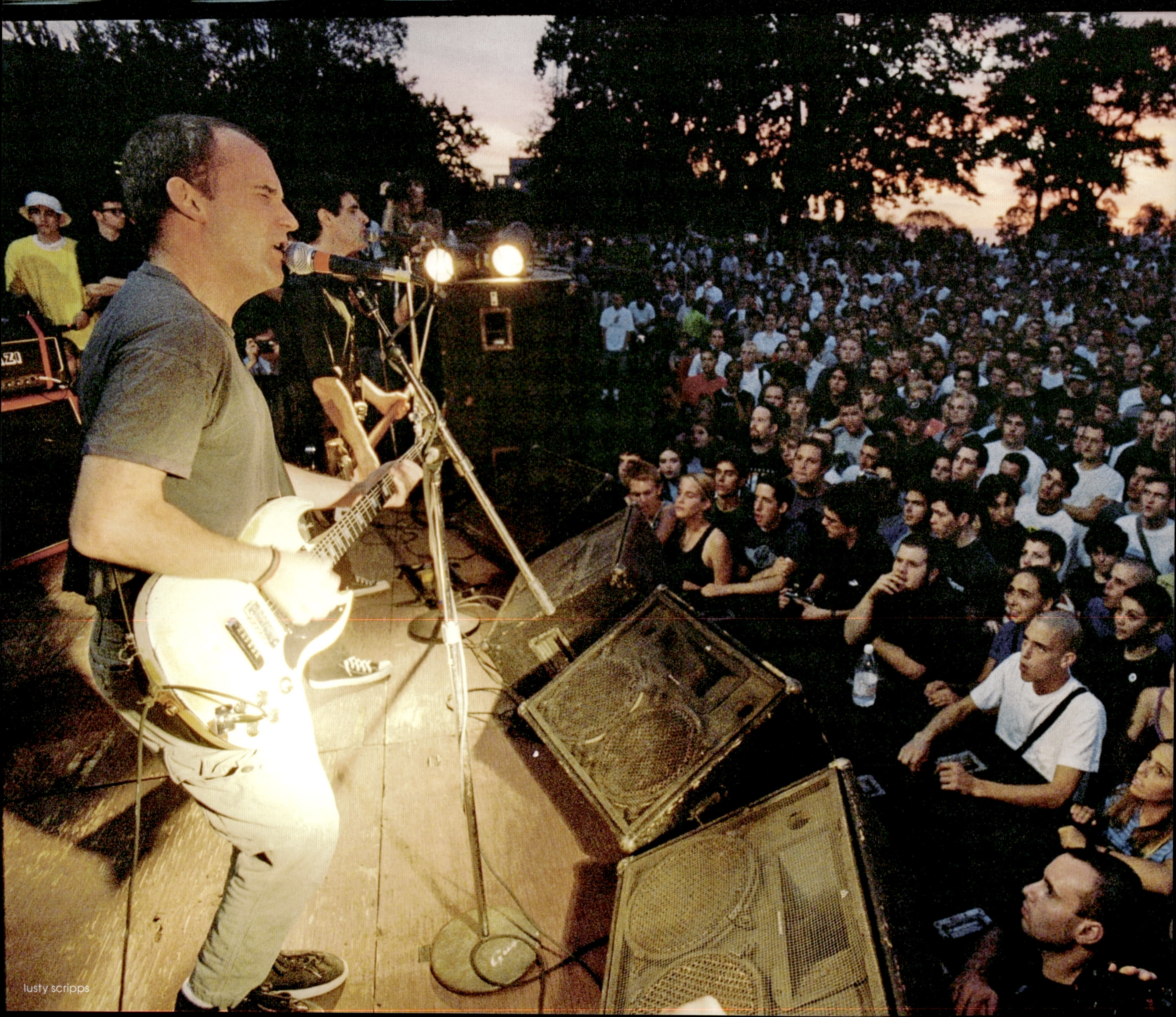

lusty scripps

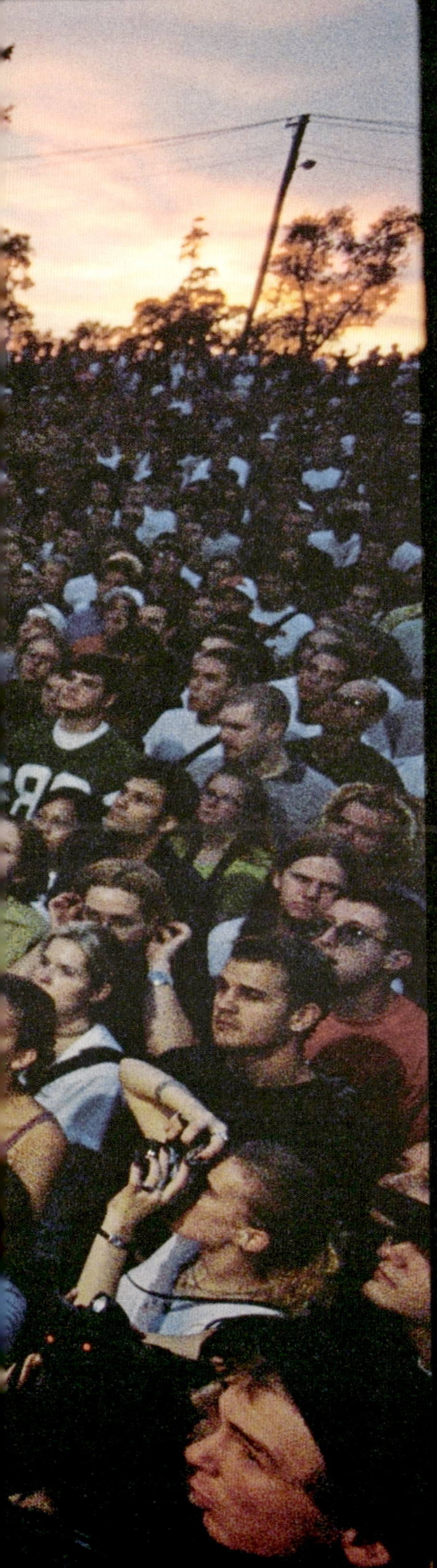

Fugazi shows at Fort Reno by this time had become a cultural event for Washingtonians.

For out-of-towners like myself, this was a pilgrimage to see our favorite band in their hometown.

Several years in a row it was anyone's bet whether the rain would come and wash out the gig.

This night the high clouds offered us nothing but beauty reflecting the sunset.

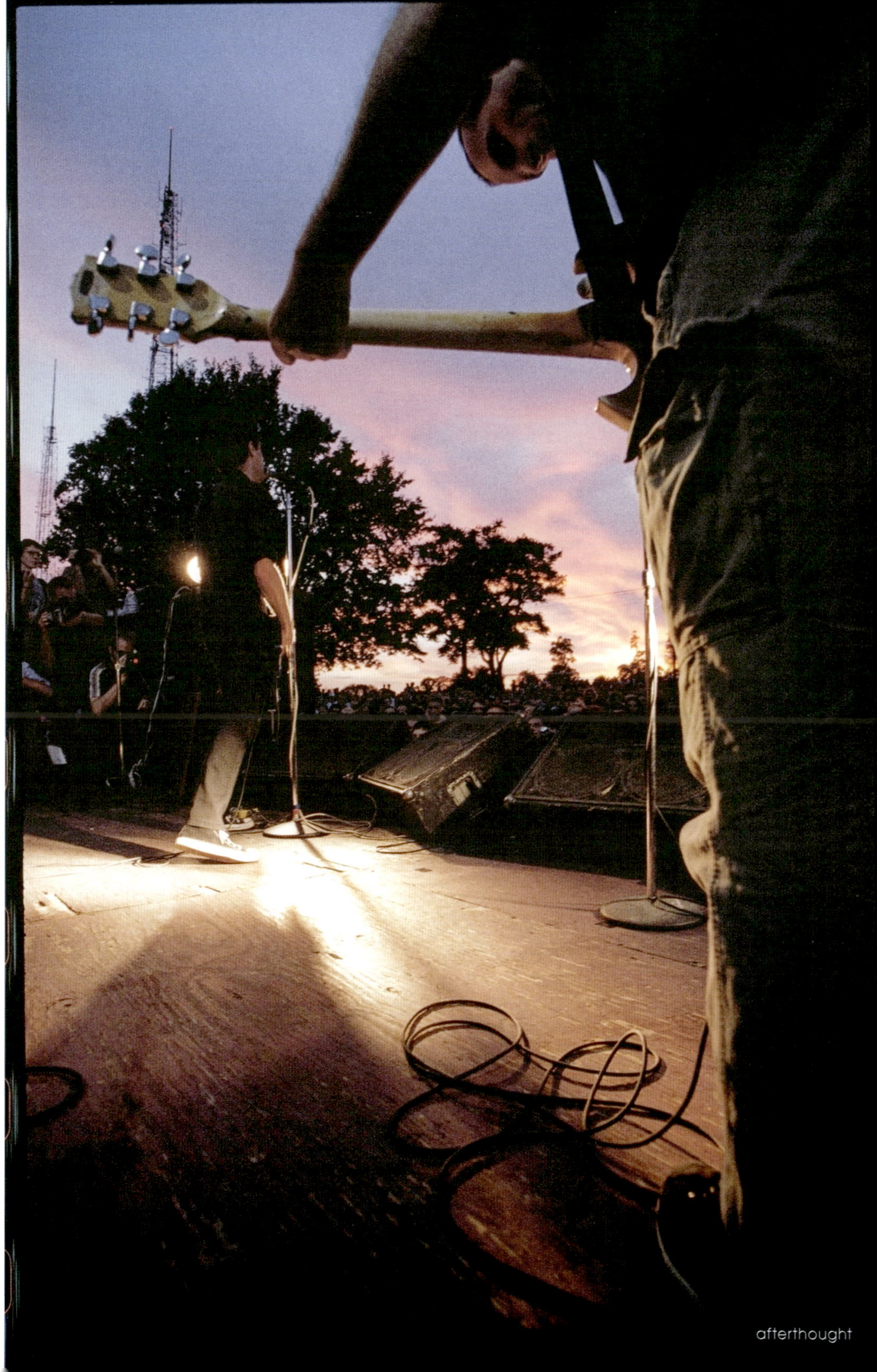

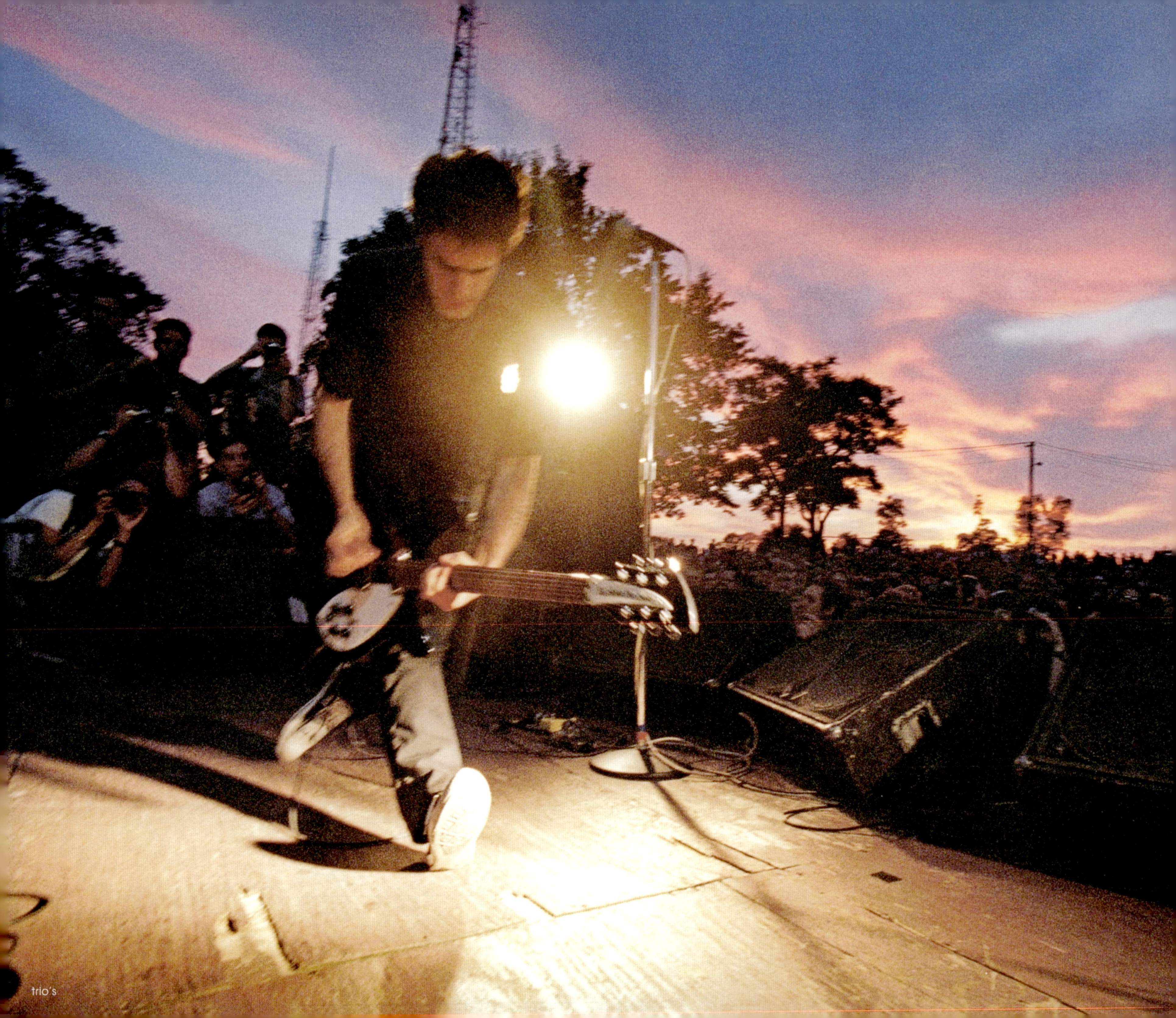

trio's

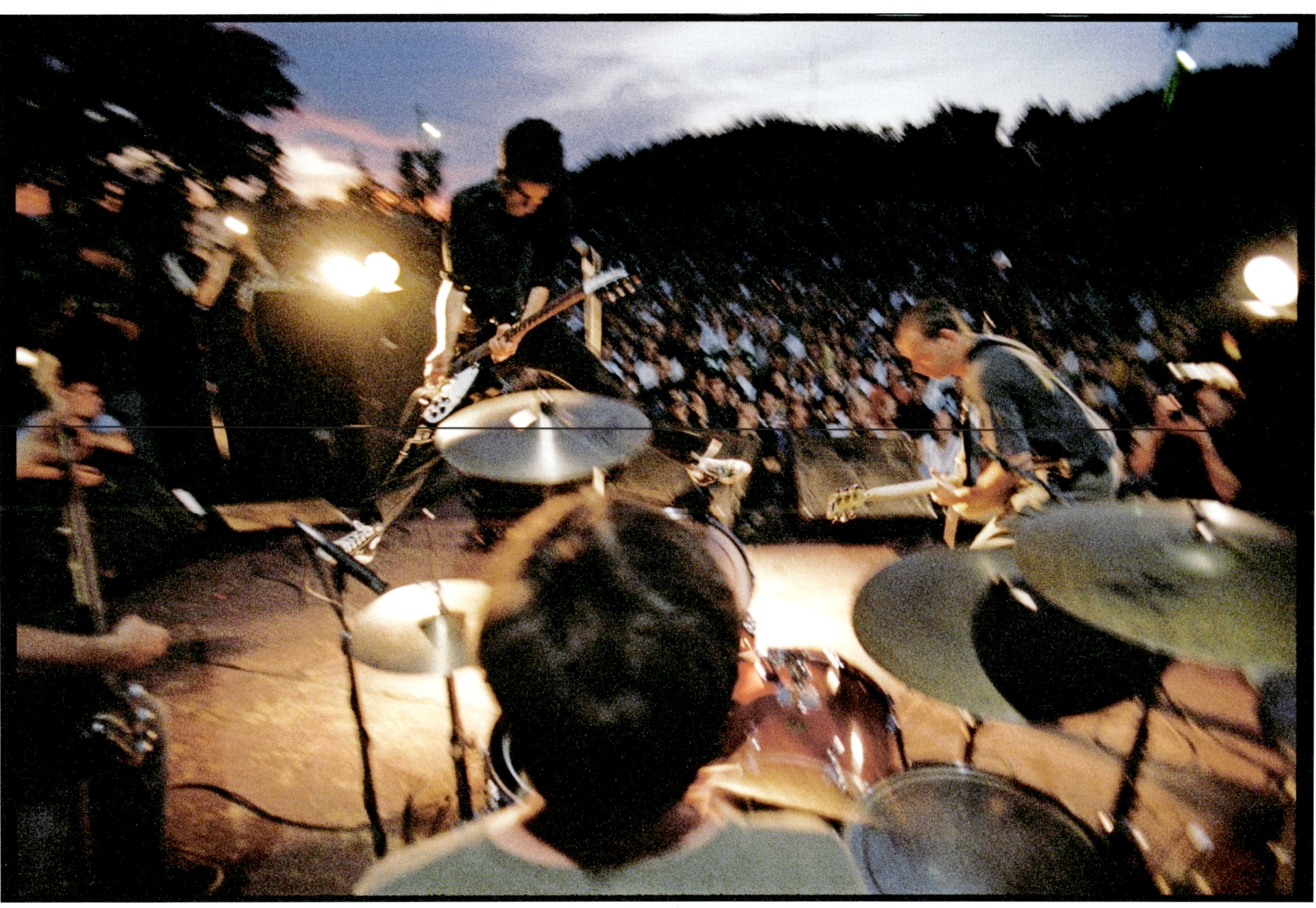

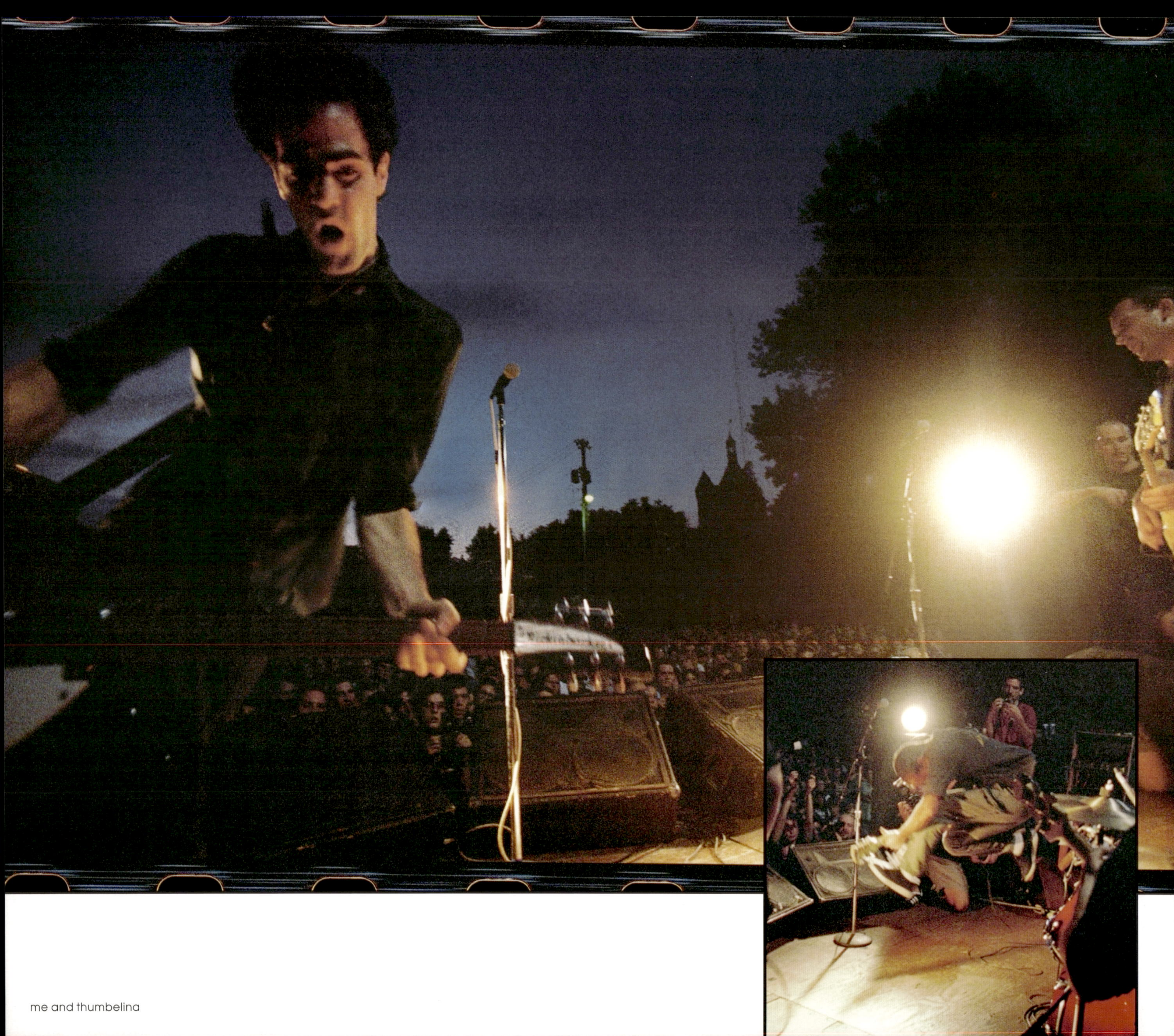

me and thumbelina

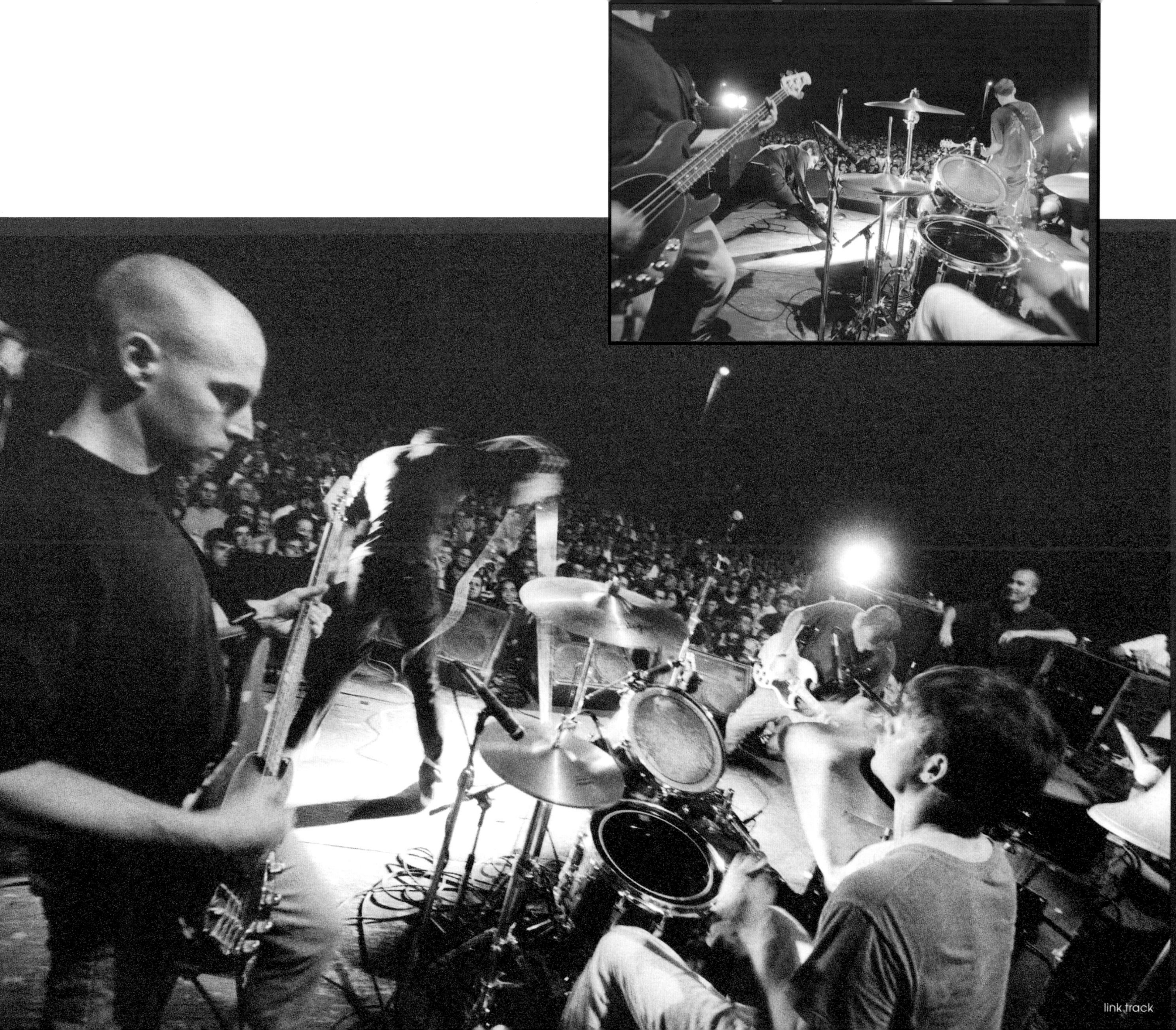

link track

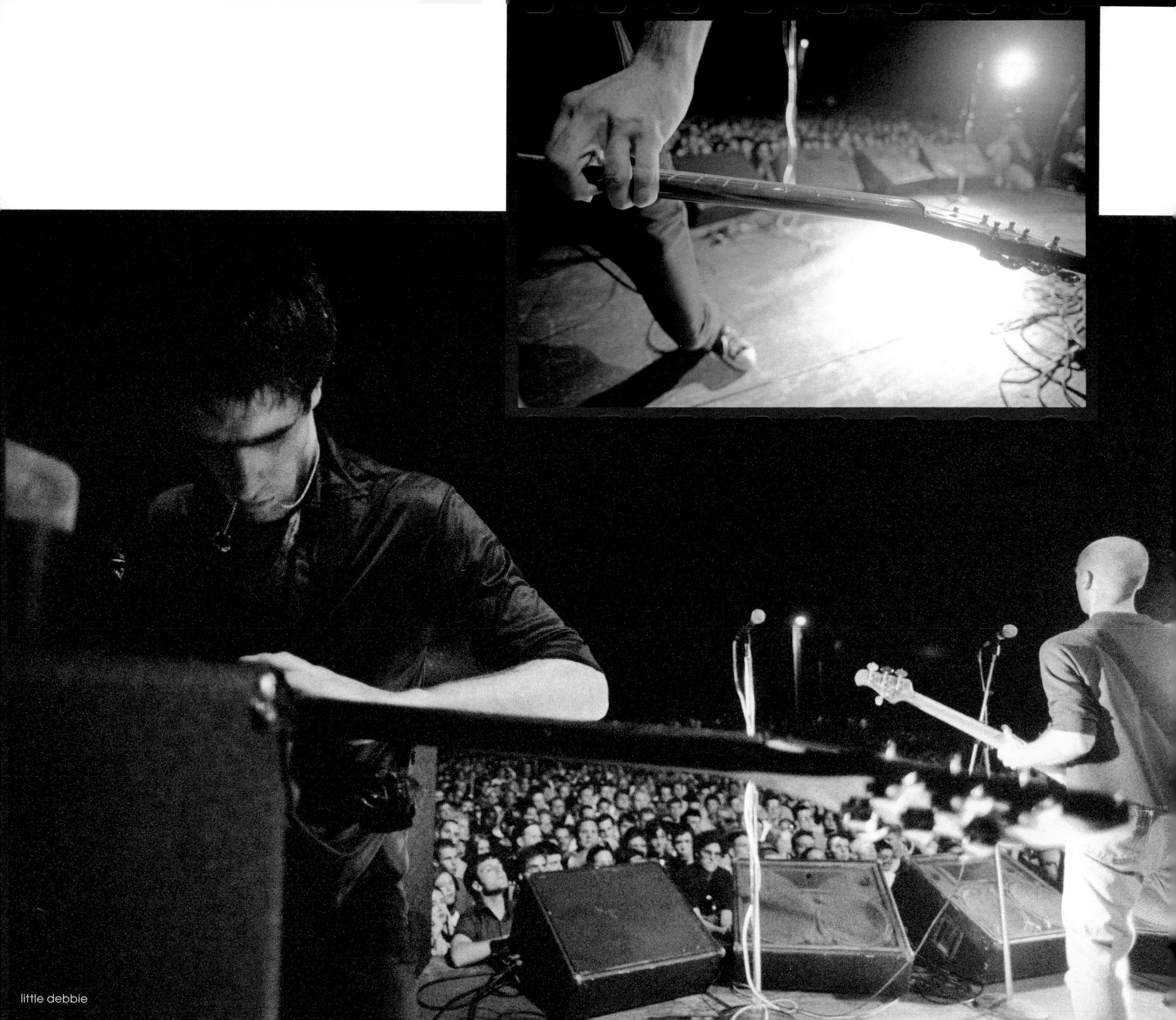

little debbie

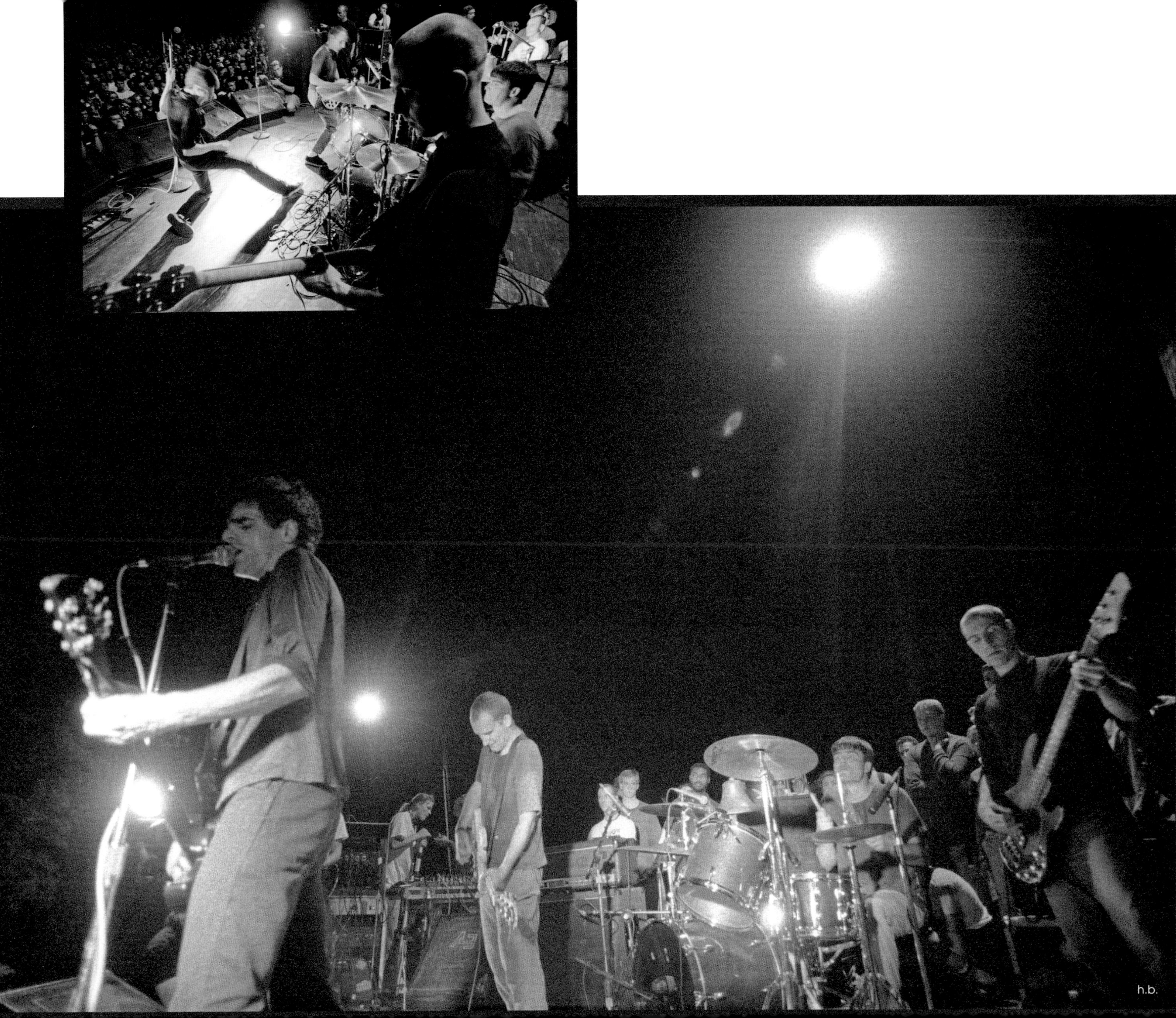

h.b.

NYC,
DECEMBER
1999

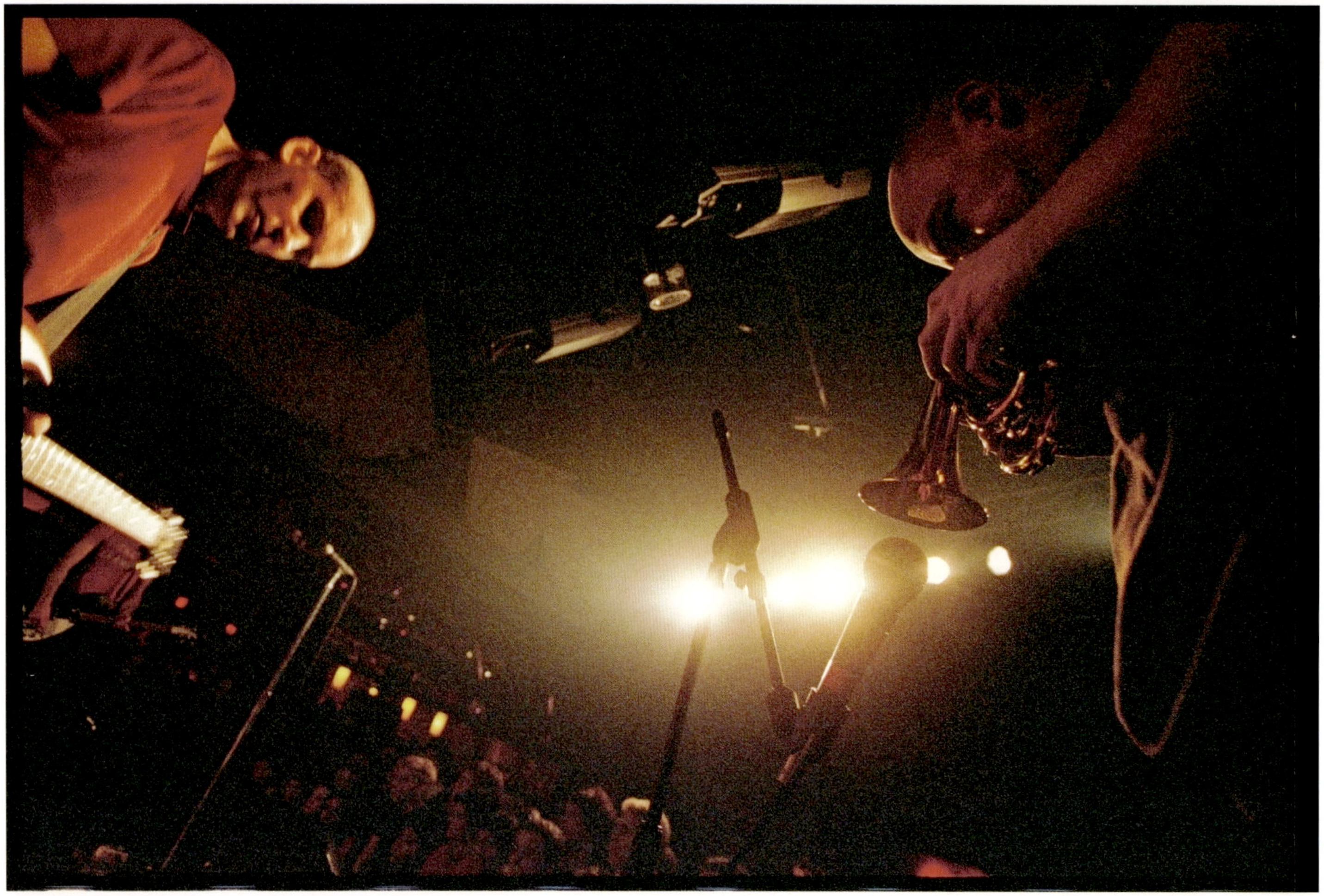

Jerry Busher joins in on the pocket trumpet.

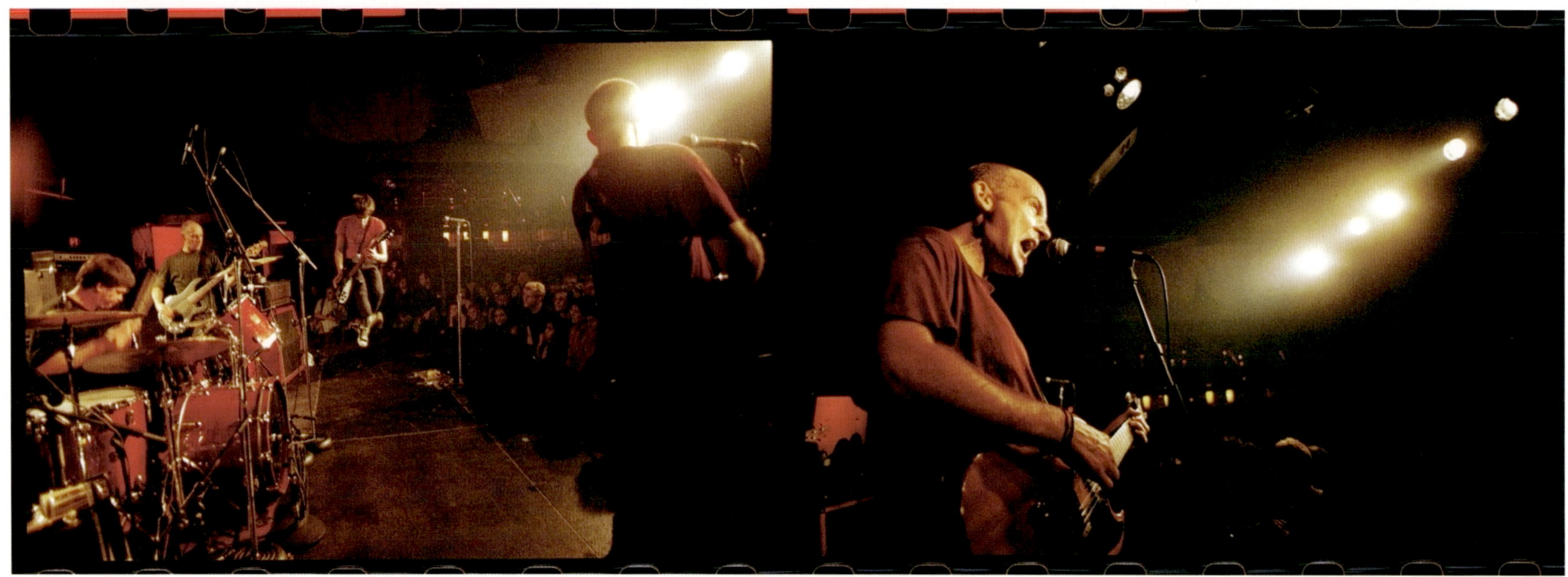

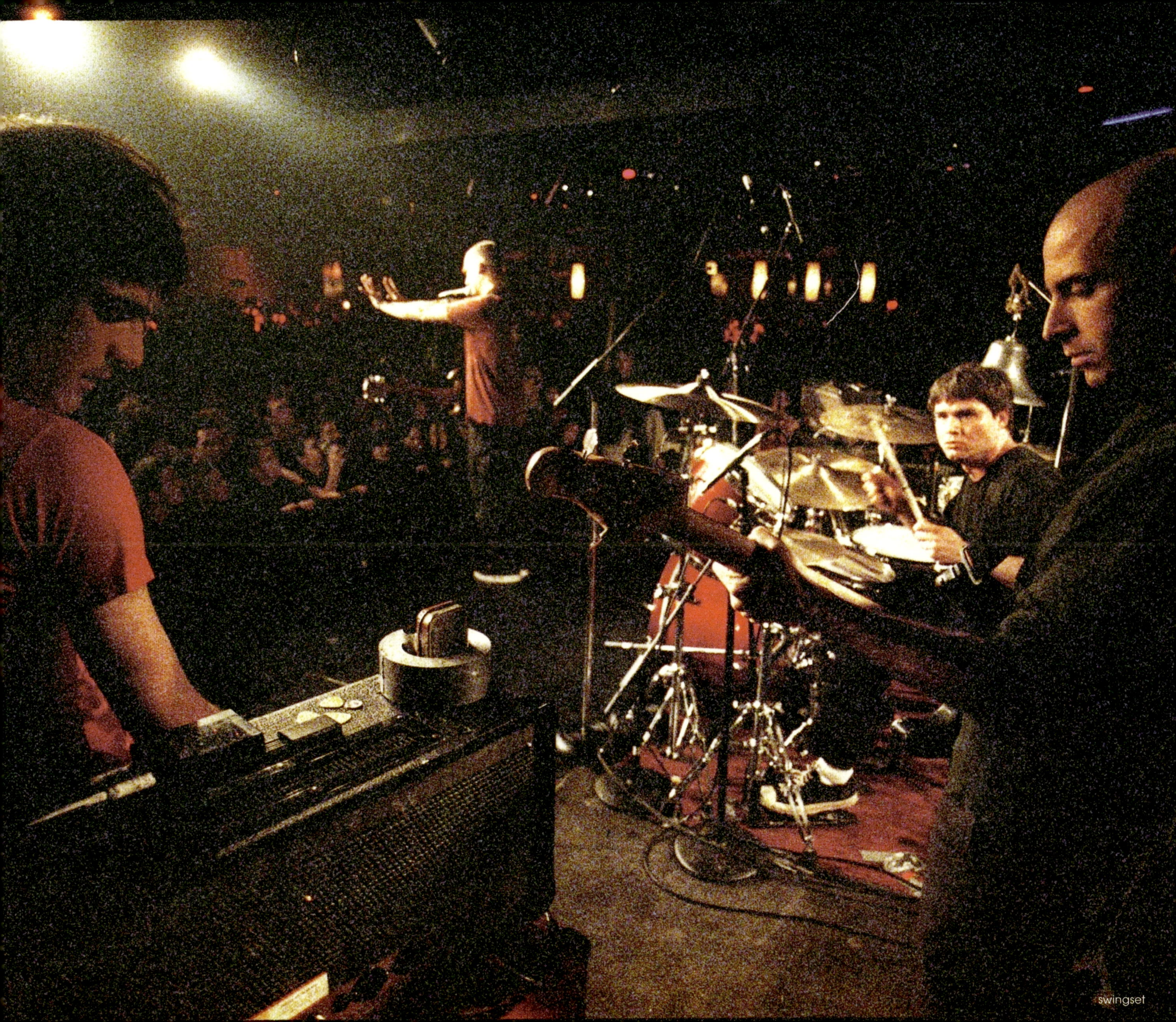
swingset

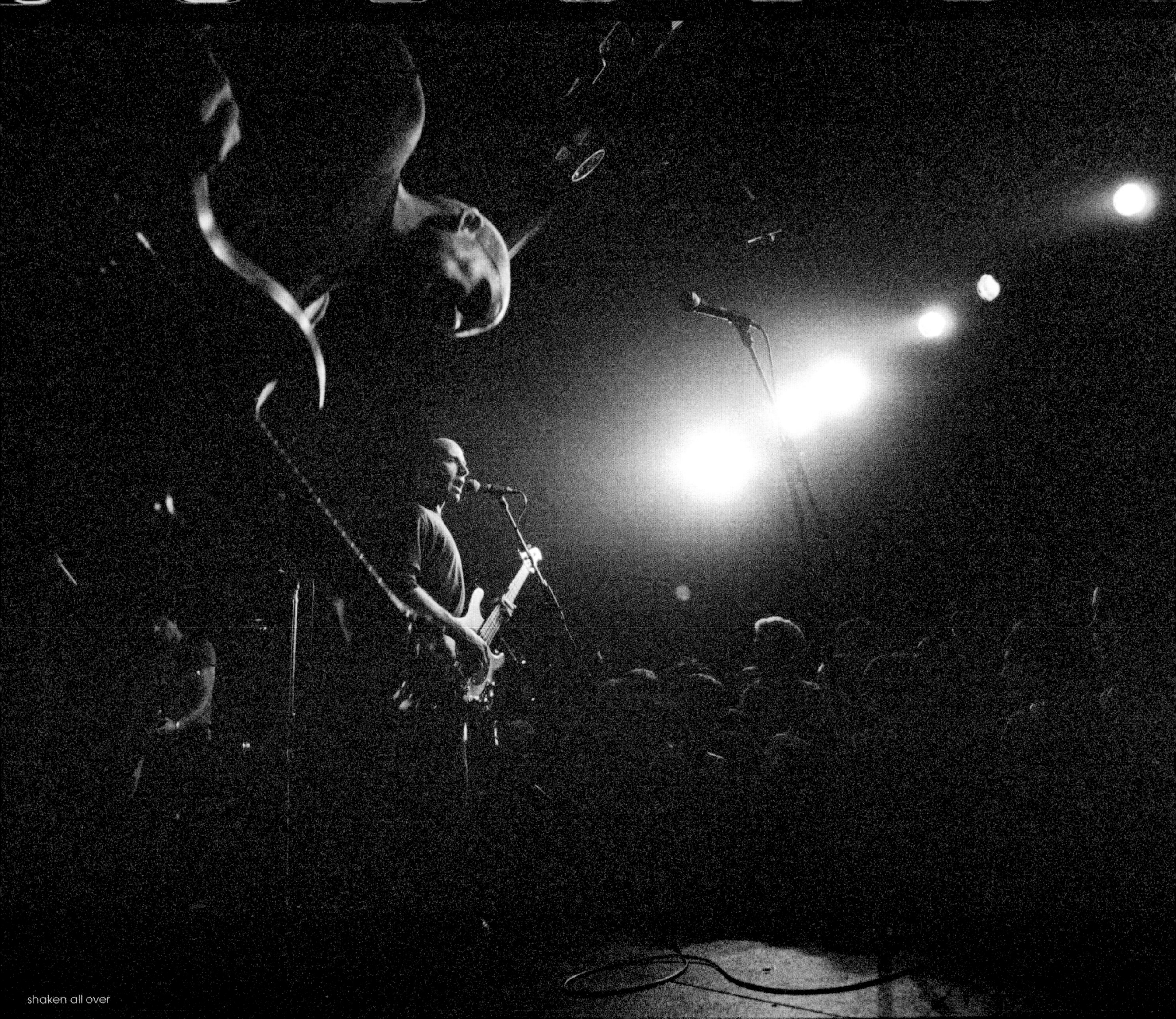

shaken all over

THE ROXY

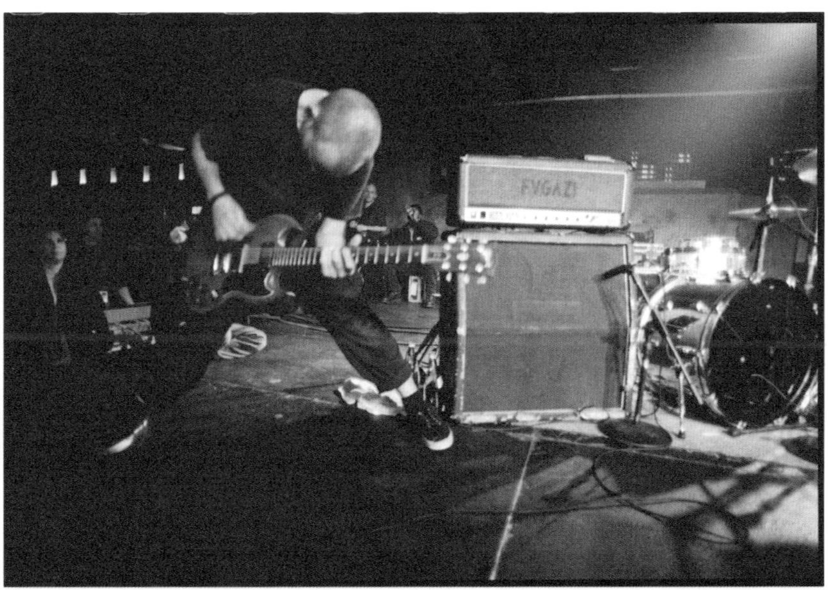

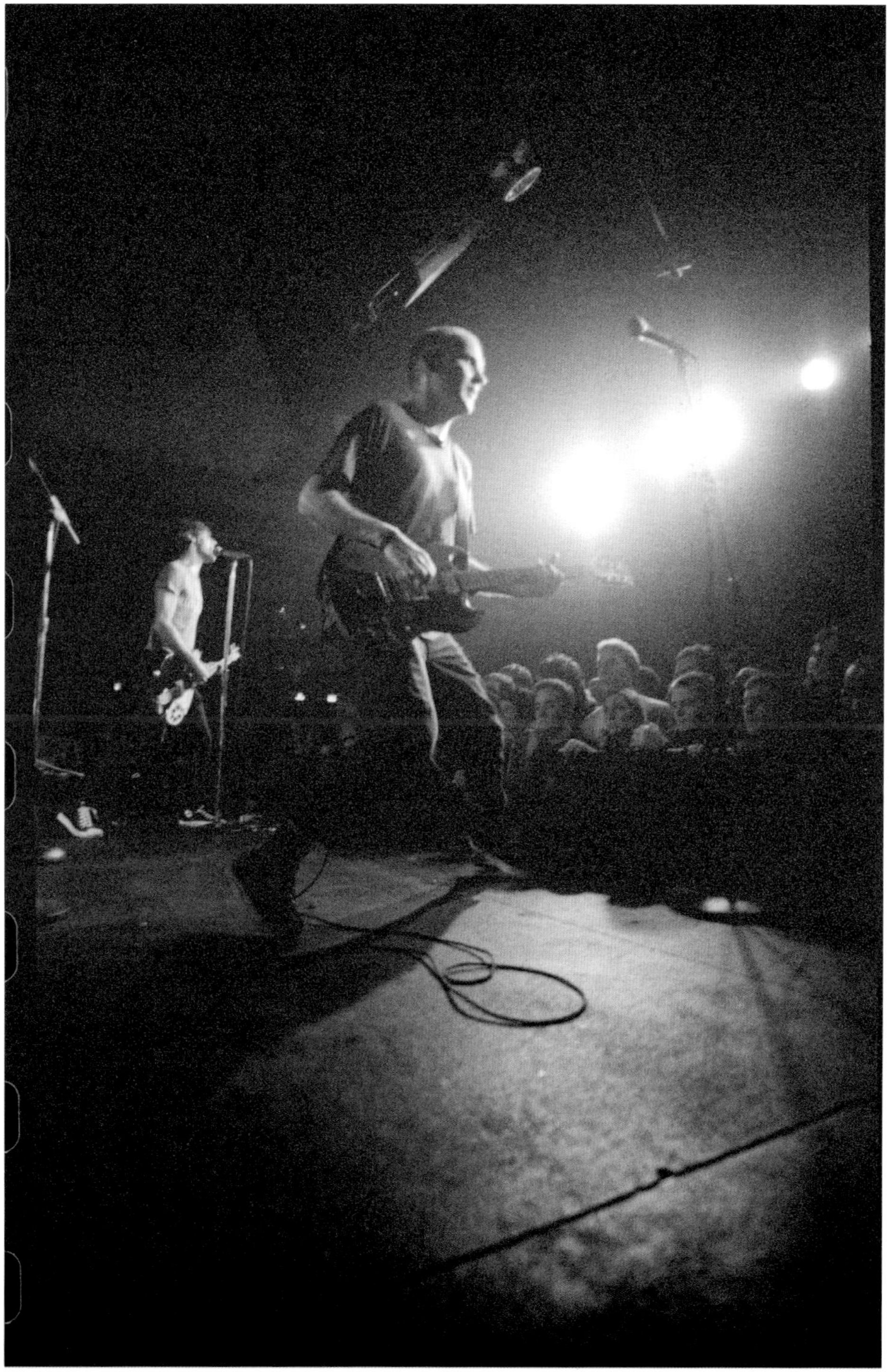

The Roxy was a roller rink that over the years had hosted an extraordinary variety of events, from straight-up roller disco to the New York premier of the Sex Pistols movie *The Great Rock 'n' Roll Swindle*. To many it was also the birthplace of hip-hop in downtown NYC.

To say the least, it was another interesting venue in the long line of peculiar locations Fugazi played over the years.

slo crostic

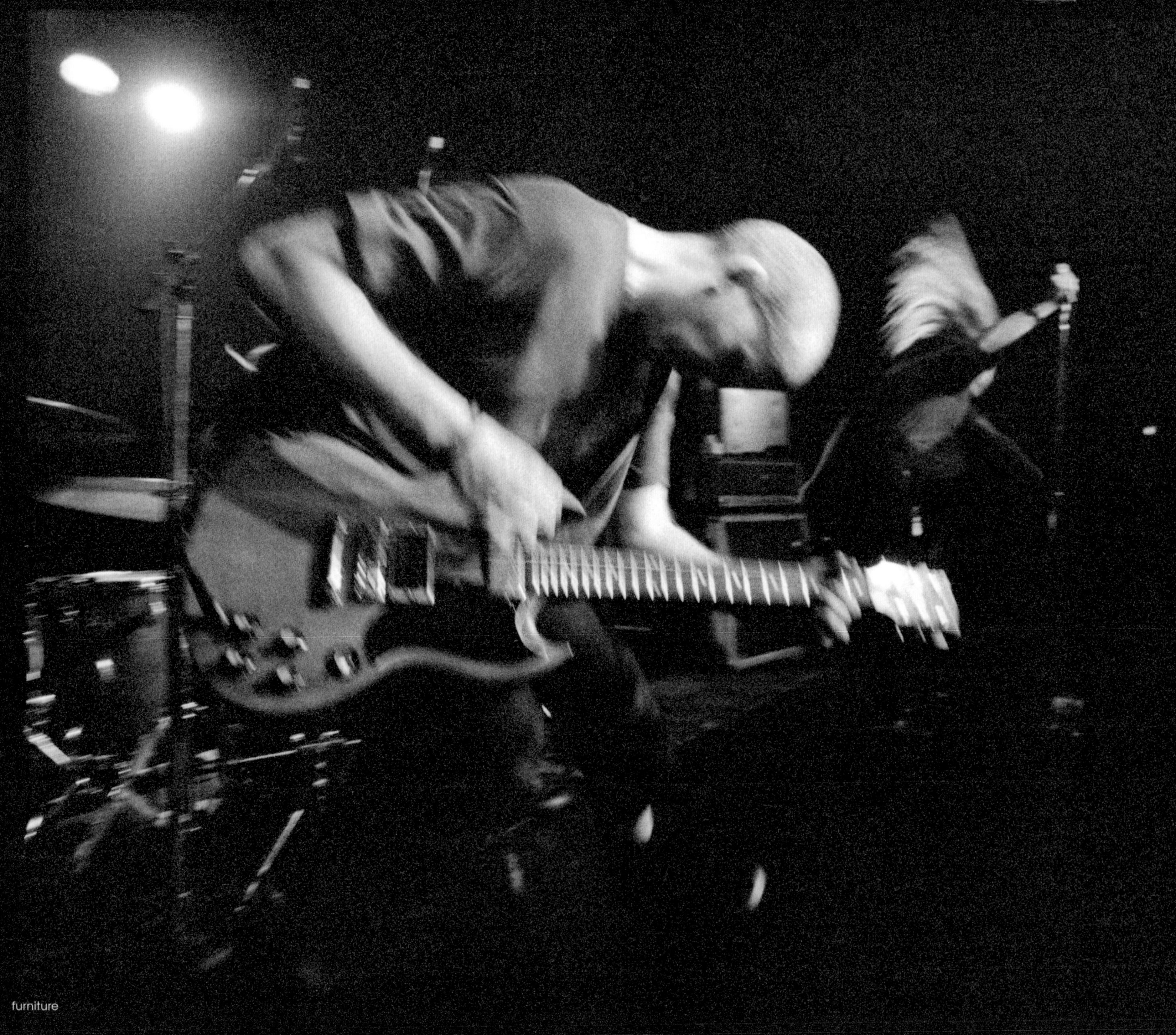

furniture

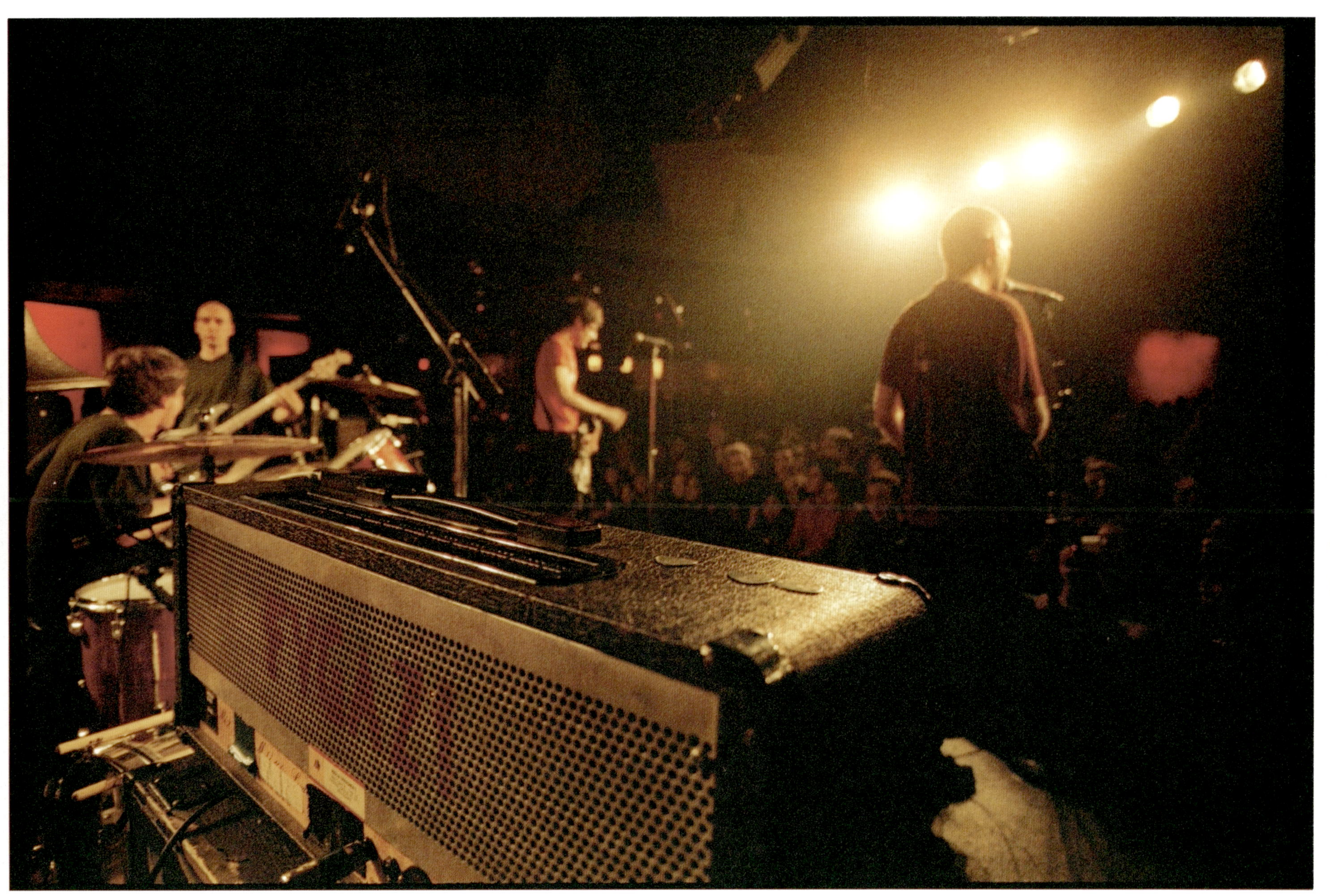

< Old DC friend Amy Pickering joining in on vocals during "Suggestion" as she often had in the past.

In Stockholm for the opening of my "FUCK YOU ALL" exhibition at the Kulturhuset (one of the most popular museums in Sweden).

Coincidentally, Fugazi was playing Stockholm at the same time, so they joined me at the opening celebration and I joined them for their gig the next night.

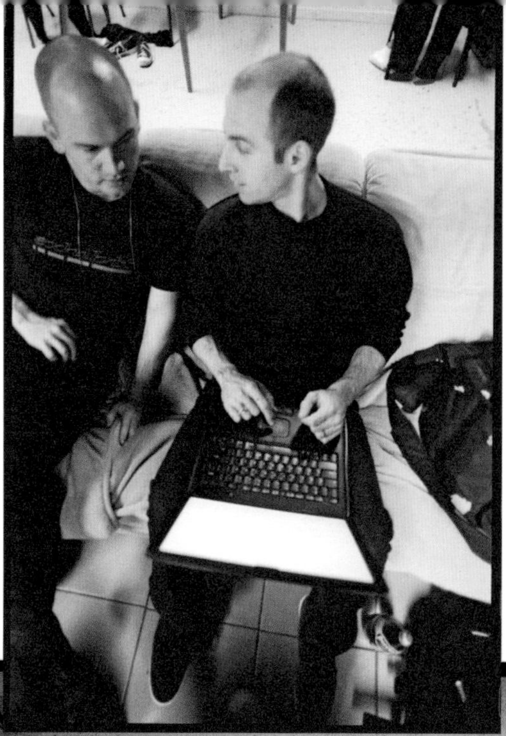

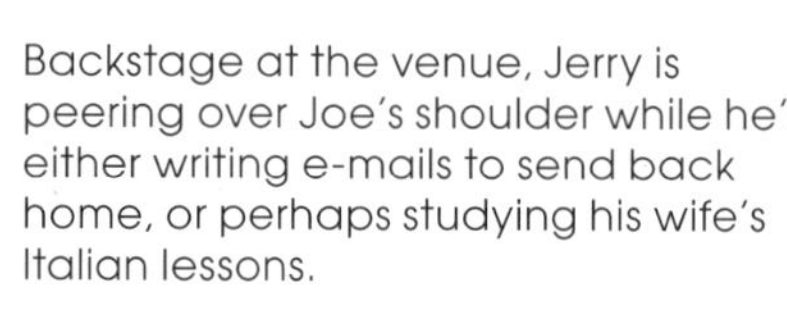

Backstage at the venue, Jerry is peering over Joe's shoulder while he's either writing e-mails to send back home, or perhaps studying his wife's Italian lessons.

Below, Brendan and Guy resting after sound check, before Fugazi gets on stage later in the evening.

STOCKHOLM, SWEDEN, 2000

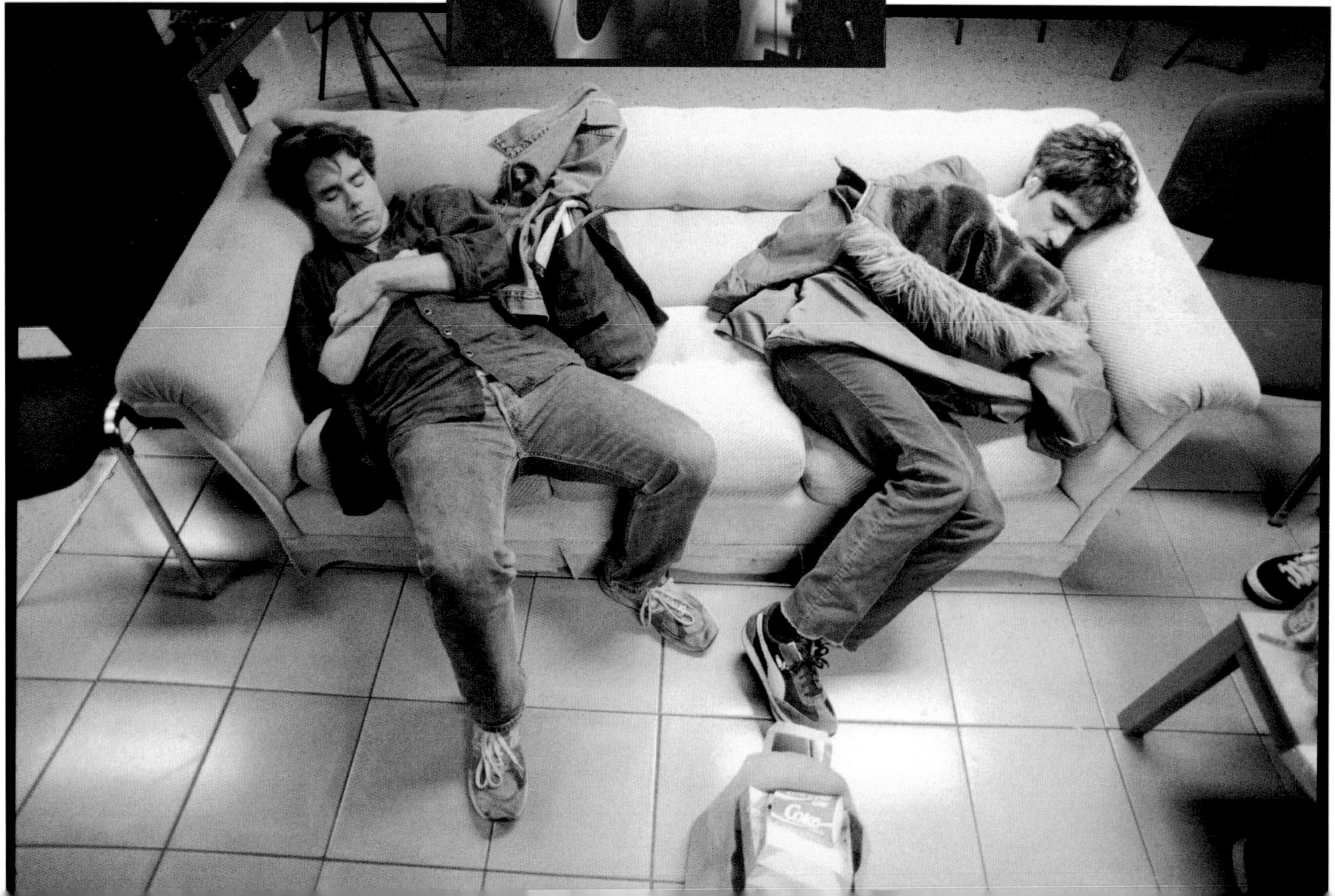

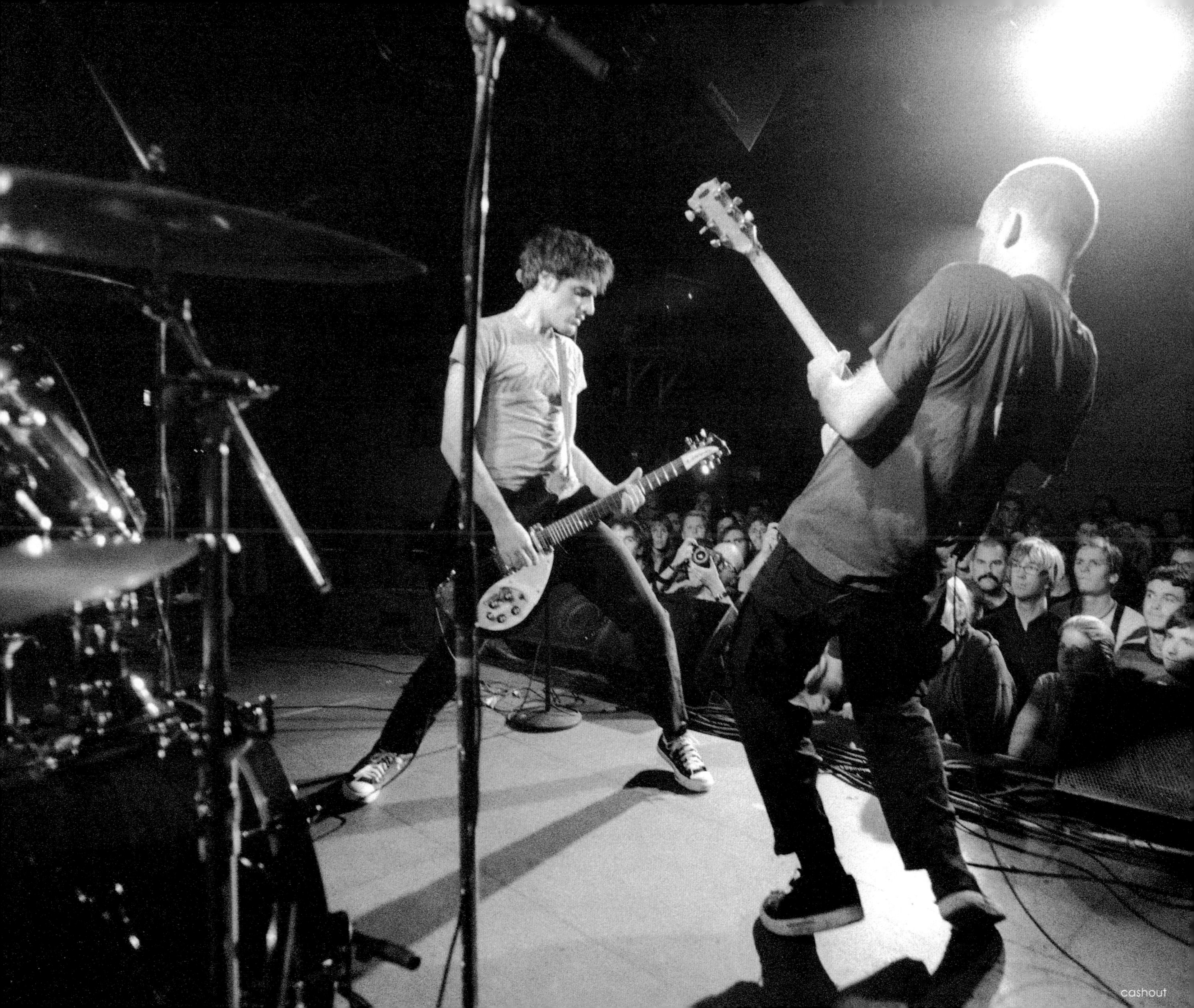
cashout

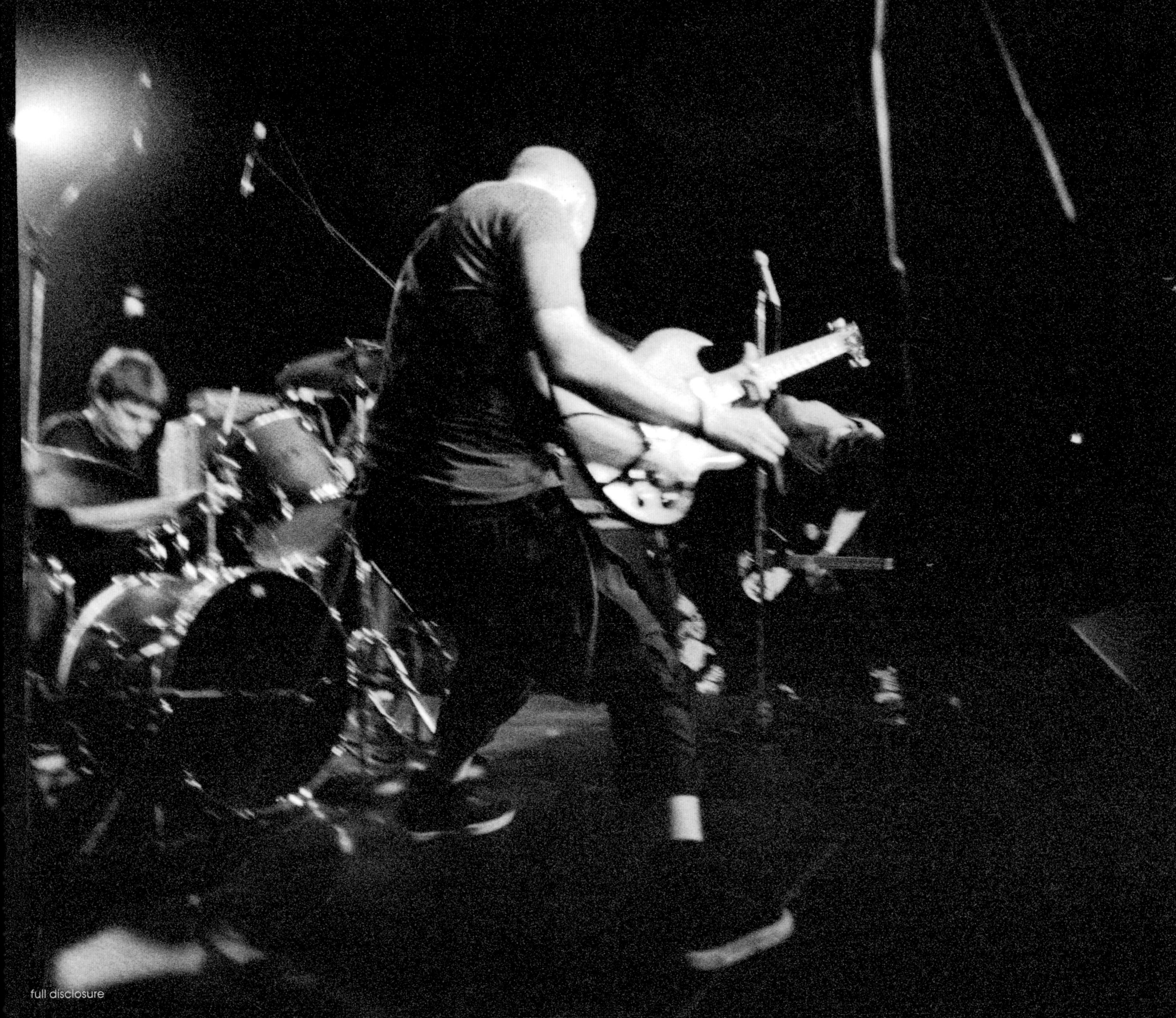

full disclosure

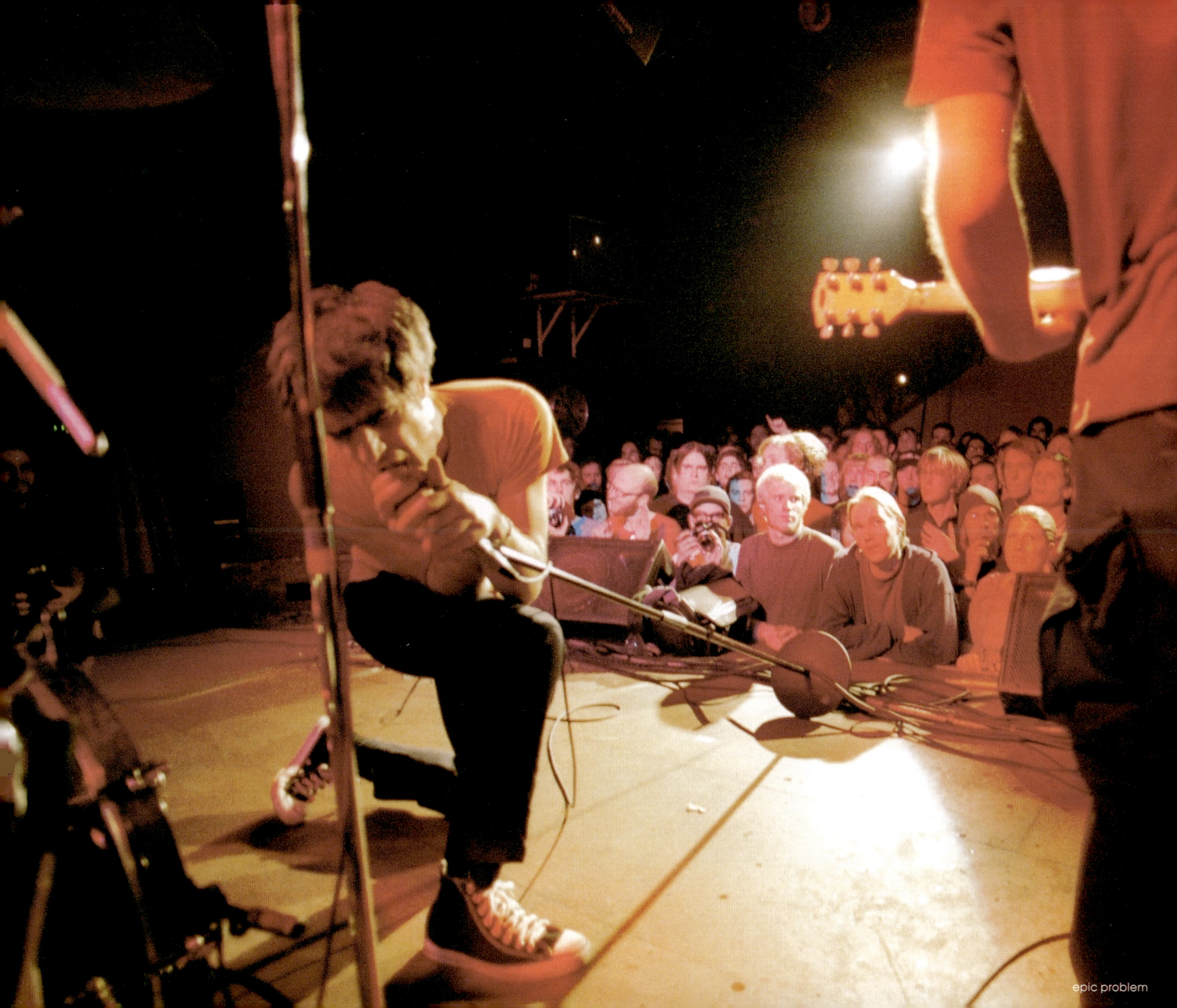

epic problem

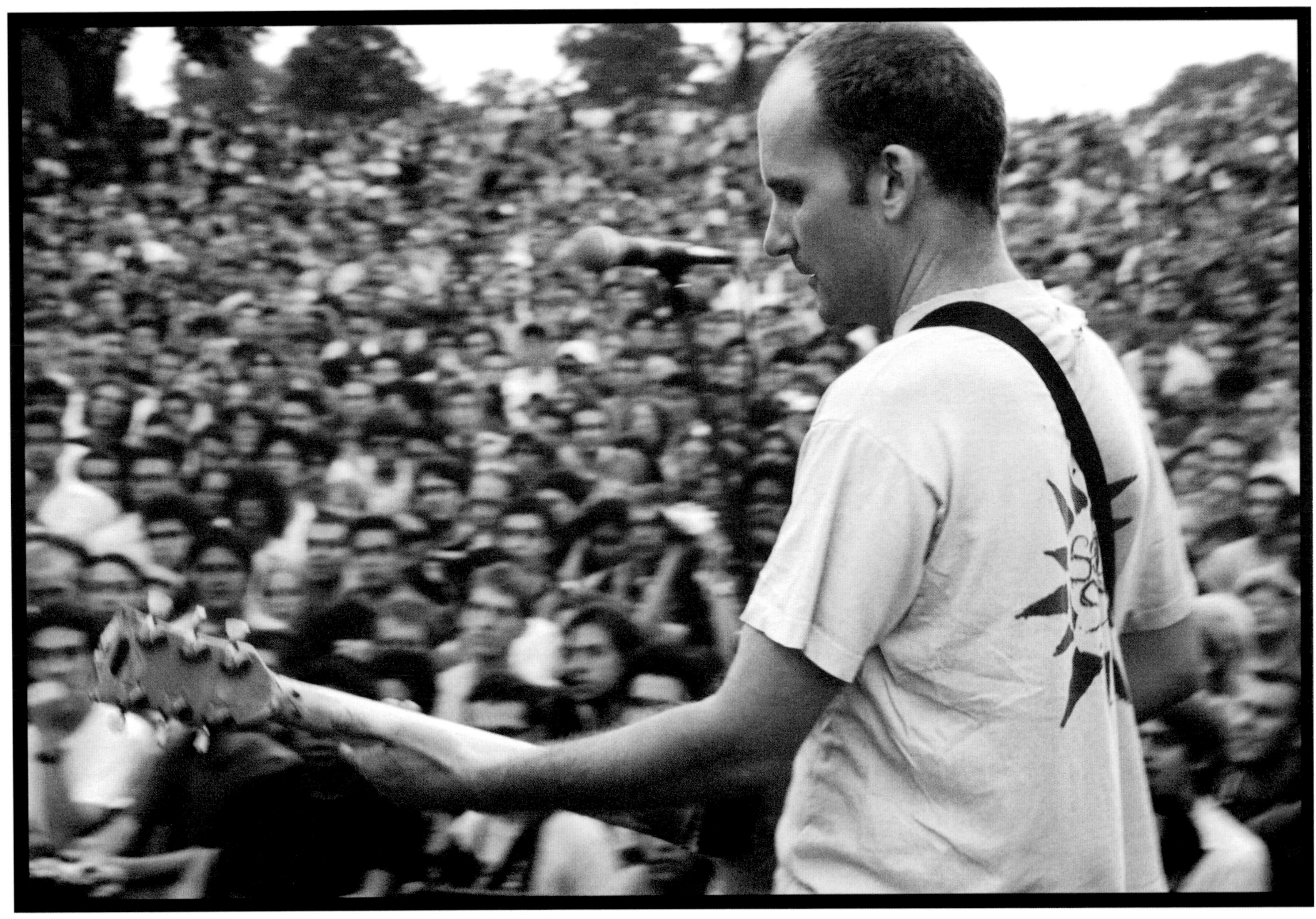

Back at Fort Reno with a remarkable crowd for the annual summer gig.
These are the last few Fugazi band photos I shot, of what would be their last show on US soil.

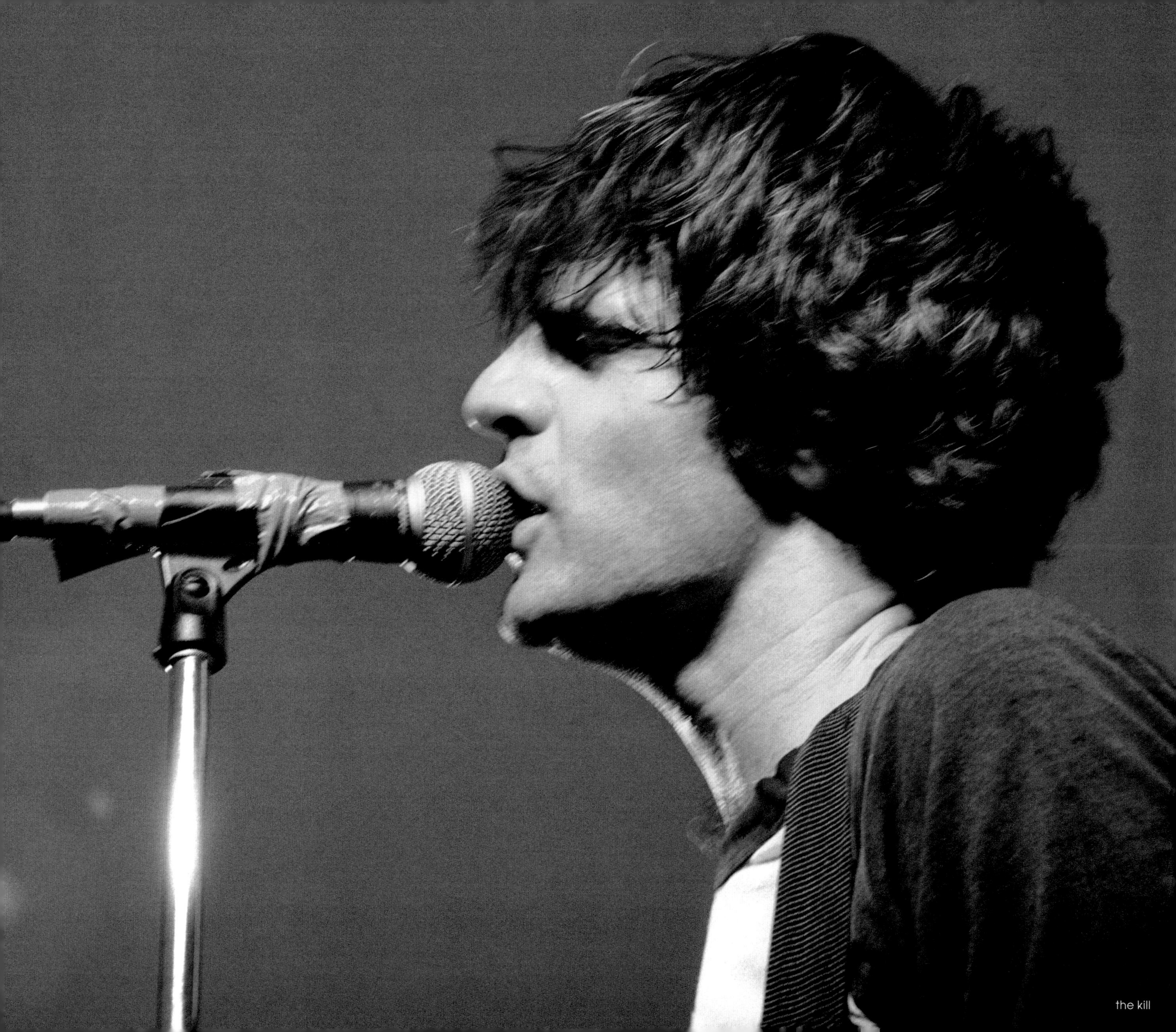

the kill

Jerry Busher here as the fifth member, standing, on drums.

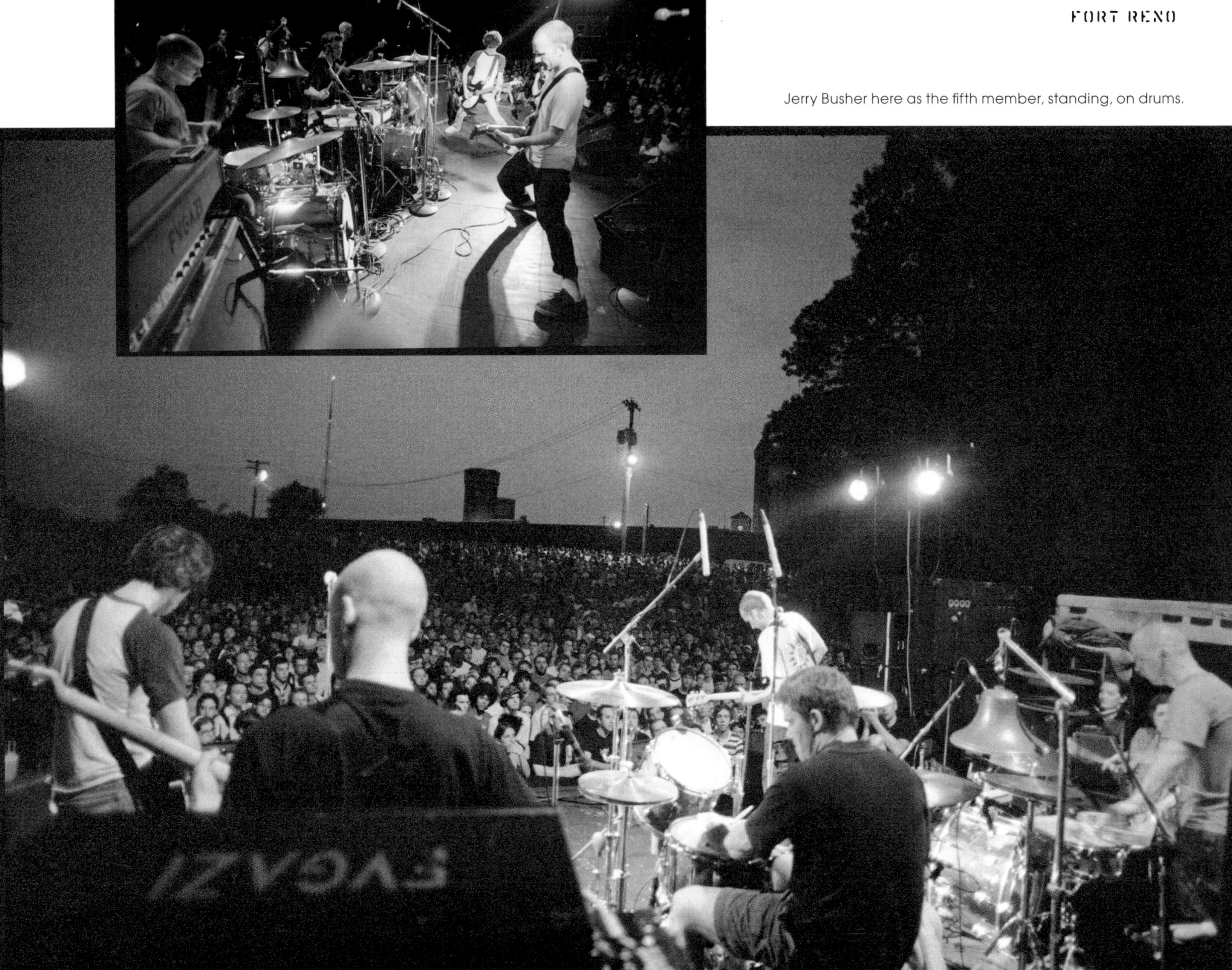

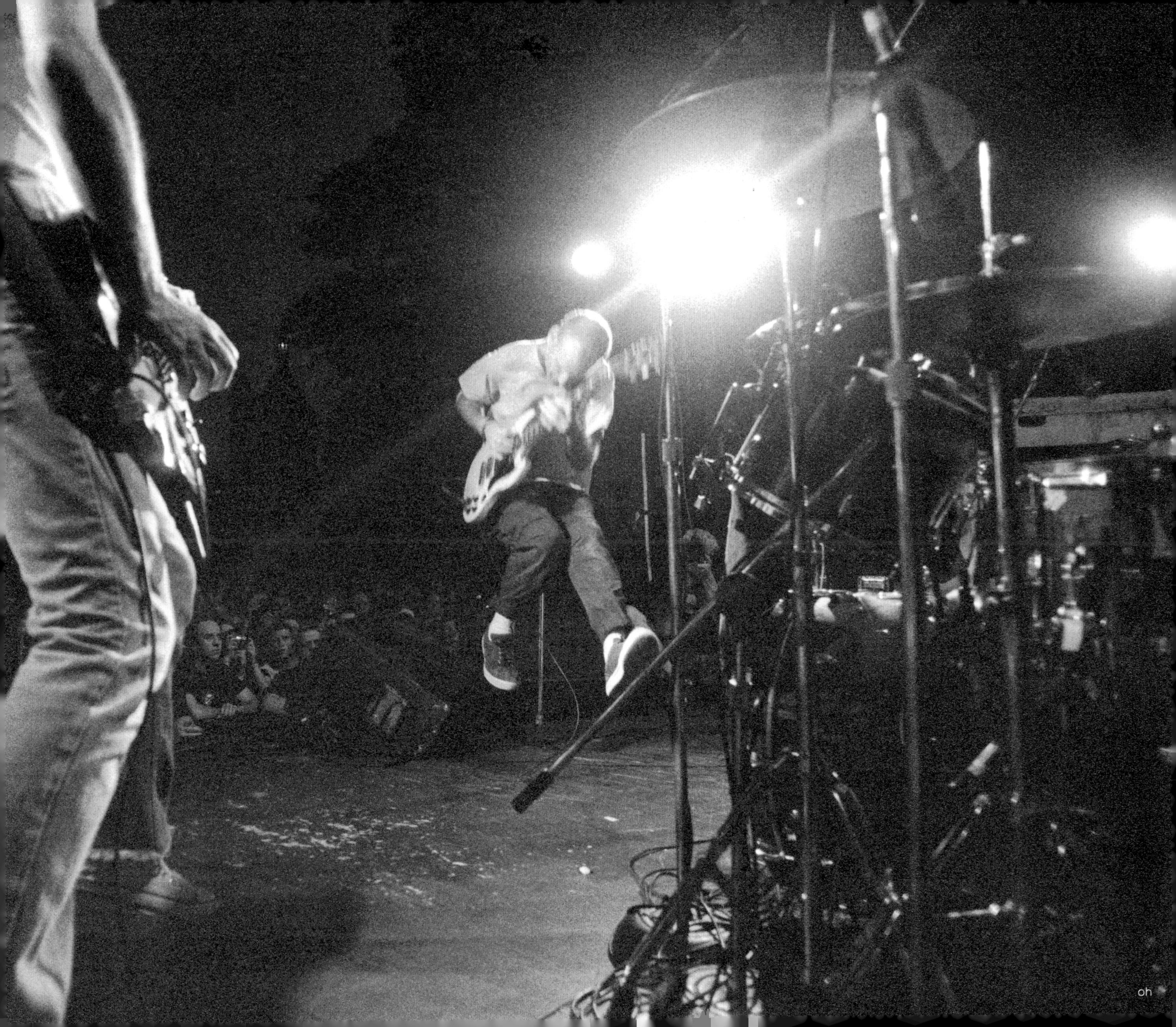
oh

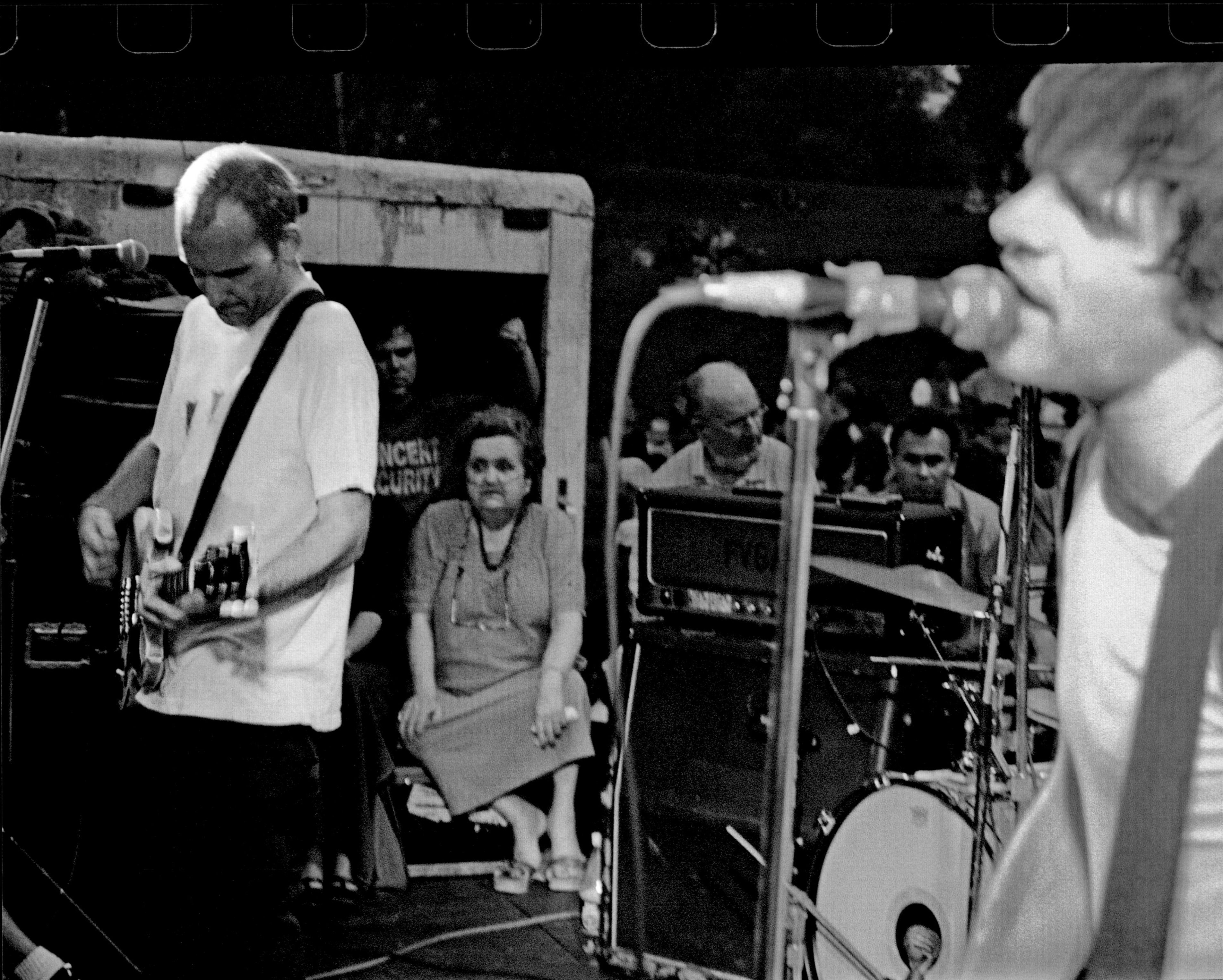

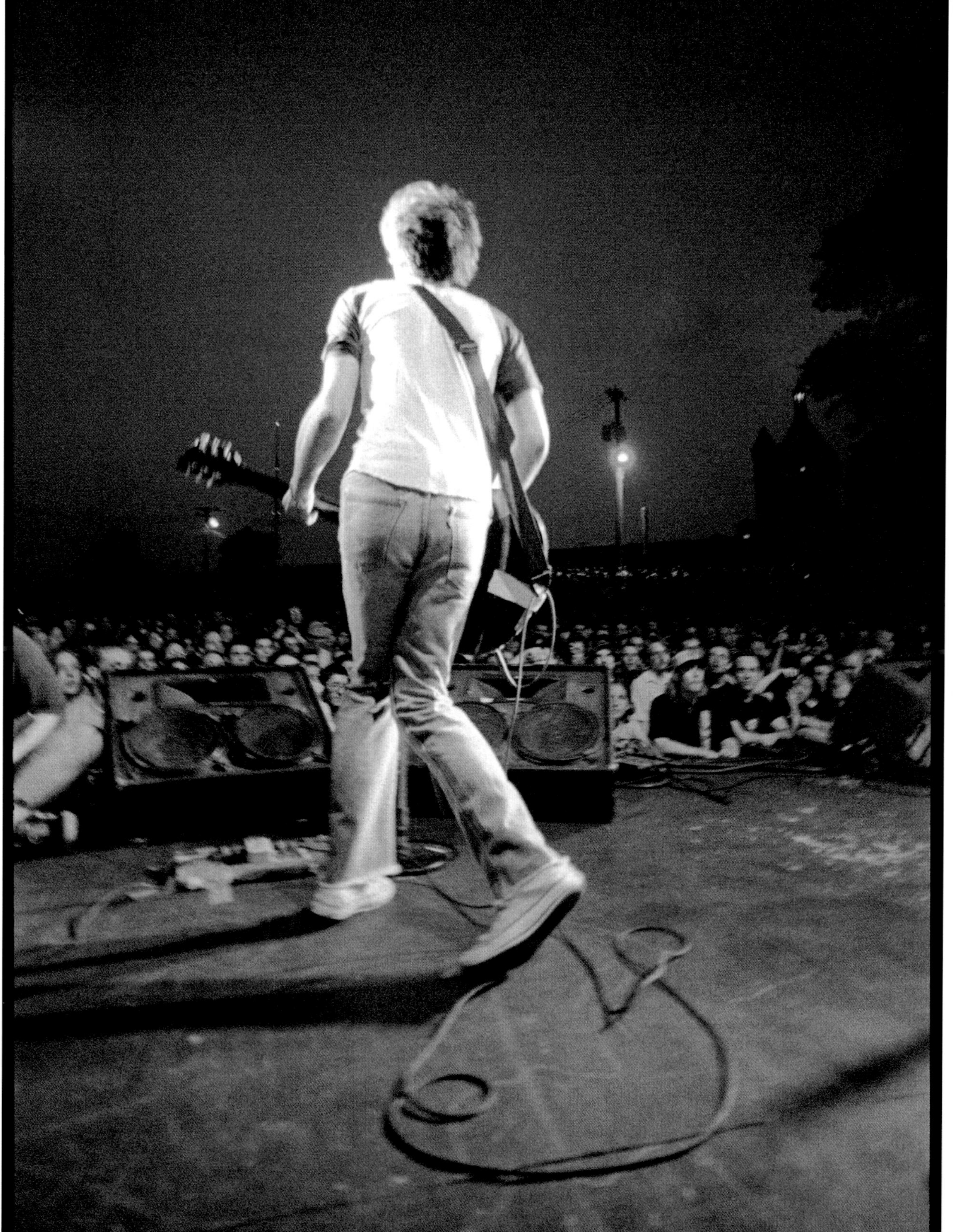

Ginger, William, and Alec MacKaye (Ian's mother, father, and brother) sitting by the side of the stage.

A few more words from the author

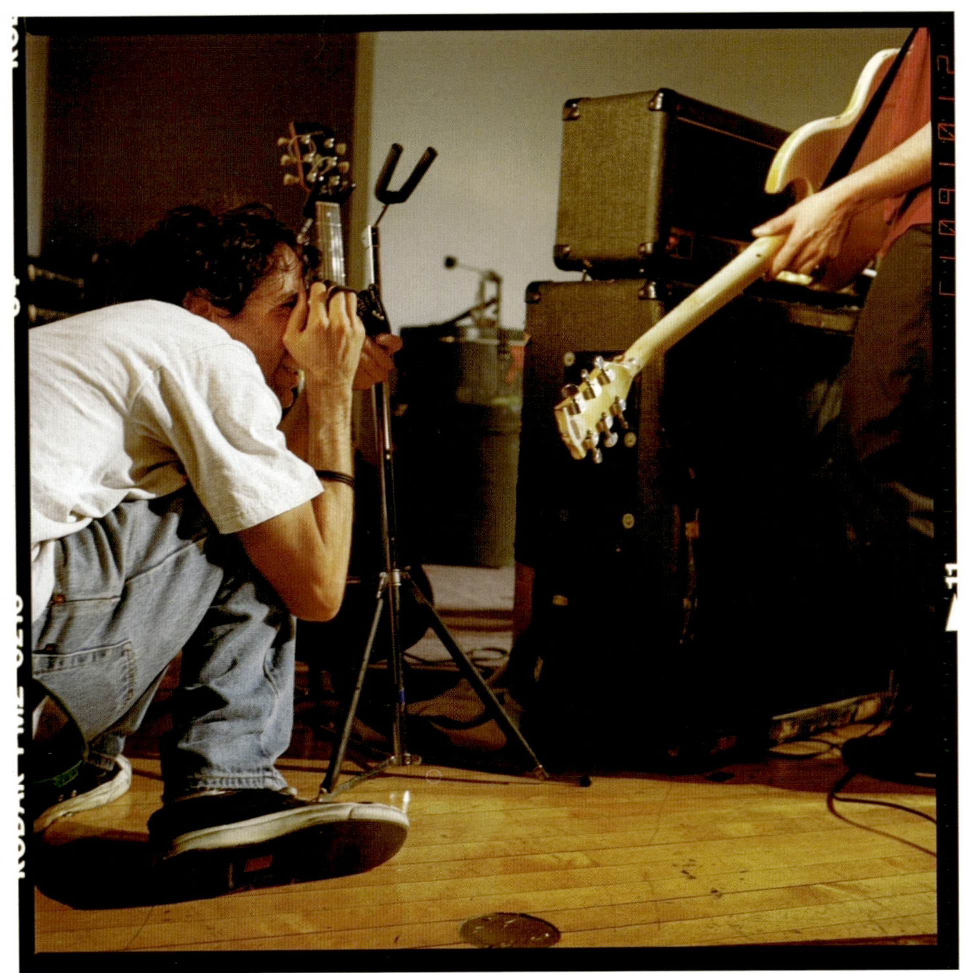

Shooting opposite photo of Ian at New York University, 1997.
Photo by Luke Hoverman

In 1987, Fugazi arrived—a band without peer who would come to personify ethics, individuality, and integrity, and who would become a rallying beacon to both those seeking sonic innovation and those striving for social justice. Fugazi wasn't just a group of DC punks who'd been around the block. Fugazi was a group of DC punks who'd been around the block and had come right back to where they'd started, ready to go somewhere new and unable to forget what punk actually meant beneath its surface. These were kids I had met at Bad Brains shows back in '81—kids who had founded phenomenal bands like Minor Threat and Rites of Spring. They questioned everything, thought their own thoughts, and spread idealism like a virus through their words, music, energy, and activism.

Fugazi's earliest shows were in small, peculiar venues—spaces that complemented the ethical standards and noncommercial attitude that the then-unknown group had fostered. The group's vision was incredible from the start—from the assurance of a low admission price to the insistence of all-ages gigs and an unwillingness to merchandise themselves, Fugazi ran the show, and they ran it on their terms to benefit the people who wanted to come out and see them play. Then there was the music—which was incredible! The venues got what they needed, the fans got what they wanted, and Fugazi humbly got their way. Everyone came out ahead and Fugazi never felt obliged to compromise with anything out of step with their ethic. Some thought it was crazy. Some still do, but what Fugazi began and stayed true to inspired countless others to follow in the footsteps of their dedication to inclusivity.

I first saw Fugazi play live at a benefit uptown at Columbia University here in New York City. It was unlike anything I had ever experienced, and the set had deafening heart. From their first chords, I remember thinking that their sound was completely unique. Par for the course, I didn't bring my camera. I usually like to scope out a band before I shoot them. But before the last drop of their sweat hit the stage that night, I vowed to take pictures of this group the next chance I had. Several months later, I got that chance at Maxwell's in Hoboken, New Jersey—about nine months after Fugazi played their very first show. I would see Fugazi play every time they toured from then on—most often in New York, New Jersey, and DC, though I've also caught up with them in Los Angeles, London, and Stockholm.

Fugazi were always so photogenic and engaging to see live, but I didn't always want to worry about my camera and sometimes preferred to enjoy the music and the company of friends without having to think about focus, shutter speed, or reloading film and missing the perfect shot. After all, I knew I had already taken some "definitive" shots very early on. Why did I need to shoot any more? So many other new and younger photographers were starting to shoot the band. The popularity of autofocus and point-and-shoot cameras was making concert photography more accessible. There were more Fugazi photos than ever! I didn't want to contribute to the further consumption of film or the waste associated with processing more than was necessary—but I loved this band . . . so much so that they changed photography for me.

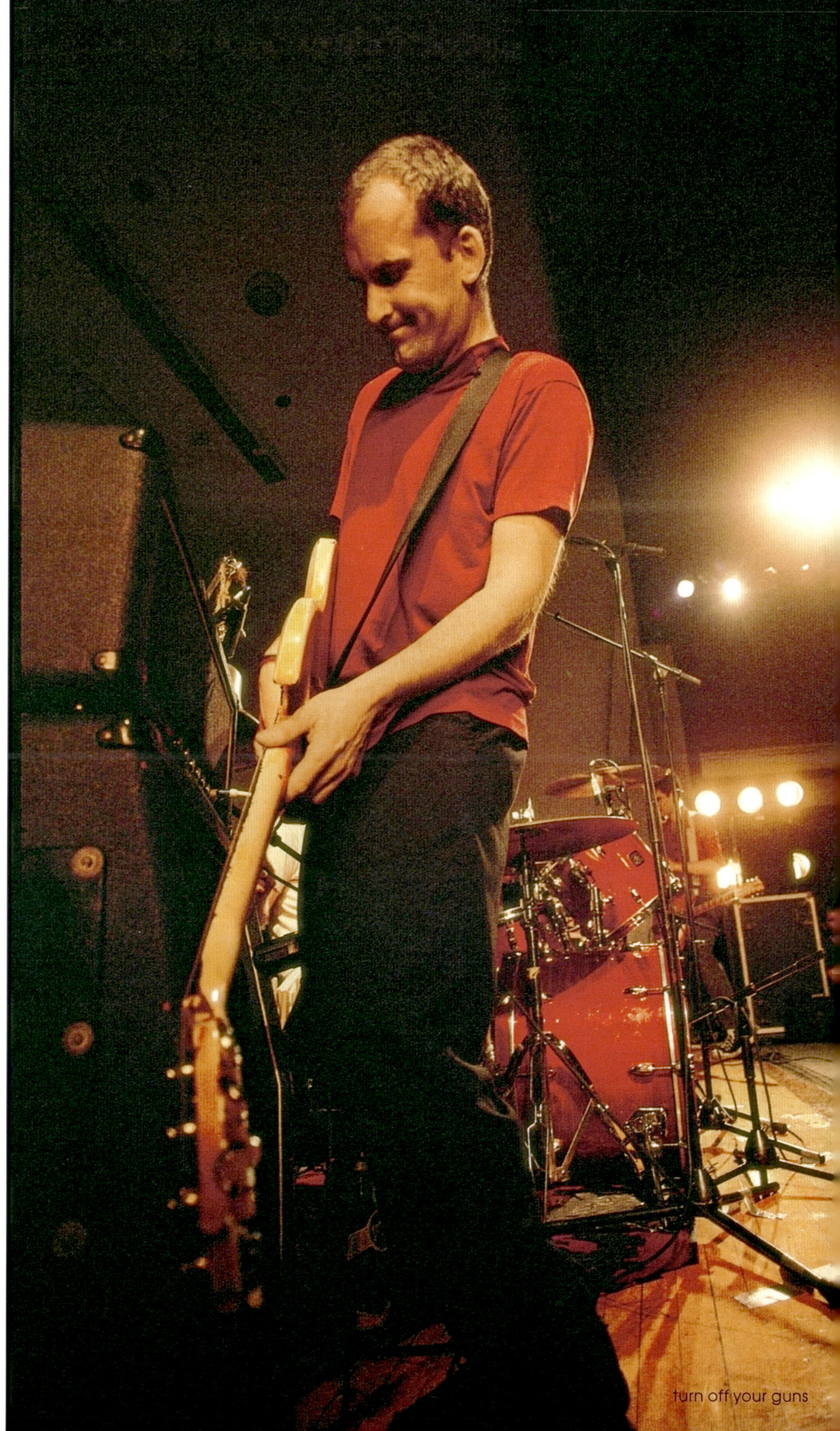
turn off your guns

It was because of the thrill of capturing Fugazi's iconic moments—or more specifically, the satisfaction brought to me by sharing those moments and the inspiration behind them with others—that I established a new paradigm in my work. As with most bands, it was just too obvious to get shots of a lead player at peak performance. What I wanted to capture more than anything, and with Fugazi in particular, was the entire band—in the same shot while accentuating that energy's relationship to the audience. This became a great challenge. Early on I also began shooting Fugazi only with available light. It took the images to the next level. Flashes, with or without time-exposures, create inorganic and flat images. I had been using those methods since the skateboarding days, and had grown bored with the unnatural and predictable results. Flash photography distracts attention from where it should be focused at a show—on the band. Composing images that technically mirrored the organic, democratic, charged, and generous ethos of Fugazi in an aesthetically sensible and symmetric style became my goal.

Fugazi shows became my laboratory for experiments with light, action, composition, and emotion. They also became a classroom for photographic etiquette. The band knew me well enough to let me position myself wherever I felt comfortable during their shows—a freedom that at moments made me feel a part of the band. At the same time, however, I was entirely aware of how potentially distracting my presence could be to the audience who came to see them. As both a kid at venues and a photographer, I've always hated photographers' reckless sense of entitlement at shows. Few things are more frustrating for an audience than an ass with a camera blocking the show just to get his or her shot. Few things belong at a Fugazi show less than an ass.

Guy, Joe, Brendan, and Ian are without a doubt four of the nicest guys anyone could ever meet. Getting to know them over the years and growing with them has been a privilege. Seeing them perform as often as I have and listening to each new record they've released has been a constant inspiration—evidenced by the number of Fugazi photos in my anthologies, dating back to *Fuck You Heroes*. I've even been fortunate enough to have some of Ian's words grace the pages of my book *The Idealist*.

Keep Your Eyes Open is dedicated only to Fugazi. The official release date of the first edition of this book was twenty years to the day after they played their very first show on September 3, 1987. It's been a number of years since they last performed together. It's been tough for all of them to be away from Fugazi, but during that hiatus, new children have been born and new groups have been formed. Like I said . . . DC punks who've been around the block—always ready to go someplace new. Their progression in one way or another is constant. When, if ever, Guy, Joe, Brendan, and Ian will get back to work and play together as Fugazi is anyone's guess. Until then, we're left with the music and the pictures.

—G.E.F.

Interview

In the fall of 2018, before this second edition of Keep Your Eyes Open *was sent off to the printer, musician/designer Sohrab Habibion sat down with Glen E. Friedman and Ian MacKaye to discuss photography, music, and their longstanding friendship.*

Sohrab: Glen, when did you first know you were going to make this book?

Glen: I think it was after the band wasn't around for a while. It was some years after the band wasn't doing gigs anymore. I'm thinking, *They're still inspiring a lot of people.* And the ethic that they kind of taught a lot of people, or that they brought to the forefront, was very important to me. And I thought, *I've got all these incredible photographs, I need to share them and continually inspire other people, hopefully.* And then I just decided, *That's what I'm going to do: I'm going to make a Fugazi book.* And it was going to be the first book of mine that concentrated on *one* subject, you know, other than *DogTown*, which is still kind of broad, relatively speaking. This is one band, and I had more photos of Fugazi than any other single subject that I had ever made photographs with.

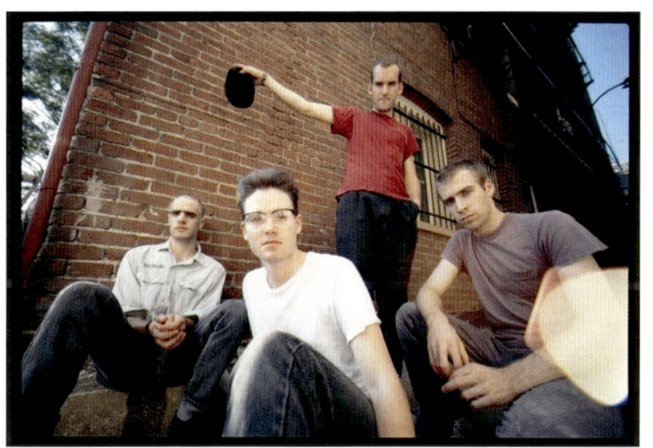

My Public Enemy photographs, and a lot of the stuff that I've done, it might be ten or fifteen rolls of any one subject, and that's it. Fugazi, it might be forty to fifty rolls at the most. Maybe even thirty—and that's over a fifteen-year period. They inspired me incredibly and were continuingly inspiring other people. So I thought a book might be appropriate, it might be in order, and I love making books. So I just started to do it, I just started fucking around with it. And then all of a sudden it started falling into place, and it's like, *Oh, this is fucking good, this is going to be really good.*

Until very recently, all of my books, I just sat there and made them. I mean, people helped me, but eventually I learned how to use Quark and design the books all by myself. And I started doing that, and the Fugazi book was just the pinnacle of all my book designing at the time. I learned a lot and had confidence in what I was doing and knew how type and photos worked. You know, I published my own books. This is all money out of my own pocket, and working with Fugazi, I'm going to sell this as inexpensively as possible. And I really did that with every book, but for this book in particular you had to be really careful because I'm dealing with a band, one group of individuals, whose ethic is like none other. Not far from mine, by the way, in most respects. My books were never about making money—they're about sharing experiences and inspiring other people. And I loved making the puzzle. And I loved showing off the work that I created because it was meant to be seen. It wasn't meant to just stay in a fucking drawer. I wanted people to see it and I want people to be inspired by it. And at that time there was no publisher waiting for it—it was me.

So I showed it to Fugazi. Their attitude, I think, at one point was like, *Who the fuck cares? Who's going to care about this? You don't need to do a book . . . maybe.* And I know that they appreciated things being documented, but I don't think it was an investment they wanted to be made—to be responsible for, almost. It was kinda like, *If you wanna do that, go ahead. But you fucking be careful. Watch your ass.*

Ian: We just didn't want you to lose money.

Glen: Yeah, no one wanted me to lose money 'cause they knew that I was doing it myself. And I'm thinking, *I believe in this, and it's okay. Let's fucking do it because I think it's worth the risk that other people will be inspired by it.*

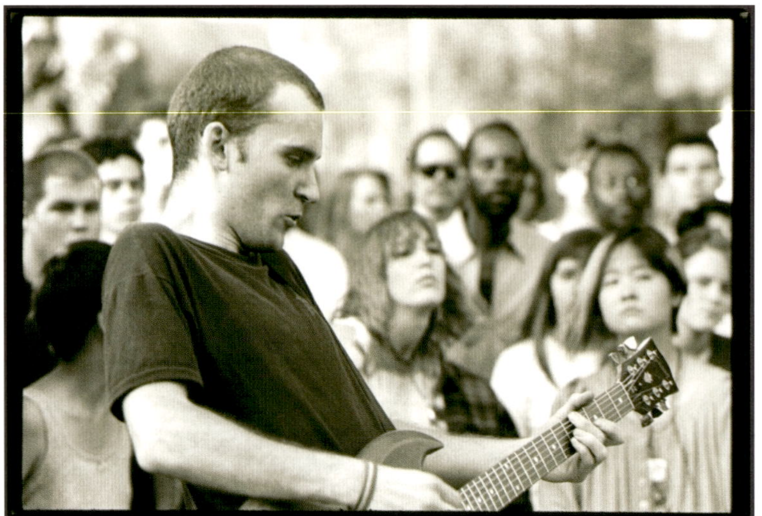

Sohrab: How many unseen Fugazi photographs have you taken that didn't make it into this book?

Glen: The photos in the book are all the best ones, for sure, other than those that appear in my other books. And the way that I can judge that—but not the way that I can with other groups of photos, like the *DogTown* stuff or the hip-hop stuff—is because these kind of came later. I mean, when's the last photo that I took in there?

Ian: 2002.

Glen: That's relatively recent in my archive of work. Most of my stuff is from '76 to '90. That's the bulk of my archive. When I took a skateboarding photo back then, it had to be radical. It had to be the peak action, otherwise it wasn't being published. Forty years later, you look at the background, look at what's going on here, look at the style, look at the environment of the era. There's so much more in this photo speaking to so many people now.

Hip-hop stuff is the same way. I'm trying to make someone look tougher than they actually are because that's the attitude of the music, of the records, and what I felt. And so I look at the pictures of LL (Cool J) now, smiling and being a sixteen-year-old. But when we published them originally, he had to look tough. Because if he looked soft, it was not good for the public image. That was the image, right? With Fugazi, it was pretty consistent all along. There was no fronting, there was no—

Ian: But the other stuff was more commercial work, in a way. You were doing record covers. You were doing covers or ads. Like you were going for magazine pages or promos.

Glen: True.

Ian: We did posed photos to some degree, but most of these photos were live. Or we were just hanging around with you and you said something like, *Let's do a picture*. You have those photos of Slick Rick up on the roof of your old apartment with the clock tower behind him. But those photos, they were really taken potentially, if not definitely, for the cover. Right, that was the idea.

Glen: That's correct.

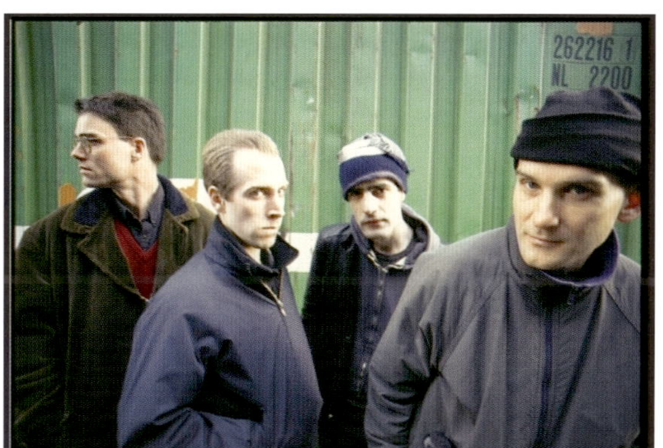

Ian: When we shot, we never felt, *Let's get a cover photo.* Ever. That was never in our mind.

Glen: No, 'cause Fugazi would never put themselves on the cover, number one.

Ian: But occasionally we did say, *Maybe we need a new publicity photo*, and we had that in mind. But we didn't say, *We have to get it TODAY.* That's absurd. That's not how we functioned. It was more like, *Hey Glen, we need to make a new publicity shot to send out. Can we use one of your group photos?*

Glen: And I'm thinking, *Of course, that would be great!* But at the same time, it was like we were artists working together, I feel, so they didn't take it for granted that they'd be able to say, *Maybe, Glen, we want to use one of these for publicity.* It was like, *What do you think about that? Do you think we could use it for that?*

Ian: We used to send the same photos to publications forever and ever and ever. And then we'd think, *Maybe we need to freshen this up.* And we're hanging out with Glen and he just took some photos. *Oh yeah, maybe we* do *need a new photo.* It wasn't the goal, ever. That is for sure.

Glen: But most of my photography was like that too. I was very rarely given assignments. And even for the record companies, the artist came to me when they wanted a cover, and then I would work out contracts later. Sometimes I would even have the photos already and people would ask to license them after the fact. But there were also record covers made, that's what we were doing. But we didn't know what it was going to look like that day. We just went and hung out and made photos and had ideas and we'd make it all work.

Sohrab: Glen, compared to other photographers, it sounds like you don't take a whole lot of photos during a shoot.

Ian: These photos, the ones you're seeing, they're not every photo Glen took, but they're pretty close. He didn't spend a lot of time in one place. So we would just walk around and stop somewhere. He'd say, "Stand over there, I'll make a picture." And then we'd make one. And it was mostly just talking and walking. It wasn't like a photo session in the normal way.

Sohrab: What are some of your favorite photos in the book?

Ian: I've always loved fisheye—wide-angled photos. This dome, this is the Canadian embassy (see page "stacks"), this is really classic.

Sohrab: Glen, how many photos do you think you would've taken on this shoot?

Glen: Maybe twenty?

Sohrab: In that location or for the full shoot?

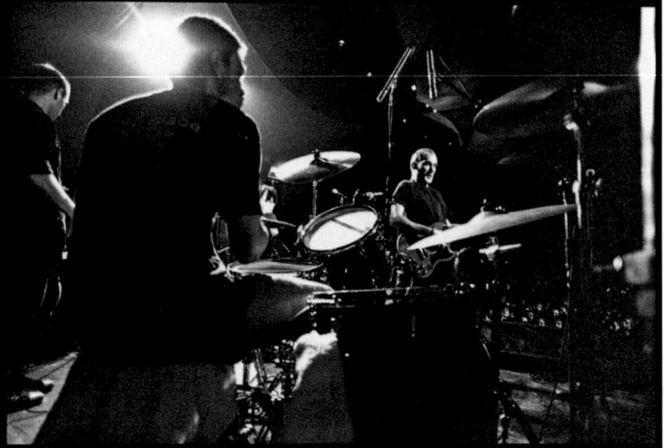

Glen: Maybe three or four images in each place, what people call a "setup." Fugazi performed at Dupont Circle that day, so we're talking about all these pictures, including the pictures that made the back cover of *Repeater*. Including the live photos, that's probably two or three rolls of film at the most. I can't imagine that I ever shot four rolls in one day of Fugazi. No way.

Ian: That was a different day.

Glen: Are you sure?

Ian: Pretty sure, yeah, because Guy's wearing a different jacket.

Glen: But sometimes I would tell people to do that.

Ian: No, we wouldn't have done that.

Glen: Guy could take off a jacket.

Ian: No—Brendan is wearing a different shirt. This is a different day.

Sohrab: Did Fugazi nix any photos or ideas from the book?

Ian: We did take out one.

Glen: Yeah, I had an idea when I was making the book to have a picture of everyone currently. Five years later, or whatever it was. And I did take a picture of Joe and his family. And then I was about to do another band member and his family. And then it got kinda shut down.

Ian: The concept of "Where are they now?"—I was not into that, for a variety of reasons. I don't like this idea of, "They toiled, and now, look, they all have families." Fuck that, I'm not into that. It just doesn't speak to me.

Glen: Well, I found it very interesting. I thought it was interesting where they had gone. And I had seen these families grow. And I thought it would be interesting to take these portraits of them at that point in time. But I eventually saw their point, or Ian's point in particular. He didn't like that type of narrative. And that's not much of a surprise. There's one page in this book that they don't like the design on because I overlaid photos on top of another image (see page "styrofoam").

Ian: Which he never did before.

Glen: It's from the Dupont Circle show. They didn't like how I covered the cymbal up in the layout.

Ian: We thought this should not have been covered. This photo is killer.

Glen: Yeah, and I told them that they were dead wrong.

Ian: No, but we were right. We were absolutely 100 percent right.

Glen: You're dead wrong. Totally wrong. It's so much blank space that I just covered it.

Ian: The intensity of the exchange that Guy and I are having in the shot is distracted by the insets.

Glen: Not hurt at all. Not hurt at all. Not hurt at all (*laughs*).

Ian: Amateur move. And there are also, I have to say, other photos in there that, like the setup—

Glen: There's one setup that he hates—

Ian: I don't like it.

Glen: There's one setup that he hates that was in *Fuck You Heroes* as well. There's one photo from that day where I used a long lens. Which I rarely ever do.

Ian: Don't like long lenses.

Glen: But it's a great portrait.

Ian: It's terrible.

Glen: For most people, a long lens is a portrait lens. I don't usually shoot with portrait lenses. But I did these shots of them in the alley behind Ford's Theatre. Behind the 9:30 Club. I know it that way 'cause I'm a tourist—I was told that it's where John Wilkes Boothe escaped from. Ian thought it looked like a Gap ad.

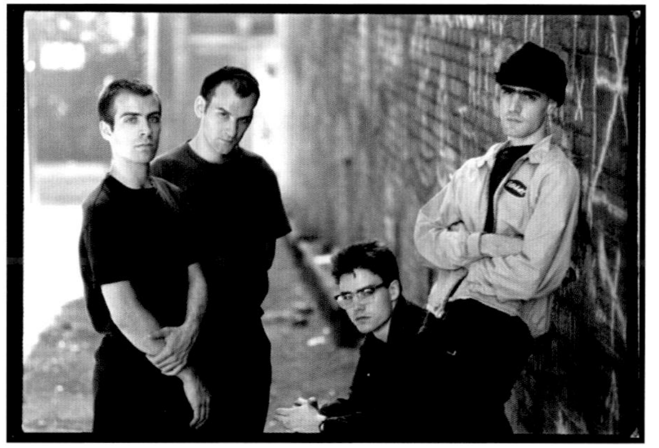

Ian: I'm not into that photo. It looks terrible.

Glen: It is too simple and too obvious for the likings of Mr. MacKaye. I'm really into compositions, and if I make a good composition, I'm an artist, I want that shit to be seen.

Ian: Ugh, yuck. And there's one more of us on Pennsylvania Avenue . . .

Glen: The very first picture in the book. The one with the Capitol in the background. Yeah, they didn't want that. I had to beg to let them let me do that.

Sohrab: It's very iconic.

Glen: That's why they hated it. They said, *We're not tourists.* It was hard. I couldn't even get them to pose. They were crossing the street. I said, *Stop, let me just take this one picture. And no one is looking.* And look how disgusted he looks.

Ian: I fucking hated it. I didn't want to do it.

Glen: And I really had to beg for permission to use it in the front of the book. And the funny thing is, everyone, *everyone* wanted to see them by the Capitol, including myself. But what Ian told me that day, and what they all told me later, was: *That is not Washington, DC.*

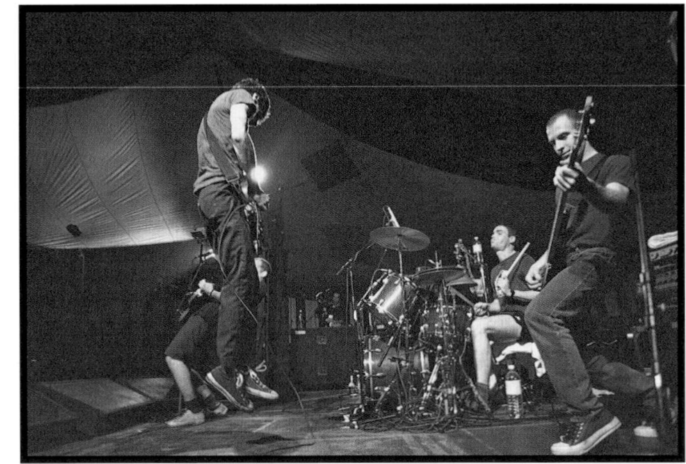

Ian: It's not.

Glen: That's Washington, DC, for tourists.

Ian: That's the federal city. That's not *our* city. That's Wall Street for New Yorkers. The US government doesn't need any advertising. Fuck them. I don't know, I feel like every time someone does something about Washington, it always starts with the Capitol or the Washington Monument or the Lincoln Memorial.

Sohrab: You do have Washington Monument on the cover of *In on the Kill Taker.*

Ian: Yeah, but it doesn't look like you usually see it—the Washington Monument isn't yellow. Everything on the cover is yellow. It's not glistening and white and marble. I really recoil at the aspect of Washington that is the touristy federal city.

Glen: That was a big fight. I mean it wasn't serious, but it was a big deal. But what was so great was that I got the picture of them there—just *one.* Even though they're totally distracted and hated posing for me that 1/125th of a second while we're literally crossing the street, not stopping even for the light to change. Half of them aren't looking at the camera. We kept on moving. I got the one shot. The exposure isn't very great. But everyone always wants to use that picture.

Ian: Who does?

Glen: When people call to use a press picture or whatever, I say, *Sorry, I cannot use that picture because the band does not like that photo.*

Ian: Because it's a locator. It's like they're looking at it and thinking, *That's what we want.* That's just so common.

Glen: People like that. They want a photo to say different things.

Ian: But fuck common, it's just common.

Sohrab: Changing topics, how did Ian Svenonius's introduction to this book come about?

Glen: I was trying to find some kind of introduction, and I am not fond of my own writing. I think when you make a book it should be respectful and it should be really good. And I don't need to show anything ugly, and I don't need to make fun of anyone. I'm making a book because it is someone that I respect and it's something to handle very seriously, for the most part. I am not a writer so I am not going to write an introduction to the book. I love Ian Svenonius's writing style. We had thought of different writers who could write something about Fugazi. But so many things at the time had been written about them, and this was before the Internet mania. I was speaking to Svenonius one day, and I was telling him I was having a tough time with the introduction, and he just said he would love to write something on Fugazi. It took at least a year or maybe longer for him to come up with that, but he had something he wanted to write. When he handed it in, I was thinking, *Man, I hope the guys like this.* 'Cause it was self-deprecating. But it was good.

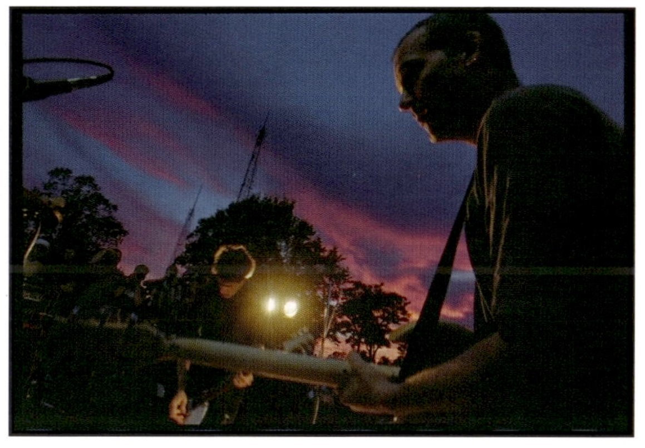

Sohrab: There's an absurd element to it.

Glen: I think he did it really well and in a nonglamorous, almost humorous way—a part of the band that people don't see in the movies or anything else about Fugazi. You don't get to see that—and they approved it, believe it or not.

Ian: We're surrealists. So in many ways we'd much rather have somebody who really has a connection with the band, who loves the band, who has a vision—have them weigh in on us. The way most people write about us is about the structural stuff—all the structural stuff that we created and we're known for. We created it *because of* the art, the music. That was the point of it. And yet people want to write about the structure. But we were actually about the art.

Sohrab: The humor of the people in the band often gets missed. And so Ian Svenonius's introduction captures a little bit of that: the absurdity.

Glen: Svenonius is the greatest conversationalist I know. And we had talked about Fugazi so many times and different aspects of Fugazi and him just being . . . I really like people who are passionate about what they do and what they believe in. You know, someone like Svenonius who still goes to shows and is still inspired by new musicians. And just musicians in general. Chuck D is a huge fan of hip-hop and of all music to this day. That's why he's still so relevant and topical. Svenonius is just a thinker and an avid reader and a lover of so many different things, particularly of politics, which is so close to activism in a weird way. He's got such a great take on things. And it's so hard to figure out, but it really makes you think and have a laugh. I couldn't imagine it being anything else at this point.

Sohrab: Glen, can you talk about your own writing at the very end of the book?

Glen: I was really thinking about adding a conclusion to the book other than the last photos from the last show in America.

Ian: Those are kind of a great.

Glen: Yeah, they are some of the best photos. That photo when you see Jerry and you see all the other people—

Ian: And my mom's in the background.

Glen: That's heavy.

Ian: Deep. That was good. That's the last time she saw us, obviously.

Glen: That's the last time *anyone* in America saw the band.

Ian: That's true.

Glen: I did eventually write something. Which took me a long time to put down . . . I don't usually go over things a lot—I mean, I do go over things a lot of times, but once it's to bed, it's done. I don't even look back at it.

Sohrab: When did the two of you first meet?

Ian: December 26, 1981, at a Bad Brains show, where my brother's band the Faith were opening, at CBGB. I have a letter from Glen from March of '82. So right after we met, we were already writing. You had gotten the SOA record from Henry (Garfield/Rollins) already. So you had met Henry. There's probably a connector in that.

Glen: When I heard Minor Threat's first record I didn't really think much of it, at first.

Ian: Right.

Glen: And I heard SOA and I liked SOA more.

Ian: All right.

Glen: Then I heard the second Minor Threat EP, *In My Eyes*. When I heard the title track, I was fucked up. And that's when I think I wrote you a letter telling you, *Wow, what you do is incredible.*

END

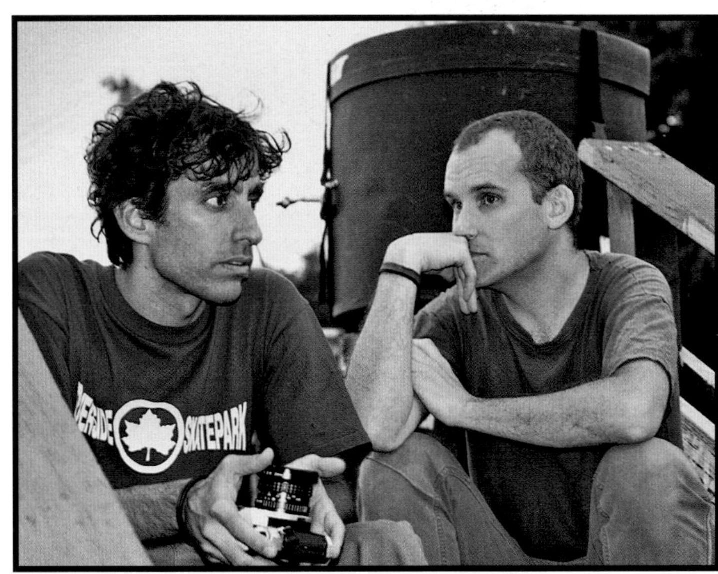

Glen and Ian at Fort Reno, Washington, DC, 1997
Photo by Kurt Sayenga

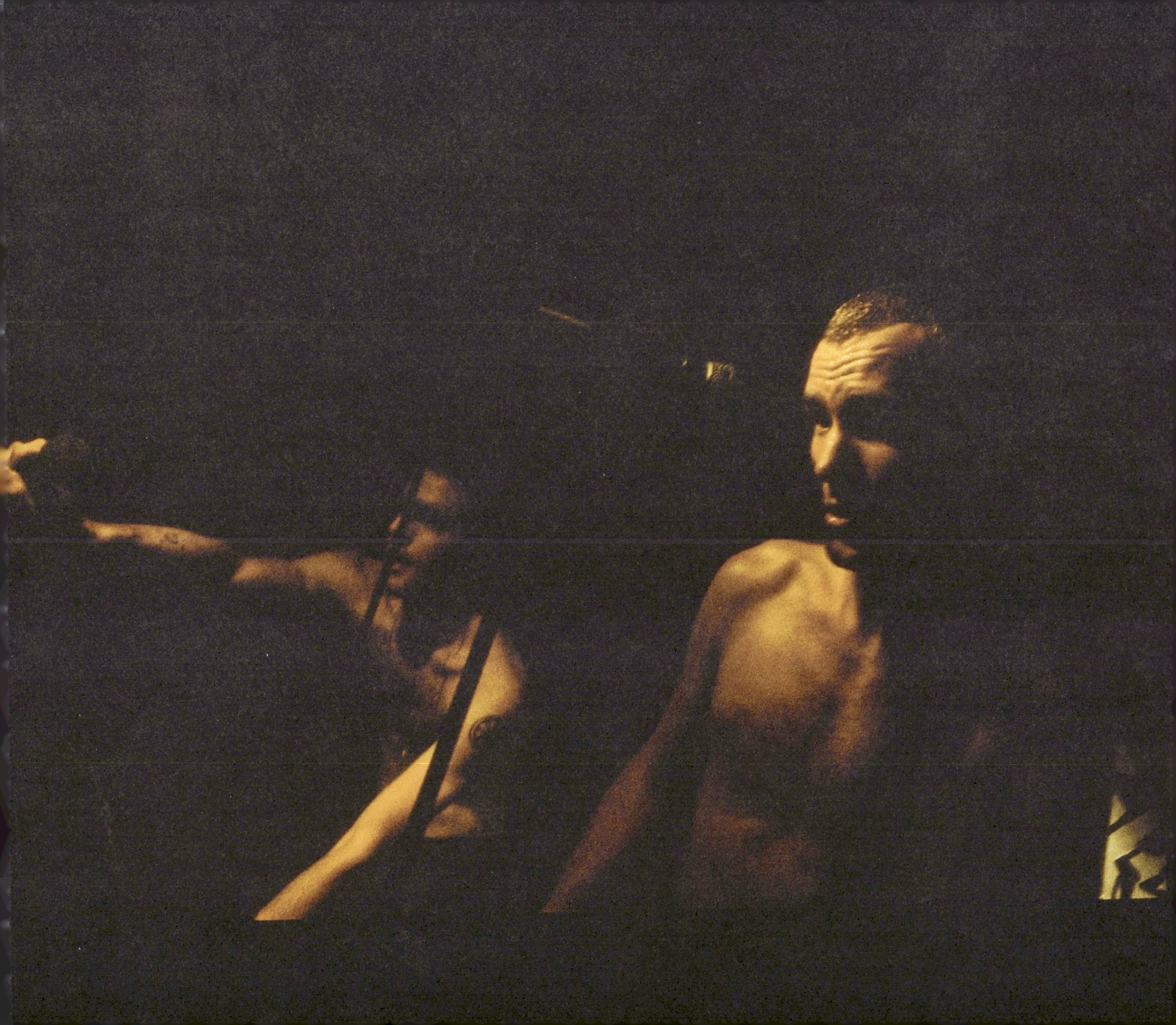

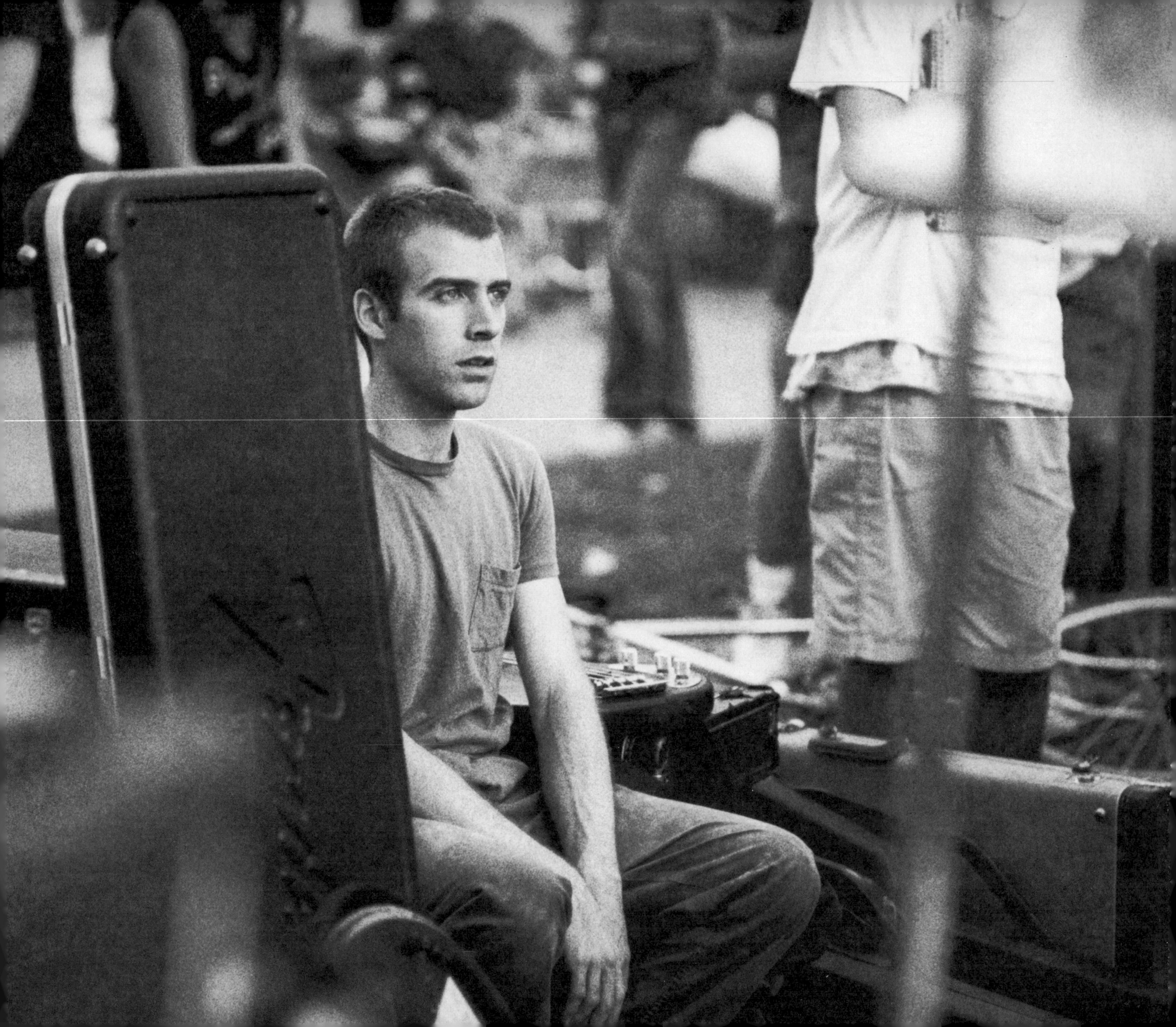